TWELVE POETS

12 POETS

WILLIAM SHAKESPEARE

JOHN DONNE

ALEXANDER POPE

WILLIAM WORDSWORTH

JOHN KEATS

ROBERT BROWNING

EMILY DICKINSON

A. E. HOUSMAN

WILLIAM BUTLER YEATS

EDWIN ARLINGTON ROBINSON

ROBERT FROST

T. S. ELIOT

Edited by Glenn Leggett

HOLT, RINEHART AND WINSTON, NEW YORK
CHICAGO SAN FRANCISCO TORONTO

Library of Congress Catalog Card Number: 58-5757
January, 1967
25199-0118

ACKNOWLEDGMENTS

EMILY DICKINSON

"I Heard a Fly Buzz When I Died," "After Great Pain a Formal Feeling Comes," "Forever Is Composed of Nows," "You'll Find It When You Come to Die," "My Life Had Stood a Loaded Gun," and "Renunciation" are from *Poems by Emily Dickinson* edited by Martha Dickinson Bianchi and Alfred Leete Hampson. Copyright 1929 by Martha Dickinson Bianchi. Reprinted by permission of Little, Brown & Co.

T. S. ELIOT

"Macavity: The Mystery Cat" is from *Old Possum's Book of Practical Cats,* copyright, 1939, by T. S. Eliot. All other poems of Mr. Eliot appearing in this volume are from *Collected Poems 1909–1935,* copyright, 1936, by Harcourt, Brace and Company, Inc. Reprinted by permission of Harcourt, Brace and Company, Inc., and Faber and Faber Limited.

ACKNOWLEDGMENTS

ROBERT FROST

All Mr. Frost's poems appearing in this volume are from *Complete Poems of Robert Frost.* Copyright, 1930, 1949, by Holt, Rinehart and Winston, Inc. Copyright, 1936, 1948, by Robert Frost. Reprinted by permission of Holt, Rinehart and Winston, Inc.

A. E. HOUSMAN

All Mr. Housman's poems appearing in this volume are from *The Collected Poems of A. E. Housman.* Copyright, 1940, by Holt, Rinehart and Winston, Inc. Reprinted by permission of Holt, Rinehart and Winston, Inc., and The Society of Authors as the Literary Representatives of the Trustees of the Estate of the late A. E. Housman, and Messrs. Jonathan Cape, Ltd., publishers of A. E. Housman's Collected Poems.

E. A. ROBINSON

"Flammonde," "Eros Turannos," "Veteran Sirens," "The Poor Relation," "Llewellyn and the Tree," "Bewick Finzer," "Thc Mill," "The Dark Hills," "Mr. Flood's Party," "Another Dark Lady," "The Sheaves," and "Erasmus" are from *Collected Poems* by Edwin Arlington Robinson. Reprinted by permission of The Macmillan Company.

"Uncle Ananias," "Miniver Cheevy," "For a Dead Lady," "Doctor of Billiards," and "How Annandale Went Out" are from *The Town Down the River* by Edwin Arlington Robinson; copyright 1910 by Charles Scribner's Sons, 1938 by Ruth Nivison. Reprinted by permission of Charles Scribner's Sons.

All other poems of Mr. Robinson appearing in this volume are from *Children of the Night* and are reprinted by permission of Charles Scribner's Sons.

WILLIAM BUTLER YEATS

All Mr. Yeats' poems appearing in this volume are from *Collected Poems* by William Butler Yeats. Reprinted by permission of The Macmillan Company, Mrs. William Butler Yeats, A. P. Watt & Son, Macmillan and Co. Ltd., London, and The Macmillan Company of Canada Limited.

PREFACE

This collection has more poems from individual poets than the usual anthology because the number of poets represented is limited to twelve, a number for which I claim no special significance. It might have been ten or fifteen or twenty or any other number; *twelve* seemed tidy and reasonable, and conventionally symbolic. More important was my feeling that the usual anthology in trying to present the best poems of a great number of poets, although aesthetically sound ("the poem is more important than the poet"), is pedagogically unwieldy, at least if the anthology is meant for freshmen and sophomores. In concentrating on a limited number of poets I do not mean that the teacher should ask students to meet their insecurity about poetry by escaping into the biography of the poet himself: the poem itself must always be the central concern of the good teacher. I mean rather that the careful reading of a number of poems by the same writer allows the students to hear enough of that poet's speaking voice to feel some security in their response. This response is not, of course, the same thing as understanding, but it is a necessary preparation for understanding, and can be treated as such in the hands of a good teacher. Is not this what we mean when we say we read "Keats" or "Pope" or "Yeats" and so on? The language of the individual poems keeps adding up and redefining itself, so that Poem 1 really doesn't come into its own with us until we hear it sounding through Poem 20, where it works simultaneously to effect our response to that poem and to others by the same poet, those read and those still to be read. "Period" anthologies, whether by conscious design or not, work on this pedagogical principle. Here I apply it more generally.

The twelve poets represented in this collection seem to satisfy better than any other group a variety of premises of selection, some of which I frankly allowed to operate more conclusively than others. In the first place, I wanted poets from whom I could select a number of good poems (twenty to twenty-five) without straining. This is why some excellent poets, such as Herbert, Marvell, Blake, Landor, and John Crowe Ransom, are omitted. It was easy to pick ten or twelve good poems by each of them; after that, my choices put me on the defensive. In the second place, though I wanted the major emphasis of the collection to fall on the short, lyric poem (as being more manageable in the classroom, *i.e.,* "more teachable"), I wished also to include some poets who worked mainly in satire and dramatic portraiture. This is the reason I chose Browning over Tennyson; it is one of the reasons I included Pope. In the third place, I wanted poets who could be presented to students with a minimum of explanatory notes. I could not allow this premise to operate fully without violating a previous one, under which I had included Pope and Browning, for the poems of these two poets need some explaining if students are to find their way around in them. But to replace them with lyric poets would have been to put the emphasis of this collection almost purely on the short poem, and a single emphasis of this sort was not my wish.

Finally I wanted poets who represented at least loosely the major periods of English poetry starting with Shakespeare—Elizabethan, Seventeenth Century, Eighteenth Century, Early Romantic, Late Romantic, Victorian, Late Victorian, and Modern. Here I permitted all the other premises of selection to operate. I chose Donne over Milton chiefly because the latter's use of classical and Biblical mythology is so pervasive and so structurally important that to prepare students for it is to have little space in a collection of this kind for anything else (I do not mean to imply that Donne is "easier"); Pope over Dryden because the latter's satires require a quite detailed understanding of his whole milieu, whereas Pope's allusions are comparatively individual and specific; Wordsworth over Coleridge because the latter's poetry, if we except a few pieces, seems unfinished and (remarkably) improvised; Keats over Shelley and Byron because Keats' work does not have to be cut up to be usefully represented; Browning over Tennyson for the reason I gave in a previous paragraph, and over Arnold because the latter does not maintain himself strongly in a sufficient number of poems; Housman over Hardy because, though the latter is certainly a greater poet, he is a less "perfect" one (I think this is the right term), and a less teachable one to freshmen and sophomores; Dickinson over Whitman because I find it hard to take any more than a few poems of the latter with complete seriousness. I chose Yeats, Robinson, Frost, and Eliot because they seem as a group to represent best the tradition we now teach as "modern poetry." Ideally, Ezra Pound, Hart Crane, Wallace Stevens, Auden, and perhaps Dylan Thomas belong here too. But complete representation was not my aim; rather it was to get the fairest representation possible with a limited number of poets. The four I included are here because they seem to be central to the modern tradition and yet to satisfy my other principles of selection.

So much for the poets. Now to the poems. Wherever possible, I wanted complete-good-brief poems: "complete" and "good" for obvious reasons, brief because of pedagogical demands. Reading a long poem is one thing; teaching it effectively is another. The accumulation of explanations, of student questions and responses, keeps wrenching it out of focus and it tends to sag between class periods. With Shakespeare, Donne, Keats, Dickinson, and Housman there were no problems in finding the proper kinds of poems; the problems were all problems of elimination. I picked the poems that my tastes told me to. With Pope the problem was more difficult, for here there are few brief poems. The question was whether to include two or three long poems in their entirety or four or five "selections." I compromised, and I have no hope that my solution will satisfy every reader. With Wordsworth the problem was of a different kind. I decided to omit his long "philosophical" poems and present him chiefly as a lyric poet, for no other reason than that I like him better this way. The selections from Browning again represent a compromise. Some of the dramatic portraits are here because they are good ("My Last Duchess"), some because they seem very teachable ("The Bishop Orders His Tomb"), some because they are strangely interesting ("Johannes Agricola"). The selections from Yeats represent, except for the first two ballads, what I think are his best poems; that most of them are brief is only coincidental. By and large, I present Frost as a lyric poet, not as a Yankee philosopher—functions which in Frost are seldom neatly separable. With Eliot another kind of question arose. The poems on which his continuing reputation rests are undoubtedly "The Wasteland" and "The Four Quartets," and yet I have omitted them both. I think them too difficult for a beginning student unless he has been prepared for them by a careful reading in the early Eliot. And because it was not possible to represent decently both the early and the late Eliot in this collection, I represented the former, in the belief that getting students to understand the early Eliot is to get them close to understanding the later Eliot in particular—and modern poetry in general. After careful attention to the Prufrock and Sweeney poems, students are almost ready for "The Wasteland" on their own; and after understanding "The Journey of the Magi," they are almost ready for "The Four Quartets." I thought it best to do first things first.

The poetry itself is the most important thing in this collection. Critical helps for the reader are limited to a brief biographical sketch of each poet and rather full notes to the "hard" words in the poems. I thought it neither wise nor necessary to supply any elaborate critical apparatus. Such devices, even when ingenious, either encumber the student with the help he can get from his own wits, his instructor, and the rest of the class he is in, or they push him in the direction of constantly tailoring his responses to what he thinks is suitable for public exhibition. In the beginning, at any rate, I think the poem and the reader ought to be kept in a pure relationship with each other. If this purity results in ambiguity (and it often does), it is best to take up the problem then, not before the poem has been allowed to do its initial work with the reader.

For help in preparing the manuscript of *Twelve Poets,* I am grateful to John Brown of the University of California at Riverside. For advice and suggestions, I am grateful to Professors Donald Emery, William Matchett, and Arnold Stein of the University of Washington. A preliminary version of the table of contents was reviewed by Professors Samuel N. Bogorad, of the University of Vermont; John Ciardi, of Rutgers University; Albert R. Kitzhaber, of the University of Kansas; William Rossky, of Temple University; and Robert H. Sproat, of Boston University, all of whom made helpful suggestions.

GLENN LEGGETT

University of Washington
Seattle · November, 1957

CONTENTS

WILLIAM WORDSWORTH [*1770–1850*]

JOHN KEATS [*1795–1821*]

ROBERT BROWNING [*1812–1889*]

EDWIN ARLINGTON ROBINSON [*1869–1935*]

ROBERT FROST [*1875–1963*]

T. S. ELIOT [*1888–1965*]

TWELVE POETS

WILLIAM SHAKESPEARE

[1564-1616]

William Shakespeare was born in the village of Stratford-on-Avon, where his father was a prosperous glover. William probably attended grammar school in Stratford, and may have spent some of his youth as a country schoolmaster. At nineteen he was married to Anne Hathaway, who bore him three children: Susanna, Hamnet and Judith.

Shakespeare's career in London as actor, poet and playwright began early in the 1590's. His first published works were VENUS AND ADONIS *(1593) and* THE RAPE OF LUCRECE *(1594). His plays, which can be dated only tentatively, are traditionally grouped according to four "periods": the early, experimental period, in which he produced* THE COMEDY OF ERRORS *(1591),* THE TWO GENTLEMEN OF VERONA *(1592), the Henry VI plays (1590–92), and* TITUS ANDRONICUS *(1592); the period of the romantic comedies, which includes* A MID-SUMMER NIGHT'S DREAM *(1595),* AS YOU LIKE IT *(1599), and* TWELFTH NIGHT *(1600), as well as the Henry IV plays and* HENRY V *(1597–99); the "tragic" period, which saw the production of the great tragedies* HAMLET *(1601),* OTHELLO *(1604),* KING LEAR *(1605), and* MACBETH *(1606), and the "dark comedies"* TROILUS AND CRESSIDA *(1602),* ALL'S WELL THAT ENDS WELL *(1602), and* MEASURE FOR MEASURE *(1604); and the final period of the tragicomedies* CYMBELINE *(1610),* THE WINTER'S TALE *(1611), and* THE TEMPEST *(1611). While the Sonnets were not published until 1609, the majority of them apparently were written between 1593 and 1596.*

Both successful and highly esteemed in his own time, Shakespeare had earned enough money by 1597 to purchase "New Place," the largest house in Stratford; and it is believed that, when he finished his career in London, he spent the remaining years of his life in retirement in the village of his birth.

Two important standard works on Shakespeare are E. K. Chambers' WILLIAM SHAKESPEARE: A STUDY OF THE FACTS AND PROBLEMS

(1930) and Hazelton Spencer's THE ART AND LIFE OF WILLIAM SHAKESPEARE *(1940). Among good recent editions of Shakespeare's complete works are those of Neilson and Hill (1942) and Hardin Craig (1951).*

SONGS FROM THE PLAYS

WHO IS SILVIA?

Who is Silvia? what is she,
  That all our swains commend her?
Holy, fair, and wise is she;
  The heaven such grace did lend her,
That she might admirèd be. 5

Is she kind as she is fair?
  For beauty lives with kindness.
Love doth to her eyes repair
  To help him of his blindness,
And, being helped, inhabits there. 10

Then to Silvia let us sing
  That Silvia is excelling;
She excels each mortal thing
  Upon the dull earth dwelling:
To her let us garlands bring. 15

FROM *The Two Gentlemen of Verona* (IV, ii, 39)

TAKE, O, TAKE THOSE LIPS AWAY

Take, O, take those lips away,
  That so sweetly were forsworn;
And those eyes, the break of day,
  Lights that do mislead the morn:
But my kisses bring again, bring again, 5
Seals of love, but sealed in vain, sealed in vain.

FROM *Measure for Measure* (IV, i, 1)

SIGH NO MORE

Sigh no more, ladies, sigh no more,
  Men were deceivers ever;
One foot in sea, and one on shore,
  To one thing constant never.
Then sigh not so, but let them go, 5
  And be you blithe and bonny,
Converting all your sounds of woe
  Into "Hey nonny, nonny!"

Sing no more ditties, sing no moe
  Of dumps so dull and heavy; 10
The fraud of men was ever so,
  Since summer first was leavy.
Then sigh not so, but let them go,
  And be you blithe and bonny,
Converting all your sounds of woe 15
  Into "Hey nonny, nonny!"

FROM *Much Ado About Nothing* (II, iii, 64)

TELL ME WHERE IS FANCY BRED

Tell me where is fancy bred,
Or in the heart or in the head?
How begot, how nourishèd?
  Reply, reply.

It is engendered in the eyes, 5
With gazing fed; and fancy dies
In the cradle where it lies.
  Let us all ring fancy's knell:
  I'll begin it,—Ding, dong, bell.

FROM *The Merchant of Venice* (III, ii, 63)

1 *fancy:* infatuation.

COME AWAY, COME AWAY, DEATH

Come away, come away, death,
  And in sad cypress let me be laid;
Fly away, fly away, breath,
  I am slain by a fair cruel maid.
My shroud of white, stuck all with yew, 5
      Oh, prepare it!
My part of death, no one so true
      Did share it.

Not a flower, not a flower sweet,
  On my black coffin let there be strown; 10
Not a friend, not a friend greet
  My poor corpse, where my bones shall be thrown.
A thousand, thousand sighs to save,
      Lay me, oh, where
Sad true lover never find my grave 15
      To weep there.

FROM *Twelfth Night* (II, iv, 52)

2 *cypress:* coffin made of cypress. 7–8: No lover so true as I has ever died before.

FEAR NO MORE

Fear no more the heat o' the sun,
  Nor the furious winter's rages;
Thou thy worldly task has done,
  Home art gone, and ta'en thy wages:
Golden lads and girls all must, 5
As chimney-sweepers, come to dust.

Fear no more the frown o' the great;
  Thou art past the tyrant's stroke;
Care no more to clothe and eat;
  To thee the reed is as the oak: 10

The sceptre, learning, physic, must
All follow this, and come to dust.

Fear no more the lightning-flash,
  Nor the all-dreaded thunder-stone;
Fear not slander, censure rash; 15
  Thou hast finished joy and moan:
All lovers young, all lovers must
Consign to thee, and come to dust.

No exorciser harm thee!
Nor no witchcraft charm thee! 20
Ghost unlaid forbear thee!
Nothing ill come near thee!
Quiet consummation have,
And renownéd be thy grave!

FROM *Cymbeline* (IV, ii, 258)

11 *physic:* medicine. 18 *consign:* submit. 19 *exorciser:* conjuror.

FULL FATHOM FIVE

Full fathom five thy father lies,
  Of his bones are coral made;
Those are pearls that were his eyes;
  Nothing of him that doth fade,
But doth suffer a sea change 5
Into something rich and strange.
Sea-nymphs hourly ring his knell:
    Ding, dong.
Hark! Now I hear them—Ding, dong, bell.

FROM *The Tempest* (I, ii, 394)

1-17 addresses young man urging him to marry

SONNETS

2

WHEN FORTY WINTERS SHALL BESIEGE THY BROW

When forty winters shall besiege thy brow
And dig deep trenches in thy beauty's field,
Thy youth's proud livery, so gazed on now,
Will be a tattered weed, of small worth held;
Then being asked where all thy beauty lies, 5
Where all the treasure of thy lusty days,
To say, within thine own deep-sunken eyes,
Were an all-eating shame and thriftless praise.
How much more praise deserved thy beauty's use,
If thou couldst answer, "This fair child of mine 10
Shall sum my count, and make my old excuse,"
Proving his beauty by succession thine!
This were to be new-made when thou art old,
And see thy blood warm when thou feel'st it cold.

4 *weed:* garment.

3

LOOK IN THY GLASS, AND TELL THE FACE THOU VIEWEST

Look in thy glass, and tell the face thou viewest
Now is the time that face should form another,
Whose fresh repair if now thou not renewest,
Thou dost beguile the world, unbless some mother.
For where is she so fair whose uneared womb 5
Disdains the tillage of thy husbandry?
Or who is he so fond will be the tomb

5 *uneared:* unplowed. 7 *fond:* foolish.

Of his self-love, to stop posterity?
Thou art thy mother's glass, and she in thee
Calls back the lovely April of her prime; 10
So thou through windows of thine age shalt see,
Despite of wrinkles, this thy golden time.
But if thou live, remembered not to be,
Die single, and thine image dies with thee.

9 *glass:* looking-glass.

12

WHEN I DO COUNT THE CLOCK THAT TELLS THE TIME

When I do count the clock that tells the time,
And see the brave day sunk in hideous night;
When I behold the violet past prime,
And sable curls, all silvered o'er with white;
When lofty trees I see barren of leaves, 5
Which erst from heat did canopy the herd,
And summer's green all girded up in sheaves,
Borne on the bier with white and bristly beard—
Then of thy beauty do I question make,
That thou among the wastes of time must go, 10
Since sweets and beauties do themselves forsake
And die as fast as they see others grow:
And nothing 'gainst Time's scythe can make defense
Save breed, to brave him when he takes thee hence.

14 *breed:* children; *brave:* defy.

perfection is only momentary, Time will cause decay

15

WHEN I CONSIDER EVERYTHING THAT GROWS

When I consider everything that grows
Holds in perfection but a little moment,
That this huge stage presenteth naught but shows

Whereon the stars in secret influence comment;
When I perceive that men as plants increase, 5
Cheered and checked e'en by the selfsame sky,
Vaunt in their youthful sap, at height decrease,
And wear their brave state out of memory—
Then the conceit of this inconstant stay
Sets you most rich in youth before my sight, 10
Where wasteful Time debateth with Decay,
To change your day of youth to sullied night:
And, all in war with Time for love of you,
As he takes from you, I engraft you new.

9 *conceit:* thought. 14 *engraft:* give you new life (in my verse).

18

SHALL I COMPARE THEE TO A SUMMER'S DAY?

Shall I compare thee to a summer's day?
Thou art more lovely and more temperate;
Rough winds do shake the darling buds of May,
And summer's lease hath all too short a date;
Sometime too hot the eye of heaven shines, 5
And often is his gold complexion dimmed;
And every fair from fair sometime declines,
By chance, or nature's changing course untrimmed.
But thy eternal summer shall not fade,
Nor lose possession of that fair thou owest, 10
Nor shall death brag thou wander'st in his shade
When in eternal lines to time thou growest:
So long as men can breathe, or eyes can see,
So long lives this, and this gives life to thee.

8 *untrimmed:* stripped of its fairness. 10 *owest:* possess.

19

DEVOURING TIME, BLUNT THOU THE LION'S PAWS

Devouring Time, blunt thou the lion's paws,
And make the earth devour her own sweet brood;
Pluck the keen teeth from the fierce tiger's jaws,
And burn the long-lived phoenix in her blood;
Make glad and sorry seasons as thou fleet'st, 5
And do whate'er thou wilt, swift-footed Time,
To the wide world and all her fading sweets,
But I forbid thee one most heinous crime:
O, carve not with thy hours my love's fair brow,
Nor draw no lines there with thine antique pen; 10
Him in thy course untainted do allow
For beauty's pattern to succeeding men.
Yet, do thy worst, old Time; despite thy wrong,
My love shall in my verse ever live young.

4 *phoenix:* a legendary Arabian bird which was believed to live five hundred years, then die in fire and be reborn from its own ashes.

29

WHEN IN DISGRACE WITH FORTUNE AND MEN'S EYES

When in disgrace with fortune and men's eyes
I all alone beweep my outcast state,
And trouble deaf heaven with my bootless cries,
And look upon myself, and curse my fate,
Wishing me like to one more rich in hope, 5
Featured like him, like him with friends possessed,
Desiring this man's art, and that man's scope,
With what I most enjoy contented least—
Yet in these thoughts myself almost despising,

3 *bootless:* futile.

Haply I think on thee, and then my state, 10
Like to the lark at break of day arising
From sullen earth, sings hymns at heaven's gate;
For thy sweet love remembered such wealth brings
That then I scorn to change my state with kings.

30

WHEN TO THE SESSIONS OF SWEET SILENT THOUGHT

When to the sessions of sweet silent thought
I summon up remembrance of things past,
I sigh the lack of many a thing I sought,
And with old woes new wail my dear time's waste;
Then can I drown an eye unused to flow 5
For precious friends hid in death's dateless night,
And weep afresh love's long since cancelled woe,
And moan the expense of many a vanished sight;
Then can I grieve at grievances foregone,
And heavily from woe to woe tell o'er 10
The sad account of fore-bemoanèd moan,
Which I new pay as if not paid before.
But if the while I think on thee, dear friend,
All losses are restored and sorrows end.

33

FULL MANY A GLORIOUS MORNING HAVE I SEEN

Full many a glorious morning have I seen
Flatter the mountain-tops with sovereign eye,
Kissing with golden face the meadows green,
Gilding pale streams with heavenly alchemy,
Anon permit the basest clouds to ride 5
With ugly rack on his celestial face,
And from the forlorn world his visage hide,
Stealing unseen to west with this disgrace:

Even so my sun one early morn did shine
With all-triumphant splendour on my brow, 10
But, out! alack! he was but one hour mine;
The region cloud hath masked him from me now.
Yet him for this my love no whit disdaineth;
Suns of the world may stain when heaven's sun staineth.

12 *region cloud:* high cloud.

55

NOT MARBLE, NOR THE GILDED MONUMENTS

Not marble, nor the gilded monuments
Of princes, shall outlive this powerful rhyme,
But you shall shine more bright in these contents
Than unswept stone, besmeared with sluttish time.
When wasteful war shall statues overturn, 5
And broils root out the work of masonry,
Nor Mars his sword nor war's quick fire shall burn
The living record of your memory.
'Gainst death and all-oblivious enmity
Shall you pace forth; your praise shall still find room 10
Even in the eyes of all posterity
That wear this world out to the ending doom.
So, till the judgment that yourself arise,
You live in this, and dwell in lovers' eyes.

4 *unswept stone:* dusty grave-stone. 13 *judgment that:* Day of Judgment when.

64

WHEN I HAVE SEEN BY TIME'S FELL HAND DEFACED

When I have seen by Time's fell hand defaced
The rich-proud cost of outworn buried age;
When sometime lofty towers I see down-razed,

And brass eternal slave to mortal rage;
When I have seen the hungry ocean gain 5
Advantage on the kingdom of the shore,
And the firm soil win of the watery main,
Increasing store with loss, and loss with store;
When I have seen such interchange of state,
Or state itself confounded to decay, 10
Ruin hath taught me thus to ruminate:
That Time will come and take my love away.
This thought is as a death, which cannot choose
But weep to have that which it fears to lose.

9 *state:* condition.

65

SINCE BRASS, NOR STONE, NOR EARTH, NOR BOUNDLESS SEA

Since brass, nor stone, nor earth, nor boundless sea
But sad mortality o'ersways their power,
How with this rage shall beauty hold a plea,
Whose action is no stronger than a flower?
O, how shall summer's honey breath hold out 5
Against the wrackful siege of battering days,
When rocks impregnable are not so stout,
Nor gates of steel so strong, but Time decays?
O fearful meditation! where, alack,
Shall Time's best jewel from Time's chest lie hid? 10
Or what strong hand can hold his swift foot back?
Or who his spoil of beauty can forbid?
O, none, unless this miracle have might,
That in black ink my love may still shine bright.

1 *Since:* Since there is no.

73

THAT TIME OF YEAR THOU MAYST IN ME BEHOLD

That time of year thou mayst in me behold
When yellow leaves, or none, or few, do hang
Upon those boughs which shake against the cold,
Bare ruined choirs, where late the sweet birds sang;
In me thou see'st the twilight of such day 5
As after sunset fadeth in the west,
Which by and by black night doth take away,
Death's second self, that seals up all in rest.
In me thou see'st the glowing of such fire
That on the ashes of his youth doth lie, 10
As the death-bed whereon it must expire,
Consumed with that which it was nourished by.
This thou perceiv'st, which makes thy love more strong,
To love that well which thou must leave ere long.

10 *his:* its.

86

WAS IT THE PROUD FULL SAIL OF HIS GREAT VERSE

Was it the proud full sail of his great verse,
Bound for the prize of all too precious you,
That did my ripe thoughts in my brain inhearse,
Making their tomb the womb wherein they grew?
Was it his spirit, by spirits taught to write 5
Above a mortal pitch, that struck me dead?
No; neither he, nor his compeers by night
Giving him aid, my verse astonishèd.
He, nor that affable familiar ghost
Which nightly gulls him with intelligence, 10

1 *his:* some scholars believe that the rival poet was George Chapman, another Elizabethan poet-dramatist. 3 *inhearse:* bury. 7 *compeers:* associates. 8 *astonished:* dismayed. 9 *ghost:* spirit. 10 *gulls:* cheats; *intelligence:* news.

As victors of my silence cannot boast;
I was not sick of any fear from thence:
But when your countenance filled up his line,
Then lacked I matter; that enfeebled mine.

87

FAREWELL! THOU ART TOO DEAR FOR MY POSSESSING

Farewell! thou art too dear for my possessing,
And, like enough, thou know'st thy estimate:
The charter of thy worth gives thee releasing;
My bonds in thee are all determinate.
For how do I hold thee but by thy granting? 5
And for that riches where is my deserving?
The cause of this fair gift in me is wanting,
And so my patent back again is swerving.
Thyself thou gav'st, thy own worth then not knowing,
Or me, to whom thou gav'st it, else mistaking; 10
So thy great gift, upon misprision growing,
Comes home again, on better judgment making.
Thus have I had thee, as a dream doth flatter,
In sleep a king, but waking, no such matter.

2 *estimate:* worth. 3 *charter:* right. 4 *determinate:* expired. 8 *patent:* privilege. 11 *upon misprision growing:* having been founded upon a mistake.

98

FROM YOU HAVE I BEEN ABSENT IN THE SPRING

From you have I been absent in the spring,
When proud-pied April, dressed in all his trim,
Hath put a spirit of youth in everything,
That heavy Saturn laughed and leaped with him.
Yet nor the lays of birds, nor the sweet smell 5

2 *proud-pied:* proud of its many colors.

Of different flowers in odor and in hue,
Could make me any summer's story tell,
Or from their proud lap pluck them where they grew;
Nor did I wonder at the lily's white,
Nor praise the deep vermilion in the rose; 10
They were but sweet, but figures of delight,
Drawn after you, you pattern of all those.
Yet seemed it winter still, and, you away,
As with your shadow, I with these did play.

106

WHEN IN THE CHRONICLE OF WASTED TIME

When in the chronicle of wasted time
I see descriptions of the fairest wights,
And beauty making beautiful old rhyme
In praise of ladies dead and lovely knights,
Then, in the blazon of sweet beauty's best, 5
Of hand, of foot, of lip, of eye, of brow,
I see their antique pen would have expressed
Even such a beauty as you master now.
So all their praises are but prophecies
Of this our time, all you prefiguring; 10
And, for they looked but with divining eyes,
They had not skill enough your worth to sing:
For we, which now behold these present days,
Have eyes to wonder, but lack tongues to praise.

2 *wights:* warriors. 5 *blazon:* technically, a description of a coat of arms; here, simply "description." 8 *master:* possess. 11 *for:* because.

109

O, NEVER SAY THAT I WAS FALSE OF HEART

O, never say that I was false of heart,
Though absence seemed my flame to qualify.
As easy might I from myself depart

As from my soul, which in thy breast doth lie;
That is my home of love: if I have ranged, 5
Like him that travels, I return again;
Just to the time, not with the time exchanged,
So that myself bring water for my stain.
Never believe, though in my nature reigned
All frailties that besiege all kinds of blood, 10
That it could so preposterously be stained,
To leave for nothing all thy sum of good;
For nothing this wide universe I call,
Save thou, my rose; in it thou art my all.

7 *Just to the time:* Just at the proper time; *exchanged:* changed. 8 *stain:* i. e., his absence.

116

LET ME NOT TO THE MARRIAGE OF TRUE MINDS

Let me not to the marriage of true minds
Admit impediments. Love is not love
Which alters when it alteration finds,
Or bends with the remover to remove;
O, no! it is an ever-fixèd mark 5
That looks on tempests and is never shaken;
It is the star to every wandering bark,
Whose worth's unknown, although his height be taken.
Love's not Time's fool, though rosy lips and cheeks
Within his bending sickle's compass come; 10
Love alters not with his brief hours and weeks,
But bears it out even to the edge of doom.
If this be error, and upon me proved,
I never writ, nor no man ever loved.

4: Or transfers its affections when its lover has transferred his. 5 *mark:* landmark, as for mariners. 8 *Whose:* i. e., the star's. 12 *doom:* Doomsday.

127

IN THE OLD AGE BLACK WAS NOT COUNTED FAIR

In the old age black was not counted fair,
Or if it were, it bore not beauty's name;
But now is black beauty's successive heir,
And beauty slandered with a bastard's shame.
For, since each hand hath put on nature's power, 5
Fairing the foul with art's false borrowed face,
Sweet beauty hath no name, no holy bower,
But is profaned, if not lives in disgrace.
Therefore my mistress' brows are raven black,
Her eyes so suited, and they mourners seem 10
At such who, not born fair, no beauty lack,
Sland'ring creation with a false esteem:
Yet so they mourn, becoming of their woe,
That every tongue says beauty should look so.

1. *black:* a dark complexion. 4 *beauty:* blonde beauty (beauty is said to be "slandered" because it was produced by cosmetics). 10 *so suited:* matching (her eyebrows). 11 *such who, not born fair, no beauty lack:* ugly women who beautify themselves artificially.

130

MY MISTRESS' EYES ARE NOTHING LIKE THE SUN

My mistress' eyes are nothing like the sun;
Coral is far more red than her lips' red:
If snow be white, why then her breasts are dun;
If hairs be wires, black wires grow on her head.
I have seen roses damasked, red and white, 5
But no such roses see I in her cheeks;
And in some perfumes is there more delight
Than in the breath that from my mistress reeks.
I love to hear her speak, yet well I know

5 *damasked:* mingled white and red.

That music hath a far more pleasing sound; 10
I grant I never saw a goddess go,
My mistress, when she walks, treads on the ground.
And yet, by heaven, I think my love as rare
As any she belied with false compare.

138

WHEN MY LOVE SWEARS THAT SHE IS MADE OF TRUTH

When my love swears that she is made of truth,
I do believe her, though I know she lies,
That she might think me some untutored youth,
Unlearnèd in the world's false subtleties.
Thus vainly thinking that she thinks me young, 5
Although she knows my days are past the best,
Simply I credit her false-speaking tongue;
On both sides thus is simple truth supprest.
But wherefore says she not she is unjust?
And wherefore say not I that I am old? 10
O, love's best habit is in seeming trust,
And age in love loves not to have years told:
Therefore I lie with her and she with me,
And in our faults by lies we flattered be.

7 *Simply I credit:* I wholly believe. 9 *unjust:* untrue. 11 *habit:* garment.

146

POOR SOUL, THE CENTER OF MY SINFUL EARTH

Poor soul, the center of my sinful earth,
Thrall to these rebel powers that thee array,
Why dost thou pine within and suffer dearth,
Painting thy outward walls so costly gay?
Why so large cost, having so short a lease, 5

Dost thou upon thy fading mansion spend?
Shall worms, inheritors of this excess,
Eat up thy charge? Is this thy body's end?
Then, soul, live thou upon thy servant's loss,
And let that pine to aggravate thy store; 10
Buy terms divine in selling hours of dross;
Within be fed, without be rich no more:
So shalt thou feed on Death, that feeds on men,
And Death once dead, there's no more dying then.

8 *charge:* expense. 10 *aggravate:* increase.

147

MY LOVE IS AS A FEVER, LONGING STILL

My love is as a fever, longing still
For that which longer nurseth the disease,
Feeding on that which doth preserve the ill,
The uncertain sickly appetite to please.
My reason, the physician to my love, 5
Angry that his prescriptions are not kept,
Hath left me, and I desperate now approve
Desire is death, which physic did except.
Past cure I am, now reason is past care,
And frantic-mad with evermore unrest; 10
My thoughts and my discourse as madmen's are,
At random from the truth vainly expressed:
For I have sworn thee fair, and thought thee bright,
Who art as black as hell, as dark as night.

7 *approve:* demonstrate (prove) through experience. 8: Desire which refuses medicine is death.

JOHN DONNE

[1573–1631]

John Donne was born in London of well-to-do Roman Catholic parents. Prevented by his Catholicism from receiving a degree from either Oxford or Cambridge—at both of which he studied—Donne became a law student at Lincoln's Inn, but never practiced law. His early witty and amorous lyrics, such as "The Good-Morrow," "The Flea," and "The Bait," were written and circulated among his friends during the 1590's, as were his "Satires" and "Elegies." A voyage to the Azores with the Earl of Essex in 1597 gave him the subject for "The Storm" and "The Calm," which were sent as verse letters to Donne's friend Christopher Brooke.

Having become secretary to Sir Thomas Egerton, Lord Keeper of the Great Seal, Donne secretly married Sir Thomas's niece Anne More (1601), and was briefly imprisoned by his indignant father-in-law. Donne's poem "The Canonization" may be read as Donne's attempt to justify this marriage, and at least two of his poems—"Sweetest Love, I Do Not Go" and "A Valediction Forbidding Mourning"—are believed to have been addressed to his wife.

From the date of his marriage until 1615, Donne sought unsuccessfully to gain preferment, and was largely dependent upon the generosity of various patrons. In 1615 he became a priest of the Anglican Church, and his famous sermons eventually earned him the position of Dean of St. Paul's (1621). The most intense statement of Donne's religious feeling is to be found in his "Holy Sonnets," most of which were apparently written toward the close of his life. His body was buried in St. Paul's Cathedral.

The chief scholarly edition of Donne is the two-volume edition published by Sir Herbert Grierson in 1912; an abridged one-volume edition of this work was published in 1933. John Hayward's edition of Donne's COMPLETE POETRY AND SELECTED PROSE *(1931) is an inexpensive edition with modernized spelling. Among the important works on Donne are Hugh I'A. Fausset's* JOHN DONNE: A STUDY IN

DISCORD (*1925*), A GARLAND FOR JOHN DONNE: 1631–1931, *edited by Theodore Spencer* (*1931*), *Doniphan Louthan's* THE POETRY OF JOHN DONNE (*1951*), *and Clay Hunt's* DONNE'S POETRY: ESSAYS IN LITERARY ANALYSIS (*1954*).

THE GOOD-MORROW

I wonder, by my troth, what thou and I
Did till we loved? Were we not weaned till then,
But sucked on country pleasures, childishly?
Or snorted we in the Seven Sleepers' den?
'Twas so; but this, all pleasures fancies be. 5
If ever any beauty I did see,
Which I desired, and got, 'twas but a dream of thee.

And now good morrow to our waking souls,
Which watch not one another out of fear;
For love all love of other sights controls, 10
And makes one little room an everywhere.
Let sea-discoverers to new worlds have gone;
Let maps to other, worlds on worlds have shown;
Let us possess one world; each hath one, and is one.

My face in thine eye, thine in mine appears, 15
And true plain hearts do in the faces rest;
Where can we find two better hemispheres
Without sharp north, without declining west?
Whatever dies was not mixed equally;
If our two loves be one, or thou and I 20
Love so alike that none do slacken, none can die.

4 *Seven Sleepers' den:* the cave in which seven Christian youths took refuge during the persecutions of Decius and, according to legend, slept for more than two hundred years. 5 *but:* except for. 19–21: here Donne alludes to the medieval belief that death comes to earthly creatures as a result of the imperfect and inharmonious combination of their elements—as opposed to the perfect and harmonious combination of elements in spiritual entities.

unfaithfulness of women

GO AND CATCH A FALLING STAR

Go and catch a falling star,
Get with child a mandrake root,
Tell me where all past years are,
Or who cleft the devil's foot,
Teach me to hear mermaids singing, 5
Or to keep off envy's stinging,
And find
What wind
Serves to advance an honest mind.

If thou be'st born to strange sights, 10
Things invisible to see,
Ride ten thousand days and nights,
Till Age snow white hairs on thee;
Thou, when thou return'st, wilt tell me
All strange wonders that befell thee, 15
And swear
No where
Lives a woman true and fair.

If thou find'st one, let me know;
Such a pilgrimage were sweet; 20
Yet do not; I would not go,
Though at next door we might meet.
Though she were true when you met her,
And last till you write your letter,
Yet she 25
Will be
False, ere I come, to two or three.

2 *mandrake root:* because of its forked shape, the root of the mandrake suggested the human body.

THE SUN RISING

Busy old fool, unruly Sun,
Why dost thou thus,
Through windows and through curtains, call on us?

Must to thy motions lovers' seasons run?
Saucy pedantic wretch, go chide 5
Late schoolboys and sour 'prentices,
Go tell court-huntsmen that the King will ride,
Call country ants to harvest offices;
Love, all alike, no season knows, nor clime,
Nor hours, days, months, which are the rags of time. 10

Thy beams, so reverend and strong
Why should'st thou think?
I could eclipse and cloud them with a wink,
But that I would not lose her sight so long.
If her eyes have not blinded thine, 15
Look, and tomorrow late, tell me,
Whether both the Indias of spice and mine
Be where thou left'st them, or lie here with me.
Ask for those Kings whom thou saw'st yesterday,
And thou shalt hear, All here in one bed lay. 20

She is all States, and all Princes, I,
Nothing else is.
Princes do but play us; compared to this,
All honor's mimic, all wealth alchemy.
Thou, sun, art half as happy as we, 25
In that the world's contracted thus;
Thine age asks ease, and since thy duties be
To warm the world, that's done in warming us.
Shine here to us, and thou art everywhere;
This bed thy center is, these walls thy sphere. 30

17 *mine:* mines of precious stones and minerals.

BREAK OF DAY

'Tis true, 'tis day; what though it be?
Oh, wilt thou therefore rise from me?
Why should we rise because 'tis light?
Did we lie down because 'twas night?
Love which in spite of darkness brought us hither 5
Should, in despite of light, keep us together.

Light hath no tongue, but is all eye;
If it could speak as well as spy,
  This were the worst that it could say:
  That, being well, I fain would stay, 10
And that I loved my heart and honor so,
That I would not from him that had them go.

Must business thee from hence remove?
Oh, that's the worst disease of love;
  The poor, the foul, the false, love can 15
  Admit, but not the busied man.
He which hath business and makes love, doth do
Such wrong as when a married man doth woo.

THE INDIFFERENT

I can love both fair and brown;
Her whom abundance melts, and her whom want betrays;
Her who loves loneness best, and her who masks and plays;
Her whom the country formed, and whom the town;
Her who believes, and her who tries; 5
Her who still weeps with spongy eyes,
And her who is dry cork and never cries.
I can love her, and her, and you, and you;
I can love any, so she be not true.

Will no other vice content you? 10
Will it not serve your turn to do as did your mothers?
Or have you all old vices spent, and now would find out others?
Or doth a fear that men are true torment you?
O, we are not, be not you so;
Let me, and do you, twenty know. 15
Rob me, but bind me not, and let me go.
Must I, who came to travail thorough you,
Grow your fixed subject because you are true?

Venus heard me sigh this song,
And by love's sweetest part, variety, she swore 20

5 *tries:* tests. 17 *thorough:* through.

She heard not this till now, and that it should be so no more.
She went, examined, and returned ere long,
And said, "Alas! some two or three
Poor heretics in love there be,
Which think to 'stablish dangerous constancy. 25
But I have told them, 'Since you be true,
You shall be true to them who are false to you.' "

THE CANONIZATION

For God's sake hold your tongue, and let me love;
Or chide my palsy, or my gout;
My five gray hairs, or ruined fortune flout;
With wealth your state, your mind with arts improve,
Take you a course, get you a place, 5
Observe His Honour, or His Grace,
Or the King's real, or his stampèd face
Contemplate; what you will, approve,
So you will let mc love.

Alas, alas, who's injured by my love? 10
What merchant's ships have my sighs drowned?
Who says my tears have overflowed his ground?
When did my colds a forward spring remove?
When did the heats which my veins fill
Add one more to the plaguey Bill? 15
Soldiers find wars, and lawyers find out still
Litigious men, which quarrels move,
Though she and I do love.

Call us what you will, we are made such by love;
Call her one, me another fly, 20
We are tapers too, and at our own cost die,
And we in us find the eagle and the dove.
The phoenix riddle hath more wit

7 *stamped:* his image on a coin. 13 *colds a forward spring remove:* chills delay an early spring. 15 *Bill:* the weekly list of victims of the plague. 21 *tapers:* candles. 22 *the eagle and the dove:* symbolic of wisdom and gentleness. 23 *phoenix riddle:* see note to Shakespeare's Sonnet 19, line 4.

By us; we two being one, are it.
So to one neutral thing both sexes fit; 25
We die and rise the same, and prove
Mysterious by this love.

We can die by it, if not live by love;
And if unfit for tombs and hearse
Our legend be, it will be fit for verse; 30
And if no piece of chronicle we prove,
We'll build in sonnets pretty rooms;
As well a well-wrought urn becomes
The greatest ashes, as half-acre tombs,
And by these hymns, all shall approve 35
Us canonized for love,

And thus invoke us: "You whom reverend love
Made one another's hermitage;
You, to whom love was peace, that now is rage;
Who did the whole world's soul contract, and drove 40
Into the glasses of your eyes
(So made such mirrors and such spies
That they did all to you epitomize)
Countries, towns, courts: beg from above
A pattern of your love!" 45

31 *chronicle:* history. 33 *becomes:* is appropriate for.

SWEETEST LOVE, I DO NOT GO

Sweetest love, I do not go
For weariness of thee,
Nor in hope the world can show
A fitter love for me;
But since that I 5
Must die at last, 'tis best
To use myself in jest
Thus by feigned deaths to die.

Yesternight the sun went hence,
And yet is here today; 10

He hath no desire nor sense,
  Nor half so short a way:
    Then fear not me,
But believe that I shall make
Speedier journeys, since I take 15
  More wings and spurs than he.

O how feeble is man's power,
  That if good fortune fall,
Cannot add another hour,
  Nor a lost hour recall! 20
    But come bad chance,
And we join it to our strength,
And we teach it art and length,
  Itself o'er us to advance.

When thou sigh'st, thou sigh'st not wind, 25
  But sigh'st my soul away;
When thou weep'st, unkindly kind,
  My life's blood doth decay.
    It cannot be
That thou lov'st me, as thou say'st, 30
If in thine my life thou waste,
  That art the best of me.

Let not thy divining heart
  Forethink me any ill;
Destiny may take thy part, 35
  And may thy tears fulfil;
    But think that we
Are but turned aside to sleep;
They who one another keep
  Alive, ne'er parted be. 40

COMMUNITY

Good we must love, and must hate ill,
For ill is ill, and good good still,
  But there are things indifferent,
Which we may neither hate, nor love,

But one, and then another prove, 5
As we shall find our fancy bent.

If then at first wise Nature had
Made women either good or bad,
Then some we might hate, and some choose;
But since she did them so create 10
That we may neither love, nor hate,
Only this rests: All, all may use.

If they were good it would be seen:
Good is as visible as green,
And to all eyes itself betrays: 15
If they were bad, they could not last,
Bad doth itself and others waste;
So, they deserve nor blame, nor praise.

But they are ours as fruits are ours,
He that but tastes, he that devours, 20
And he that leaves all, doth as well:
Changed loves are but changed sorts of meat,
And when he hath the kernel eat,
Who doth not fling away the shell?

THE FLEA

Mark but this flea, and mark in this
How little that which thou deny'st me is;
It sucked me first, and now sucks thee,
And in this flea our two bloods mingled be;
Thou know'st that this cannot be said 5
A sin, nor shame, nor loss of maidenhead;
Yet this enjoys before it woo,
And pampered swells with one blood made of two,
And this, alas, is more than we would do.

Oh stay, three lives in one flea spare, 10
Where we almost, yea, more than married are.
This flea is you and I, and this
Our marriage bed, and marriage temple is;

Though parents grudge, and you, we are met
And cloistered in these living walls of jet. 15
Though use make you apt to kill me,
Let not to that, self-murder added be,
And sacrilege, three sins in killing three.

Cruel and sudden, hast thou since
Purpled thy nail in blood of innocence? 20
Wherein could this flea guilty be,
Except in that drop which it sucked from thee?
Yet thou triumph'st and say'st that thou
Find'st not thyself, nor me the weaker now.
'Tis true. Then learn how false fears be: 25
Just so much honor, when thou yield'st to me,
Will waste, as this flea's death took life from thee.

A NOCTURNAL UPON SAINT LUCY'S DAY, BEING THE SHORTEST DAY

'Tis the year's midnight, and it is the day's,
Lucy's, who scarce seven hours herself unmasks;
The sun is spent, and now his flasks
Send forth light squibs, no constant rays;
The whole world's sap is sunk; 5
The general balm the hydroptic earth hath drunk,
Whither, as to the bed's feet, life is shrunk,
Dead and interred; yet all these seem to laugh,
Compared with me, who am their epitaph.

Study me then, you who shall lovers be 10
At the next world (that is, at the next spring),
For I am every dead thing
In whom love wrought new alchemy.
For his art did express
A quintessence even from nothingness, 15
From dull privations, and lean emptiness;
He ruined me, and I am re-begot
Of absence, darkness, death: things which are not.

All others from all things draw all that's good,
Life, soul, form, spirit, whence they being have; 20
I, by love's limbec, am the grave
Of all that's nothing. Oft a flood
Have we two wept, and so
Drowned the whole world, us two; oft did we grow
To be two chaoses, when we did show 25
Care to aught else; and often absences
Withdrew our souls, and made us carcases.

But I am by her death (which word wrongs her)
Of the first nothing the elixir grown;
Were I a man, that I were one 30
I needs must know; I should prefer,
If I were any beast,
Some ends, some means; yea plants, yea stones detest
And love; all, all some properties invest;
If I an ordinary nothing were, 35
As shadow, a light and body must be here.

But I am none; nor will my sun renew.
You lovers, for whose sake the lesser sun
At this time to the Goat is run
To fetch new lust, and give it you, 40
Enjoy your summer all;
Since she enjoys her long night's festival,
Let me prepare towards her, and let me call
This hour her vigil, and her eve, since this
Both the year's and the day's deep midnight is. 45

21 *limbec:* alembic, still. 39 *Goat:* Capricorn.

A VALEDICTION FORBIDDING MOURNING

As virtuous men pass mildly away,
And whisper to their souls to go,
Whilst some of their sad friends do say,
"The breath goes now," and some say, "No,"

So let us melt, and make no noise, 5
  No tear-floods, nor sigh-tempests move;
'Twere profanation of our joys
  To tell the laity our love.

Moving of the earth brings harms and fears,
  Men reckon what it did, and meant; 10
But trepidation of the spheres,
  Though greater far, is innocent.

Dull sublunary lovers' love
  —Whose soul is sense—cannot admit
Absence, because it doth remove 15
  Those things which elemented it.

But we by a love so much refined
  That ourselves know not what it is,
Inter-assurèd of the mind,
  Care less eyes, lips and hands to miss. 20

Our two souls therefore, which are one,
  Though I must go, endure not yet
A breach, but an expansion,
  Like gold to airy thinness beat.

If they be two, they are two so 25
  As stiff twin compasses are two;
Thy soul, the fixed foot, makes no show
  To move, but doth, if the other do.

And though it in the center sit,
  Yet, when the other far doth roam, 30
It leans, and hearkens after it,
  And grows erect, as that comes home.

Such wilt thou be to me, who must
  Like the other foot, obliquely run;
Thy firmness draws my circle just, 35
  And makes me end, where I begun.

11–12: a reference to the notion of the Ptolemaic astronomers that the "innocent" variation in the date of the equinoxes was caused by the motion ("trepidation") of the ninth sphere. 16 *elemented:* constituted.

THE ECSTASY

Where, like a pillow on a bed,
  A pregnant bank swelled up to rest
The violet's reclining head,
  Sat we two, one another's best.
Our hands were firmly cèmented 5
  With a fast balm, which thence did spring;
Our eye-beams twisted, and did thread
  Our eyes upon one double string;
So to entergraft our hands, as yet
  Was all the means to make us one, 10
And pictures in our eyes to get
  Was all our propagation.
As, 'twixt two equal armies, fate
  Suspends uncertain victory,
Our souls, which to advance their state 15
  Were gone out, hung 'twixt her and me.
And whilst our souls negotiate there,
  We like sepulchral statues lay;
All day, the same our postures were,
  And we said nothing, all the day. 20
If any, so by love refined
  That he soul's language understood,
And by good love were grown all mind,
  Within convenient distance stood,
He, though he knew not which soul spake, 25
  Because both meant, both spake the same,
Might thence a new concoction take
  And part far purer than he came.
This ecstasy doth unperplex,
  We said, and tell us what we love: 30
We see by this it was not sex,
  We see we saw not what did move;
But as all several souls contain
  Mixture of things, they know not what,
Love these mixed souls doth mix again 35
  And makes both one, each this and that.
A single violet transplant,
  The strength, the color, and the size,

All which before was poor and scant,
  Redoubles still, and multiplies. 40
When love with one another so
  Interinanimates two souls,
That abler soul, which thence doth flow,
  Defects of loneliness controls.
We then, who are this new soul, know 45
  Of what we are composed, and made,
For the atomies of which we grow
  Are souls, whom no change can invade.
But O alas! so long, so far,
  Our bodies why do we forbear? 50
They are ours, though they are not we; we are
  The intelligences, they the spheres.
We owe them thanks, because they thus
  Did us, to us, at first convey,
Yielded their forces, sense, to us, 55
  Nor are dross to us, but allay.
On man heaven's influence works not so,
  But that it first imprints the air;
So soul into the soul may flow,
  Though it to body first repair. 60
As our blood labors to beget
  Spirits, as like souls as it can,
Because such fingers need to knit
  That subtle knot, which makes us man,
So must pure lovers' souls descend 65
  To affections, and to faculties,
Which sense may reach and apprehend;
  Else a great prince in prison lies.
To our bodies turn we then, that so
  Weak men on love revealed may look; 70
Love's mysteries in souls do grow,
  But yet the body is his book.
And if some lover, such as we,
  Have heard this dialogue of one,
Let him still mark us, he shall see 75
  Small change when we're to bodies gone.

33–48: see note to "The Good-Morrow," lines 19–21. 47 *atomies:* atoms. 51–52: an allusion to the medieval theory that each of the "spheres" was controlled and moved by an "intelligence," or angel. 56 *allay:* alloy.

LOVE'S DEITY

I long to talk with some old lover's ghost
  Who died before the god of love was born;
I cannot think that he who then loved most,
  Sunk so low as to love one which did scorn.
But since this god produced a destiny 5
And that vice-nature, custom, lets it be,
  I must love her that loves not me.

Sure, they which made him god, meant not so much,
  Nor he in his young godhead practiced it.
But when an even flame two hearts did touch, 10
  His office was indulgently to fit
Actives to passives. Correspondency
Only, his subject was; it cannot be
  Love, till I love her who loves me.

But every modern god will not extend 15
  His vast prerogative as far as Jove.
To rage, to lust, to write to, to commend,
  All is the purlieu of the god of love.
O! were we wakened by this tyranny
To ungod this child again, it could not be 20
  I should love her who loves not me.

Rebel and atheist too, why murmur I,
  As though I felt the worse that love could do?
Love may make me leave loving, or might try
  A deeper plague, to make her love me too; 25
Which, since she loves before, I'm loath to see.
Falsehood is worse than hate; and that must be,
  If she whom I love, should love me.

26 *loves before:* i. e., already loves another.

THE FUNERAL

Whoever comes to shroud me, do not harm
Nor question much
That subtle wreath of hair about mine arm;
The mystery, the sign you must not touch,
For 'tis my outward soul, 5
Viceroy to that which, unto heaven being gone,
Will leave this to control
And keep these limbs, her provinces, from dissolution.

For if the sinewy thread my brain lets fall
Through every part 10
Can tie those parts, and make me one of all,
Those hairs, which upward grew, and strength and art
Have from a better brain,
Can better do it: except she meant that I
By this should know my pain, 15
As prisoners then are manacled, when they're condemned to die.

Whate'er she meant by it, bury it with me,
For since I am
Love's martyr, it might breed idolatry
If into other hands these reliques came. 20
As it was humility
To afford to it all that a soul can do,
So it is some bravery
That, since you would have none of me, I bury some of you.

6 *Viceroy:* i. e., acting as representative.

THE RELIC

When my grave is broke up again
Some second guest to entertain

Donne uses the term "relic" in its ecclesiastical sense, to denote a part of the body of a saint which is preserved and venerated as a memento of the saint.

(For graves have learned that womanhead
To be to more than one a bed),
And he that digs it, spies 5
A bracelet of bright hair about the bone,
Will he not let us alone,
And think that there a loving couple lies,
Who thought that this device might be some way
To make their souls, at the last busy day, 10
Meet at this grave, and make a little stay?

If this fall in a time, or land,
Where mis-devotion doth command,
Then he that digs us up will bring
Us to the Bishop and the King, 15
To make us Relics; then
Thou shalt be a Mary Magdalen, and I
A something else thereby;
All women shall adore us, and some men;
And since at such time, miracles are sought, 20
I would have that age by this paper taught
What miracles we harmless lovers wrought.

First, we loved well and faithfully,
Yet knew not what we loved, nor why;
Difference of sex no more we knew 25
Than our guardian angels do;
Coming and going, we
Perchance might kiss, but not between those meals;
Our hands ne'er touched the seals
Which nature, injured by late law, sets free: 30
These miracles we did; but now, alas,
All measure, and all language, I should pass,
Should I tell what a miracle she was.

3 *womanhead:* womanly trick. 13 *misdevotion:* i. e., Roman Catholicism, which approved of the preservation and veneration of relics, as the English Protestants did not.

FALL OF A WALL

Under an undermined, and shot-bruised wall
A too-bold captain perished by the fall,
Whose brave misfortune happiest men envied,
That had a town for tomb, his bones to hide.

ELEGY 17

On His Mistress

By our first strange and fatal interview,
By all desires which thereof did ensue,
By our long starving hopes, by that remorse
Which my words' masculine persuasive force
Begot in thee, and by the memory 5
Of hurts which spies and rivals threatened me,
I calmly beg; but by thy father's wrath,
By all pains which want and divorcement hath,
I conjure thee; and all the oaths which I
And thou have sworn to seal joint constancy, 10
Here I unswear, and overswear them thus:
Thou shalt not love by ways so dangerous.
Temper, O fair love, love's impetuous rage,
Be my true mistress still, not my feigned page;
I'll go, and by thy kind leave, leave behind 15
Thee, only worthy to nurse in my mind
Thirst to come back; oh, if thou die before,
My soul from other lands to thee shall soar.
Thy (else almighty) beauty cannot move
Rage from the seas, nor thy love teach them love, 20
Nor tame wild Boreas' harshness; thou hast read
How roughly he in pieces shiverèd
Fair Orithea, whom he swore he loved.
Fall ill or good, 'tis madness to have proved

21–23: Boreas, the north wind, fell in love with the nymph Orithea; unable to play the part of a gentle lover, he seized Orithea and carried her away.

Dangers unurged; feed on this flattery, 25
That absent lovers one in the other be.
Dissemble nothing, not a boy, nor change
Thy body's habit, nor mind's; be not strange
To thyself only; all will spy in thy face
A blushing womanly discovering grace. 30
Richly clothed apes are called apes; and as soon
Eclipsed as bright, we call the moon the moon.
Men of France, changeable chameleons,
Spitals of diseases, shops of fashions,
Love's fuellers, and the rightest company 35
Of players which upon the world's stage be,
Will quickly know thee, and no less, alas!
The indifferent Italian, as we pass
His warm land, well content to think thee page,
Will hunt thee with such lust and hideous rage 40
As Lot's fair guests were vexed. But none of these,
Nor spongy hydroptic Dutch shall thee displease,
If thou stay here. Oh, stay here! for, for thee,
England is only a worthy gallery
To walk in expectation, till from thence 45
Our greatest King call thee to his presence.
When I am gone, dream me some happiness,
Nor let thy looks our long hid love confess,
Nor praise, nor dispraise me, nor bless nor curse
Openly love's force, nor in bed fright thy nurse 50
With midnight's startings, crying out, "Oh, oh,
Nurse, oh, my love is slain, I saw him go
O'er the white Alps alone; I saw him, I,
Assailed, fight, taken, stabbed, bleed, fall, and die."
Augur me better chance, except dread Jove 55
Think it enough for me to have had thy love.

34 *Spitals:* hospitals. 41 *As Lot's fair guests were vexed:* see Genesis 19.
55 *Augur:* foresee; *except:* unless.

THE CALM

Our storm is past, and that storm's tyrannous rage,
A stupid calm, but nothing it, doth 'suage.
The fable is inverted, and far more
A block afflicts, now, than a stork before.
Storms chafe, and soon wear out themselves, or us; 5
In calms, Heaven laughs to see us languish thus.
As steady as I can wish that my thoughts were,
Smooth as my mistress' glass, or what shines there,
The sea is now. And, as the isles which we
Seek, when we can move, our ships rooted be. 10
As water did in storms, now pitch runs out:
As lead, when a fired church becomes one spout;
And all our beauty, and our trim, decays,
Like courts removing, or like ended plays.
The fighting place now seamen's rags supply; 15
And all the tackling is a frippery.
No use of lanthorns; and in one place lay
Feathers and dust, today and yesterday.
Earth's hollownesses, which the world's lungs are,
Have no more wind than the upper vault of air. 20
We can nor lost friends, nor sought foes recover,
But meteor-like, save that we move not, hover.
Only the calenture together draws
Dear friends, which meet dead in great fishes' jaws;
And on the hatches as on altars lies 25
Each one, his own priest and own sacrifice.
Who live, that miracle do multiply
Where walkers in hot ovens do not die.
If, in despite of these, we swim, that hath
No more refreshing than our brimstone bath, 30
But from the sea into the ship we turn,
Like parboiled wretches, on the coals to burn.

4 *block:* the log in Aesop's fable of King Log and King Stork. 16 *frippery:* a selling-place for cast-off clothes. 17 *lanthorns:* lanterns, used by each ship to indicate its position to other ships in the fleet. 23 *calenture:* a tropical madness which drove men to leap into the sea. 28: see Daniel 3.

Like Bajazet encaged, the shepherds' scoff,
Or like slack-sinewed Samson, his hair off,
Languish our ships. Now, as a myriad 35
Of ants, durst the emperor's loved snake invade,
The crawling galleys, sea-gaols, finny chips,
Might brave our pinnaces, now bed-rid ships.
Whether a rotten state, and hope of gain,
Or to disuse me from the queasy pain 40
Of being beloved, and loving, or the thirst
Of honor, or fair death, out-pushed me first,
I lose my end; for here, as well as I,
A desperate may live, and a coward die.
Stag, dog, and all which from or towards flies, 45
Is paid with life, or prey, or doing, dies.
Fate grudges us all, and doth subtly lay
A scourge, 'gainst which we all forget to pray;
He that at sea prays for more wind, as well
Under the poles may beg cold, heat in hell. 50
What are we then? How little more, alas,
Is man now, than before he was? He was
Nothing; for us, we are for nothing fit;
Chance or ourselves still disproportion it.
We have no power, no will, no sense; I lie, 55
I should not then thus feel this misery.

33 *Bajazet:* an emperor who is imprisoned in a cage and subjected to the scorn of the commoners in Marlowe's *Tamburlaine.* 36: The emperor Tiberius was once about to enter Rome when his beloved pet snake was eaten by ants. Taking this as an omen, Tiberius turned back.

HOLY SONNETS

5

I AM A LITTLE WORLD MADE CUNNINGLY

I am a little world made cunningly
Of elements, and an angelic sprite,
But black sin hath betrayed to endless night
My world's both parts, and oh, both parts must die.
You which beyond that heaven which was most high 5
Have found new spheres, and of new lands can write,
Pour new seas in mine eyes, that so I might
Drown my world with my weeping earnestly,
Or wash it if it must be drowned no more;
But oh it must be burnt! Alas, the fire 10
Of lust and envy have burnt it heretofore,
And made it fouler; let their flames retire,
And burn me, O Lord, with a fiery zeal
Of Thee and Thy house, which doth in eating heal.

2 *sprite:* spirit.

7

AT THE ROUND EARTH'S IMAGINED CORNERS

At the round earth's imagined corners, blow
Your trumpets, angels, and arise, arise
From death, you numberless infinities
Of souls, and to your scattered bodies go;
All whom the flood did, and fire shall o'erthrow, 5
All whom war, dearth, age, agues, tyrannies,
Despair, law, chance, hath slain, and you whose eyes
Shall behold God, and never taste death's woe.
But let them sleep, Lord, and me mourn a space,
For if, above all these, my sins abound, 10
'Tis late to ask abundance of Thy grace
When we are there; here on this lowly ground,
Teach me how to repent; for that's as good
As if Thou hadst sealed my pardon with Thy blood.

9

IF POISONOUS MINERALS

If poisonous minerals, and if that tree
Whose fruit threw death on else immortal us,
If lecherous goats, if serpents envious
Cannot be damned, alas, why should I be?
Why should intent or reason, born in me, 5
Make sins, else equal, in me more heinous?
And mercy being easy and glorious
To God, in his stern wrath why threatens He?
But who am I that dare dispute with Thee,
O God? O, of thine only worthy blood 10
And my tears make a heavenly Lethean flood,
And drown in it my sins' black memory.
That thou remember them, some claim as debt;
I think it mercy if thou wilt forget.

11 *Lethean:* Lethe was the river of forgetfulness in the Greek underworld.

10

DEATH BE NOT PROUD

Death be not proud, though some have callèd thee
Mighty and dreadful, for thou art not so;
For those whom thou think'st thou dost overthrow
Die not, poor Death; nor yet canst thou kill me.
From rest and sleep, which but thy pictures be, 5
Much pleasure, then from thee much more must flow;
And soonest our best men with thee do go,
Rest of their bones and soul's delivery.
Thou'rt slave to fate, chance, kings, and desperate men,
And dost with poison, war, and sickness dwell; 10
And poppy or charms can make us sleep as well
And better than thy stroke. Why swell'st thou then?
One short sleep past, we wake eternally,
And Death shall be no more; Death, thou shalt die.

14

BATTER MY HEART, THREE-PERSONED GOD

Batter my heart, three-personed God, for you
As yet but knock, breathe, shine, and seek to mend;
That I may rise and stand, o'erthrow me, and bend
Your force to break, blow, burn and make me new.
I, like an usurped town, to another due, 5
Labour to admit you, but oh, to no end;
Reason your viceroy in me, me should defend,
But is captived, and proves weak or untrue.
Yet dearly I love you, and would be loved fain,
But am betrothed unto your enemy: 10
Divorce me, untie, or break that knot again,
Take me to you, imprison me, for I
Except you enthrall me, never shall be free,
Nor ever chaste, except you ravish me.

13, 14 *except:* unless.

17

SINCE SHE WHOM I LOVED HATH PAID HER LAST DEBT

Since she whom I loved hath paid her last debt
To Nature, and to her and my good is dead,
And her soul early into heaven ravishèd,
Wholly on heavenly things my mind is set.
Here the admiring her my mind did whet 5
To seek Thee, God; so streams do show their head;
But though I have found Thee, and Thou my thirst hast fed,
A holy thirsty dropsy melts me yet.
But why should I beg more love, whenas Thou
Dost woo my soul for hers, offering all Thine: 10
And dost not only fear lest I allow
My Love to saints and angels, things divine,
But in Thy tender jealousy dost doubt
Lest the world, flesh, yea devil put Thee out.

9 *whenas:* when.

ALEXANDER POPE

[1688–1744]

Alexander Pope, like John Donne, was born in London of Roman Catholic parents; unlike Donne, he was physically stunted and deformed. Both his Catholicism and his deformity prevented him from attending a university, and he spent his youth reading widely at his parents' home in Windsor Forest. He began writing poetry in his childhood. His PASTORALS *appeared in 1709, when he was only twenty-one, and they were followed in the next year by his* ESSAY ON CRITICISM, *which won him considerable fame. He became the friend of Addison, Gay, Swift, and other leading men-of-letters.* THE RAPE OF THE LOCK, *his most popular poem, was published in a short version in 1712, and enlarged in 1714. In it Pope burlesques all the major devices of classical epic; it is generally regarded as the finest mock-heroic poem in the English language.*

Through his immensely successful translation of Homer's ILIAD *(1715–20), Pope earned enough money to retire to Twickenham. After translating the* ILIAD, *he went on to translate—with the help of two hack-poets—Homer's* ODYSSEY, *and to edit Shakespeare's plays. Under constant attack for his religion, for his presumptuousness in translating Homer, and for the defects of his editing of Shakespeare, Pope replied savagely to his detractors in* THE DUNCIAD *(1728), in which he depicts one of his chief critics, Lewis Theobald, as the "hero" and darling of the Goddess Dullness. Pope's last years were spent in revising and enlarging* THE DUNCIAD *and in writing the* ESSAY ON MAN *(1733–34), the* MORAL ESSAYS *(1731–35), and the* IMITATIONS OF HORACE *(1733–39).*

The chief scholarly edition of Pope's writings is THE TWICKENHAM EDITION, *in six volumes, under the general editorship of John Butt (1939–54). A more convenient edition is Henry W. Boynton's* THE COMPLETE POETICAL WORKS *(1931); a good selection from the works is made by W. K. Wimsatt in his edition of Pope's* SELECTED POETRY AND PROSE *(1951).*

source of guidance for literature

AN ESSAY ON CRITICISM

(*Part I*)

'Tis hard to say, if greater want of skill
Appear in writing or in judging ill;
But, of the two, less dangerous is th' offence
To tire our patience, than mislead our sense.
Some few in that, but numbers err in this, 5
Ten censure wrong for one who writes amiss;
A fool might once himself alone expose,
Now one in verse makes many more in prose.
  'Tis with our judgments as our watches, none
Go just alike, yet each believes his own. 10
In Poets as true genius is but rare,
True Taste as seldom is the Critic's share;
Both must alike from Heaven derive their light,
These born to judge, as well as those to write.
Let such teach others who themselves excel, 15
And censure freely who have written well.
Authors are partial to their wit, 'tis true,
But are not Critics to their judgment too?
  Yet if we look more closely, we shall find
Most have the seeds of judgment in their mind: 20
Nature affords at least a glimmering light;
The lines, though touched but faintly, are drawn right.
But as the slightest sketch, if justly traced,
Is by ill colouring but the more disgraced,
So by false learning is good sense defaced: 25
Some are bewildered in the maze of schools,
And some made coxcombs Nature meant but fools.
In search of wit these lose their common sense,
And then turn Critics in their own defence:
Each burns alike, who can, or cannot write, 30
Or with a Rival's, or an Eunuch's spite.
All fools have still an itching to deride,
And fain would be upon the laughing side.
If Mævius scribble in Apollo's spite,

34 *Mævius:* a poet of Virgil's time who was considered a prime example of the poor poet; *Apollo:* Greek God who was the patron of poetry.

There are who judge still worse than he can write. 35
  Some have at first for Wits, then Poets past,
Turned Critics next, and proved plain fools at last.
Some neither can for Wits nor Critics pass,
As heavy mules are neither horse nor ass.
Those half-learned witlings, numerous in our isle, 40
As half-formed insects on the banks of Nile;
Unfinished things, one knows not what to call,
Their generation's so equivocal:
To tell 'em, would a hundred tongues require,
Or one vain wit's, that might a hundred tire. 45
  But you who seek to give and merit fame,
And justly bear a Critic's noble name,
Be sure yourself and your own reach to know,
How far your genius, taste, and learning go;
Launch not beyond your depth, but be discreet, 50
And mark that point where sense and dulness meet.
  Nature to all things fixed the limits fit,
And wisely curbed proud man's pretending wit.
As on the land while here the ocean gains,
In other parts it leaves wide sandy plains; 55
Thus in the soul while memory prevails,
The solid power of understanding fails;
Where beams of warm imagination play,
The memory's soft figures melt away.
One science only will one genius fit; 60
So vast is art, so narrow human wit:
Not only bounded to peculiar arts,
But oft in those confined to single parts.
Like Kings we lose the conquests gained before,
By vain ambition still to make them more; 65
Each might his several province well command,
Would all but stoop to what they understand.
  First follow Nature, and your judgment frame
By her just standard, which is still the same:
Unerring NATURE, still divinely bright, 70
One clear, unchanged, and universal light,

41: it was believed that the sun's heat generated insects in the mud of the Nile. 44 *tell:* count.

Life, force, and beauty, must to all impart,
At once the source, and end, and test of Art.
Art from that fund each just supply provides,
Works without show, and without pomp presides: 75
In some fair body thus th' informing soul
With spirits feeds, with vigour fills the whole,
Each motion guides, and every nerve sustains;
Itself unseen, but in the effects, remains.
Some, to whom Heaven in wit has been profuse, 80
Want as much more, to turn it to its use;
For wit and judgment often are at strife,
Though meant each other's aid, like man and wife.
'Tis more to guide, than spur the Muse's steed;
Restrain his fury, than provoke his speed; 85
The wingèd courser, like a generous horse,
Shows most true mettle when you check his course.
Those RULES of old discovered, not devised,
Are Nature still, but Nature methodized;
Nature, like Liberty, is but restrained 90
By the same Laws which first herself ordained.
Hear how learned Greece her useful rules indites,
When to repress, and when indulge our flights:
High on Parnassus' top her sons she showed,
And pointed out those arduous paths they trod; 95
Held from afar, aloft, th' immortal prize,
And urged the rest by equal steps to rise.
Just precepts thus from great examples given,
She drew from them what they derived from Heaven.
The generous Critic fanned the Poet's fire, 100
And taught the world with reason to admire.
Then Criticism the Muses' handmaid proved,
To dress her charms, and make her more beloved:
But following wits from that intention strayed,
Who could not win the mistress, wooed the maid; 105
Against the Poets their own arms they turned,
Sure to hate most the men from whom they learned.
So modern 'Pothecaries, taught the art
By Doctor's bills to play the Doctor's part,

109 *Doctor's bills:* prescriptions.

Bold in the practice of mistaken rules, 110
Prescribe, apply, and call their masters fools.
Some on the leaves of ancient authors prey,
Nor time nor moths e'er spoiled so much as they.
Some drily plain, without invention's aid,
Write dull receipts how poems may be made. 115
These leave the sense, their learning to display,
And those explain the meaning quite away.
  You then whose judgment the right course would steer,
Know well each ANCIENT's proper character;
His Fable, Subject, scope in every page; 120
Religion, Country, genius of his Age:
Without all these at once before your eyes,
Cavil you may, but never criticize.
Be Homer's works your study and delight,
Read them by day, and meditate by night; 125
Thence form your judgment, thence your maxims bring,
And trace the Muses upward to their spring.
Still with itself compared, his text peruse;
And let your comment be the Mantuan Muse.
  When first young Maro in his boundless mind 130
A work t' outlast immortal Rome designed,
Perhaps he seem'd above the Critic's law,
And but from Nature's fountains scorned to draw:
But when t' examine every part he came,
Nature and Homer were, he found, the same. 135
Convinced, amazed, he checks the bold design;
And rules as strict his laboured work confine,
As if the Stagyrite o'erlooked each line.
Learn hence for ancient rules a just esteem;
To copy nature is to copy them. 140
  Some beauties yet no Precepts can declare,
For there's a happiness as well as care.
Music resembles Poetry, in each
Are nameless graces which no methods teach,

119 *Ancient's:* classical author's. 129 *Mantuan Muse:* Virgil. The meaning of line 129 is: "Read Virgil's *Aeneid* as a commentary on Homer's *Iliad* and *Odyssey*." 130 *Maro:* Virgil. His full name was Publius Vergilius Maro. 138 *the Stagyrite:* Aristotle, who was born at Stagira in Macedonia, and whose *Poetics* is the first great work of literary criticism.

And which a master hand alone can reach. 145
If, where the rules not far enough extend,
(Since rules were made but to promote their end)
Some lucky Licence answer to the full
Th' intent proposed, that Licence is a rule.
Thus Pegasus, a nearer way to take, 150
May boldly deviate from the common track;
From vulgar bounds with brave disorder part,
And snatch a grace beyond the reach of art,
Which without passing through the judgment, gains
The heart, and all its end at once attains. 155
In prospects thus, some objects please our eyes,
Which out of nature's common order rise,
The shapeless rock, or hanging precipice.
Great Wits sometimes may gloriously offend,
And rise to faults true Critics dare not mend. 160
But though the Ancients thus their rules invade,
(As Kings dispense with laws themselves have made)
Moderns, beware! or if you must offend
Against the precept, ne'er transgress its End;
Let it be seldom, and compelled by need; 165
And have, at least, their precedent to plead.
The Critic else proceeds without remorse,
Seizes your fame, and puts his laws in force.
I know there are, to whose presumptuous thoughts
Those freer beauties, even in them, seem faults. 170
Some figures monstrous and misshaped appear,
Considered singly, or beheld too near,
Which, but proportioned to their light, or place,
Due distance reconciles to form and grace.
A prudent chief not always must display 175
His powers in equal ranks, and fair array,
But with th' occasion and the place comply,
Conceal his force, nay seem sometimes to fly.
Those oft are stratagems which error seem,
Nor is it Homer nods, but we that dream. 180
Still green with bays each ancient Altar stands,
Above the reach of sacrilegious hands;
Secure from Flames, from Envy's fiercer rage,
Destructive War, and all-involving Age.

addresses classical poets

See, from each clime the learned their incense bring! 185
Hear, in all tongues concenting Pæans ring!
In praise so just let every voice be joined,
And fill the general chorus of mankind.
Hail, Bards triumphant! born in happier days;
Immortal heirs of universal praise! 190
Whose honours with increase of ages grow,
As streams roll down, enlarging as they flow;
Nations unborn your mighty names shall sound,
And worlds applaud that must not yet be found!
Oh may some spark of your celestial fire, 195
The last, the meanest of your sons inspire,
(That on weak wings, from far, pursues your flights;
Glows while he reads, but trembles as he writes)
To each vain Wits a science little known,
T' admire superior sense, and doubt their own! 200

THE RAPE OF THE LOCK

(*1717 Version*)

CANTO I

What dire offence from amorous causes springs,
What mighty contests rise from trivial things,
I sing—This verse to CARYLL, Muse! is due:
This, even Belinda may vouchsafe to view:
Slight is the subject, but not so the praise, 5
If She inspire, and He approve my lays.
Say what strange motive, Goddess! could compel
A well-bred Lord t' assault a gentle Belle?
O say what stranger cause, yet unexplored,
Could make a gentle Belle reject a Lord? 10
In tasks so bold, can little men engage,

Pope wrote this poem to help bring an end to a quarrel which had arisen between two families of his acquaintance when Lord Petre (the "Baron" of the poem) snipped a lock of hair from the head of Miss Arabella Fermor ("Belinda").

3 *Caryll:* a friend of Pope's, who suggested to him that he write the poem.

And in soft bosoms dwells such mighty Rage?
  Sol through white curtains shot a timorous ray,
And oped those eyes that must eclipse the day:
Now lap dogs give themselves the rousing shake, 15
And sleepless lovers, just at twelve, awake:
Thrice rung the bell, the slipper knocked the ground,
And the pressed watch returned a silver sound.
Belinda still her downy pillow prest,
Her guardian SYLPH prolonged the balmy rest: 20
'Twas He had summoned to her silent bed
The morning dream that hovered o'er her head;
A Youth more glittering than a Birth-night Beau,
(That even in slumber caused her cheek to glow)
Seemed to her ear his winning lips to lay, 25
And thus in whispers said, or seemed to say:
  "Fairest of mortals, thou distinguished care
Of thousand bright Inhabitants of Air!
If e'er one Vision touched thy infant thought,
Of all the Nurse and all the Priest have taught; 30
Of airy Elves by moonlight shadows seen,
The silver token, and the circled green,
Or virgins visited by Angel powers,
With golden crowns and wreaths of heavenly flowers;
Hear and believe! thy own importance know, 35
Nor bound thy narrow views to things below.
Some secret truths, from learnèd pride concealed,
To Maids alone and Children are revealed:
What though no credit doubting Wits may give?
The Fair and Innocent shall still believe. 40
Know, then, unnumbered Spirits round thee fly,
The light Militia of the lower sky:
These, though unseen, are ever on the wing,
Hang o'er the Box, and hover round the Ring.

17–19: Belinda awakens, summons her maid, and then goes back to sleep again. 20 *Sylph:* a friendly spirit; a kind of "guardian angel." In the Rosicrucian system which Pope makes use of in this poem, four orders of spirits are distinguished: Sylphs, Salamanders, Nymphs, and Gnomes. 23 *Birth-night Beau:* a young man dressed in his finest clothes for the celebration of a royal birthday. 44 *Box:* a box at the theater; *Ring:* a fashionable drive in Hyde Park in London.

Think what an equipage thou hast in Air, 45
And view with scorn two Pages and a Chair.
As now your own, our beings were of old,
And once enclosed in Woman's beauteous mould;
Thence, by a soft transition, we repair
From earthly Vehicles to these of air. 50
Think not, when a Woman's transient breath is fled,
That all her vanities at once are dead;
Succeeding vanities she still regards,
And though she plays no more, o'erlooks the cards.
Her joy in gilded Chariots, when alive, 55
And love of Ombre, after death survive.
For when the Fair in all their pride expire,
To their first Elements their Souls retire:
The Sprites of fiery Termagants in Flame
Mount up, and take a Salamander's name. 60
Soft yielding minds to water glide away,
And sip, with Nymphs, their elemental tea.
The graver Prude sinks downward to a Gnome,
In search of mischief still on Earth to roam.
The light Coquettes in Sylphs aloft repair, 65
And sport and flutter in the fields of Air.
"Know further yet; whoever fair and chaste
Rejects mankind, is by some Sylph embraced:
For Spirits, freed from mortal laws, with ease
Assume what sexes and what shapes they please. 70
What guards the purity of melting Maids,
In courtly balls, and midnight masquerades,
Safe from the treacherous friend, the daring spark,
The glance by day, the whisper in the dark,
When kind occasion prompts their warm desires, 75
When music softens, and when dancing fires?
'Tis but their Sylph, the wise Celestials know,
Though Honour is the word with Men below.
"Some nymphs there are, too conscious of their face,
For life predestined to the Gnomes' embrace. 80

50 *Vehicles:* bodies. 56 *Ombre:* a card game. 59 *Termagants:* scolding, abusive women. 60, 62 *Salamander, Nymphs:* see note to line 20. 73 *spark:* beau.

These swell their prospects and exalt their pride,
When offers are disdained, and love denied:
Then gay Ideas crowd the vacant brain,
While Peers, and Dukes, and all their sweeping train,
And Garters, Stars, and Coronets appear, 85
And in soft sounds, Your Grace salutes their ear.
'Tis these that early taint the female soul,
Instruct the eyes of young Coquettes to roll,
Teach Infant cheeks a bidden blush to know,
And little hearts to flutter at a Beau. 90
"Oft, when the world imagine women stray,
The Sylphs through mystic mazes guide their way,
Through all the giddy circle they pursue,
And old impertinence expel by new.
What tender maid but must a victim fall 95
To one man's treat, but for another's ball?
When Florio speaks what virgin could withstand,
If gentle Damon did not squeeze her hand?
With varying vanities, from every part,
They shift the moving Toyshop of their heart; 100
Where wigs with wigs, with sword-knots sword-knots strive,
Beaux banish beaux, and coaches coaches drive.
This erring mortals levity may call,
Oh, blind to truth! the sylphs contrive it all.
"Of these am I, who thy protection claim, 105
A watchful sprite, and Ariel is my name.
Late, as I ranged the crystal wilds of air,
In the clear Mirror of thy ruling Star
I saw, alas! some dread event impend,
Ere to the main this morning sun descend, 110
But heaven reveals not what, or how, or where:
Warned by the Sylph, oh pious maid, beware!
This to disclose is all thy guardian can:
Beware of all, but most beware of Man!"
He said; when Shock, who thought she slept too long, 115
Leaped up, and waked his mistress with his tongue.

85 *Garters, Stars, and Coronets:* the insignia of knights, peers, and dukes. 94 *impertinence:* folly. 101 *sword-knots:* ribbons on sword-hilts. 115 *Shock:* Belinda's dog.

'Twas then, Belinda, if report say true,
Thy eyes first opened on a Billet doux;
Wounds, Charm, and Ardors were no sooner read,
But all the Vision vanished from thy head. 120
And now, unveiled, the Toilet stands displayed,
Each silver Vase in mystic order laid.
First, robed in white, the Nymph intent adores,
With head uncovered, the Cosmetic powers.
A heavenly image in the glass appears, 125
To that she bends, to that her eyes she rears;
Th' inferior Priestess, at her altar's side,
Trembling, begins the sacred rites of Pride.
Unnumbered treasures ope at once, and here
The various offerings of the world appear; 130
From each she nicely culls with curious toil,
And decks the Goddess with the glittering spoil.
This casket India's glowing gems unlocks,
And all Arabia breathes from yonder box.
The Tortoise here and Elephant unite, 135
Transformed to combs, the speckled, and the white.
Here files of pins extend their shining rows,
Puffs, Powders, Patches, Bibles, Billet-doux.
Now awful Beauty puts on all its arms;
The fair each moment rises in her charms, 140
Repairs her smiles, awakens every grace,
And calls forth all the wonders of her face;
Sees by degrees a purer blush arise,
And keener lightnings quicken in her eyes.
The busy Sylphs surround their darling care, 145
These set the head, and those divide the hair,
Some fold the sleeve, whilst others plait the gown;
And Betty's praised for labours not her own.

127 *Priestess:* Belinda's maid, Betty.

CANTO II

Not with more glories, in th' etherial plain,
The Sun first rises o'er the purpled main,
Than, issuing forth, the rival of his beams
Launched on the bosom of the silver Thames.

Fair Nymphs, and well-dressed Youths around her shone, 5
But every eye was fixed on her alone.
On her white breast a sparkling Cross she wore,
Which Jews might kiss, and Infidels adore.
Her lively looks a sprightly mind disclose,
Quick as her eyes, and as unfixed as those: 10
Favours to none, to all she smiles extends;
Oft she rejects, but never once offends.
Bright as the sun, her eyes the gazers strike,
And, like the sun, they shine on all alike.
Yet graceful ease, and sweetness void of pride, 15
Might hide her faults, if Belles had faults to hide:
If to her share some female errors fall,
Look on her face, and you'll forget 'em all.
  This Nymph, to the destruction of mankind,
Nourished two Locks, which graceful hung behind 20
In equal curls, and well conspired to deck
With shining ringlets the smooth ivory neck.
Love in these labyrinths his slaves detains,
And mighty hearts are held in slender chains.
With hairy springes we the birds betray, 25
Slight lines of hair surprise the finny prey,
Fair tresses man's imperial race ensnare,
And beauty draws us with a single hair.
  Th' adventurous Baron the bright locks admired;
He saw, he wished, and to the prize aspired. 30
Resolved to win, he meditates the way,
By force to ravish, or by fraud betray;
For when success a Lover's toil attends,
Few ask, if fraud or force attained his ends.
  For this, ere Phœbus rose, he had implored 35
Propitious Heaven, and every power adored:
But chiefly Love—to Love an Altar built,
Of twelve vast French Romances, neatly gilt.
There lay three garters, half a pair of gloves;
And all the trophies of his former loves: 40
With tender Billet-doux he lights the pyre,
And breathes three amorous sighs to raise the fire.

35 *Phœbus:* the sun.

Then prostrate falls, and begs with ardent eyes
Soon to obtain, and long possess the prize:
The powers gave ear, and granted half his prayer, 45
The rest, the winds dispersed in empty air.
  But now secure the painted vessel glides,
The sunbeams trembling on the floating tides:
While melting music steals upon the sky,
And softened sounds along the waters die; 50
Smooth flow the waves, the Zephyrs gently play,
Belinda smiled, and all the world was gay.
All but the Sylph—with careful thoughts opprest,
Th' impending woe sat heavy on his breast.
He summons strait his Denizens of air; 55
The lucid squadrons round the sails repair:
Soft o'er the shrouds aërial whispers breathe,
That seemed but Zephyrs to the train beneath.
Some to the sun their insect wings unfold,
Waft on the breeze, or sink in clouds of gold; 60
Transparent forms, too fine for mortal sight,
Their fluid bodies half dissolved in light,
Loose to the wind their airy garments flew,
Thin glittering textures of the filmy dew,
Dipped in the richest tincture of the skies, 65
Where light disports in ever-mingling dyes,
While every beam new transient colours flings,
Colours that change whene'er they wave their wings.
Amid the circle, on the gilded mast,
Superior by the head, was Ariel placed; 70
His purple pinions opening to the sun,
He raised his azure wand, and thus begun:
  "Ye Sylphs and Sylphids, to your chief give ear!
Fays, Fairies, Genii, Elves, and Dæmons, hear!
Ye know the spheres and various tasks assigned 75
By laws eternal to th' aërial kind.
Some in the fields of purest Æther play,
And bask and whiten in the blaze of day.
Some guide the course of wandering orbs on high,
Or roll the planets through the boundless sky. 80

70 *Superior by the head:* taller by a head than any of the others.

Some less refined, beneath the moon's pale light
Pursue the stars that shoot athwart the night,
Or suck the mists in grosser air below,
Or dip their pinions in the painted bow,
Or brew fierce tempests on the wintry main, 85
Or o'er the glebe distil the kindly rain.
Others on earth o'er human race preside,
Watch all their ways, and all their actions guide:
Of these the chief the care of Nations own,
And guard with Arms divine the British Throne. 90
"Our humbler province is to tend the Fair,
Not a less pleasing, though less glorious care;
To save the powder from too rude a gale,
Nor let th' imprisoned essences exhale;
To draw fresh colours from the vernal flowers; 95
To steal from rainbows e'er they drop in showers
A brighter wash; to curl their waving hairs,
Assist their blushes, and inspire their airs;
Nay oft, in dreams, invention we bestow,
To change a Flounce, or add a Furbelow. 100
"This day, black Omens threat the brightest Fair
That e'er deserved a watchful spirit's care;
Some dire disaster, or by force, or slight;
But what, or where, the fates have wrapped in night.
Whether the nymph shall break Diana's law, 105
Or some frail China jar receive a flaw;
Or stain her honour, or her new brocade;
Forget her prayers, or miss a masquerade;
Or lose her heart, or necklace, at a ball;
Or whether Heaven has doomed that Shock must fall. 110
Haste, then, ye spirits! to your charge repair:
The fluttering fan be Zephyretta's care;
The drops to thee, Brillante, we consign;
And, Momentilla, let the watch be thine;
Do thou, Crispissa, tend her favorite Lock; 115
Ariel himself shall be the guard of Shock.

97 *wash:* lotion. 103 *slight:* cunning. 105 *Diana's law:* the moon-goddess's rule of chastity. 112 *Zephyretta:* "fluttering." 113 *drops:* ear-rings; *Brillante:* "sparkling." 114 *Momentilla:* "timing." 115 *Crispissa:* "curling."

"To fifty chosen Sylphs, of special note,
We trust th' important charge, the Petticoat:
Oft have we known that sevenfold fence to fail,
Though stiff with hoops, and armed with ribs of whale; 120
Form a strong line about the silver bound,
And guard the wide circumference around.
"Whatever spirit, careless of his charge,
His post neglects, or leaves the fair at large,
Shall feel sharp vengeance soon o'ertake his sins, 125
Be stopp'd in vials, or transfixed with pins;
Or plunged in lakes of bitter washes lie,
Or wedged whole ages in a bodkin's eye:
Gums and Pomatums shall his flight restrain,
While clogged he beats his silken wings in vain; 130
Or Alum styptics with contracting power
Shrink his thin essence like a rivelled flower:
Or, as Ixion fixed, the wretch shall feel
The giddy motion of the whirling Mill,
In fumes of burning Chocolate shall glow, 135
And tremble at the sea that froths below!"
He spoke; the spirits from the sails descend;
Some, orb in orb, around the nymph extend;
Some thrid the mazy ringlets of her hair;
Some hang upon the pendants of her ear; 140
With beating hearts the dire event they wait,
Anxious, and trembling for the birth of Fate.

132 *rivelled:* shriveled. 134 *Mill:* beater for hot chocolate. 139 *thrid:* thread.

CANTO III

Close by those meads, for ever crowned with flowers,
Where Thames with pride surveys his rising towers,
There stands a structure of majestic frame,
Which from the neighboring Hampton takes it name.
Here Britain's statesmen oft the fall foredoom 5
Of foreign Tyrants, and of Nymphs at home;
Here thou, great ANNA! whom three realms obey,

7 *Anna:* Queen Anne of England.

Dost sometimes counsel take—and sometimes Tea.
  Hither the heroes and the nymphs resort,
To taste awhile the pleasures of a Court; 10
In various talk th' instructive hours they past,
Who gave the ball, or paid the visit last;
One speaks the glory of the British Queen,
And one describes a charming Indian screen;
A third interprets motions, looks, and eyes; 15
At every word a reputation dies.
Snuff, or the fan, supply each pause of chat,
With singing, laughing, ogling, *and all that.*
  Meanwhile, declining from the noon of day,
The sun obliquely shoots his burning ray; 20
The hungry Judges soon the sentence sign,
And wretches hang that jurymen may dine;
The merchant from th' Exchange returns in peace,
And the long labours of the Toilet cease.
Belinda now, whom thirst of fame invites, 25
Burns to encounter two adventurous Knights,
At Ombre singly to decide their doom;
And swells her breast with conquests yet to come.
Straight the three bands prepare in arms to join,
Each band the number of the sacred nine. 30
Soon as she spreads her hand, th' aërial guard
Descend, and sit on each important card:
First Ariel perched upon a Matadore,
Then each, according to the rank they bore;
For Sylphs, yet mindful of their ancient race, 35
Are, as when women, wondrous fond of place.
  Behold, four Kings in majesty revered,
With hoary whiskers and a forky beard;
And four fair Queens whose hands sustain a flower,
Th' expressive emblem of their softer power; 40
Four Knaves in garbs succinct, a trusty band,
Caps on their heads, and halberts in their hand;
And particoloured troops, a shining train,
Draw forth to combat on the velvet plain.

29 *bands:* hands of cards. 30 *the sacred nine:* the Muses. 33 *Matadore:* one of the three highest trump cards. 41 *succinct:* tucked up. 44 *velvet plain:* velvet covering of the card table.

The skilful Nymph reviews her force with care: 45
"Let Spades be trumps!" she said, and trumps they were.
Now move to war her sable Matadores,
In show like leaders of the swarthy Moors.
Spadillio first, unconquerable Lord!
Led off two captive trumps, and swept the board. 50
As many more Manillio forced to yield,
And marched a victor from the verdant field.
Him Basto followed, but his fate more hard
Gained but one trump and one Plebian card.
With his broad sabre next, a chief in years, 55
The hoary Majesty of Spades appears,
Puts forth one manly leg, to sight revealed,
The rest, his many-coloured robe concealed.
The rebel Knave, who dares his prince engage,
Proves the just victim of his royal rage. 60
Even mighty Pam, that Kings and Queens o'erthrew
And mowed down armies in the fights of Lu,
Sad chance of war! now destitute of aid,
Falls undistinguished by the victor Spade!
Thus far both armies to Belinda yield; 65
Now to the Baron fate inclines the field.
His warlike Amazon her host invades,
Th' imperial consort of the crown of Spades.
The Club's black Tyrant first her victim died
Spite of his haughty mien, and barbarous pride: 70
What boots the regal circle on his head,
His giant limbs, in state unwieldy spread;
That long behind he trails his pompous robe,
And, of all monarchs, only grasps the globe?
The Baron now his Diamonds pours apace; 75
Th' embroidered King who shows but half his face,
And his refulgent Queen, with powers combined
Of broken troops an easy conquest find.
Clubs, Diamonds, Hearts, in wild disorder seen,
With throngs promiscuous strew the level green. 80

49 *Spadillio:* the ace of spades. 51 *Manillio:* the two of spades: the second Matadore. 53 *Basto:* the ace of clubs: the third Matadore. 61 *Pam:* the jack of clubs, top trump in the game of Lu.

Thus when dispersed a routed army runs,
Of Asia's troops, and Afric's sable sons,
With like confusion different nations fly,
Of various habit, and of various dye,
The pierced battalions disunited fall, 85
In heaps on heaps; one fate o'erwhelms them all.
The Knave of Diamonds tries his wily arts,
And wins (oh shameful chance!) the Queen of Hearts.
At this, the blood the virgin's cheek forsook,
A livid paleness spreads o'er all her look; 90
She sees, and trembles at th' approaching ill,
Just in the jaws of ruin, and Codille.
And now (as oft in some distempered State)
On one nice Trick depends the general fate.
An Ace of Hearts steps forth: The King unseen 95
Lurked in her hand, and mourned his captive Queen:
He springs to vengeance with an eager pace,
And falls like thunder on the prostrate Ace.
The nymph exulting fills with shouts the sky;
The walls, the woods, and long canals reply. 100
Oh thoughtless mortals! ever blind to fate,
Too soon dejected, and too soon elate.
Sudden, these honours shall be snatched away,
And cursed for ever this victorious day.
For lo! the board with cups and spoons is crowned, 105
The berries crackle, and the mill turns round;
On shining Altars of Japan they raise
The silver lamp; the fiery spirits blaze:
From silver spouts the grateful liquors glide,
While China's earth receives the smoking tide: 110
At once they gratify their scent and taste,
And frequent cups prolong the rich repast.
Straight hover round the Fair her airy band;
Some, as she sipped, the fuming liquor fanned,
Some o'er her lap their careful plumes displayed, 115
Trembling, and conscious of the rich brocade.

92 *Codille:* being "set." 95 *The King:* highest card in red suits in Ombre. 106 *berries:* coffee beans.

Coffee, (which makes the politician wise,
And see through all things with his half-shut eyes)
Sent up in vapours to the Baron's brain
New stratagems, the radiant Lock to gain. 120
Ah cease, rash youth! desist ere 'tis too late,
Fear the just Gods, and think of Scylla's Fate!
Changed to a bird, and sent to flit in air,
She dearly pays for Nisus' injured hair!
  But when to mischief mortals bend their will, 125
How soon they find fit instruments of ill!
Just then, Clarissa drew with tempting grace
A two-edged weapon from her shining case:
So Ladies in Romance assist their Knight,
Present the spear, and arm him for the fight. 130
He takes the gift with reverence, and extends
The little engine on his fingers' ends;
This just behind Belinda's neck he spread,
As o'er the fragrant steams she bends her head.
Swift to the Lock a thousand Sprites repair, 135
A thousand wings, by turns, blow back the hair;
And thrice they twitched the diamond in her ear;
Thrice she looked back, and thrice the foe drew near.
Just in that instant, anxious Ariel sought
The close recesses of the Virgin's thought; 140
As on the nosegay in her breast reclined,
He watched th' Ideas rising in her mind,
Sudden he viewed, in spite of all her art,
An earthly Lover lurking at her heart.
Amazed, confused, he found his power expired, 145
Resigned to fate, and with a sigh retired.
  The Peer now spreads the glittering Forfex wide,
T' enclose the Lock; now joins it, to divide.
Even then, before the fatal engine closed,
A wretched Sylph too fondly interposed; 150

122 *Scylla's Fate:* Scylla plucked from the head of her father, Nisus, a purple hair on which the prosperity of his kingdom was said to depend, in order to give it to an enemy of Nisus with whom she was in love. The enemy repudiated her for this act, and both Scylla and Nisus were changed into birds.
147 *Forfex:* scissors.

Fate urged the shears, and cut the Sylph in twain,
(But airy substance soon unites again)
The meeting points the sacred hair dissever
From the fair head, for ever, and for ever!
  Then flashed the living lightning from her eyes, 155
And screams of horror rend th' affrighted skies.
Not louder shrieks to pitying heaven are cast,
When husbands, or when lap dogs breathe their last;
Or when rich China vessels fallen from high,
In glittering dust, and painted fragments lie! 160
  "Let wreaths of triumph now my temples twine,
(The Victor cried) the glorious Prize is mine!
While fish in streams, or birds delight in air,
Or in a coach and six the British Fair,
As long as Atalantis shall be read, 165
Or the small pillow grace a Lady's bed,
While visits shall be paid on solemn days,
When numerous wax-lights in bright order blaze,
While nymphs take treats, or assignations give,
So long my honour, name, and praise shall live! 170
What Time would spare, from Steel receives its date,
And monuments, like men, submit to fate!
Steel could the labour of the Gods destroy,
And strike to dust th' imperial towers of Troy;
Steel could the works of mortal pride confound, 175
And hew triumphal arches to the ground.
What wonder then, fair nymph! thy hairs should feel,
The conquering force of unresisted steel?"

165 *Atalantis: The New Atalantis,* a slanderous but very popular book of the day.

CANTO IV

But anxious cares the pensive nymph oppressed,
And secret passions laboured in her breast.
Not youthful kings in battle seized alive,
Not scornful virgins who their charms survive,
Not ardent lovers robbed of all their bliss, 5
Not ancient ladies when refused a kiss,
Not tyrants fierce that unrepenting die,

Not Cynthia when her manteau's pinned awry,
E'er felt such rage, resentment, and despair,
As thou, sad Virgin! for thy ravised hair. 10
For, that sad moment, when the Sylphs withdrew,
And Ariel weeping from Belinda flew,
Umbriel, a dusky, melancholy sprite,
As ever sullied the fair face of light,
Down to the central earth, his proper scene, 15
Repaired to search the gloomy Cave of Spleen.
Swift on his sooty pinions flits the Gnome,
And in a vapour reached the dismal dome.
No cheerful breeze this sullen region knows,
The dreaded East is all the wind that blows. 20
Here in a grotto, sheltered close from air,
And screened in shades from day's detested glare,
She sighs for ever on her pensive bed,
Pain at her side, and Megrim at her head.
Two handmaids wait the throne: alike in place, 25
But differing far in figure and in face.
Here stood Ill Nature like an ancient maid,
Her wrinkled form in black and white arrayed;
With store of prayers, for mornings, nights, and noons,
Her hand is filled; her bosom with lampoons. 30
There Affectation, with a sickly mien,
Shows in her cheek the roses of eighteen,
Practised to lisp, and hang the head aside,
Faints into airs, and languishes with pride,
On the rich quilt sings with becoming woe, 35
Wrapped in a gown, for sickness, and for show.
The fair ones feel such maladies as these,
When each new nightdress gives a new disease.
A constant Vapour o'er the palace flies;
Strange phantoms rising as the mists arise; 40
Dreadful, as hermit's dreams in haunted shades,
Or bright, as visions of expiring maids.

18 *vapour:* used here in two senses: "mist" and "peevishness." 20 *The dreaded East:* the east wind was supposed to cause the "spleen." 24 *Megrim:* a migraine headache. 39: with this line begins a description of the delusions of one suffering from the "spleen."

Now glaring fiends, and snakes on rolling spires,
Pale spectres, gaping tombs, and purple fires:
Now lakes of liquid gold, Elysian scenes, 45
And crystal domes, and Angels in machines.
  Unnumbered throngs on every side are seen
Of bodies changed to various forms by Spleen.
Here living teapots stand, one arm held out,
One bent; the handle this, and that the spout: 50
A Pipkin there, like Homer's Tripod walks;
Here sighs a Jar, and there a Goose Pie talks;
Men prove with child, as powerful fancy works,
And maids turned bottles, call aloud for corks.
  Safe passed the Gnome through his fantastic band, 55
A branch of healing Spleenwort in his hand.
Then thus addressed the power: "Hail, wayward Queen!
Who rule the sex to fifty from fifteen:
Parent of vapours, and of female wit,
Who give th' hysteric, or poetic fit, 60
On various tempers act by various ways,
Make some take physic, others scribble plays;
Who cause the proud their visits to delay,
And send the godly in a pet to pray.
A nymph there is, that all thy power disdains, 65
And thousands more in equal mirth maintains.
But oh! if e'er thy Gnome could spoil a grace,
Or raise a pimple on a beauteous face,
Like Citron waters matrons' cheeks inflame,
Or change complexions at a losing game; 70
If e'er with airy horns I planted heads,
Or rumpled petticoats, or tumbled beds,
Or caused suspicion when no soul was rude,
Or discomposed the headdress of a Prude,
Or e'er to costive lap dog gave disease, 75
Which not the tears of brightest eyes could ease:
Hear me, and touch Belinda with chagrin,
That single act gives half the world the spleen."
  The Goddess with a discontented air

69 *Citron waters:* a mild orange-flavored brandy. 71 *airy horns:* the symbol of cuckolds.

Seems to reject him, though she grants his prayer. 80
A wondrous Bag with both her hands she binds,
Like that where once Ulysses held the winds;
There she collects the force of female lungs,
Sighs, sobs, and passions, and the war of tongues.
A Vial next she fills with fainting fears, 85
Soft sorrows, melting griefs, and flowing tears.
The Gnome rejoicing bears her gifts away,
Spreads his black wings, and slowly mounts to day.
  Sunk in Thalestris' arms the nymph he found,
Here eyes dejected and her hair unbound. 90
Full o'er their heads the swelling bag he rent,
And all the Furies issued at the vent.
Belinda burns with more than mortal ire,
And fierce Thalestris fans the rising fire.
"O wretched maid!" she spread her hands, and cried, 95
(While Hampton's echoes, "Wretched maid!" replied)
"Was it for this you took such constant care
The bodkin, comb, and essence to prepare?
For this your locks in paper durance bound,
For this with torturing irons wreathed around? 100
For this with fillets strained your tender head,
And bravely bore the double loads of lead?
Gods! shall the ravisher display your hair,
While the Fops envy, and the Ladies stare!
Honour forbid! at whose unrivalled shrine 105
Ease, pleasure, virtue, all our sex resign.
Methinks already I your tears survey,
Already hear the horrid things they say,
Already see you a degraded toast,
And all your honour in a whisper lost! 110
How shall I, then, your helpless fame defend?
'Twill then be infamy to seem your friend!
And shall this prize, th' inestimable prize,
Exposed through crystal to the gazing eyes,

89 *Thalestris:* the queen of the Amazons. Here the name is applied to Belinda's friend. 98 *bodkin:* in this case, a hairpin. 99 *durance:* curlers. 100–101: Belinda used curl-papers stiffened with lead. 114–116: Thalestris conjectures that the Baron will have the lock of hair set in a ring, which he will wear.

And heightened by the diamond's circling rays, 115
On that rapacious hand for ever blaze?
Sooner shall grass in Hyde Park Circus grow,
And wits take lodgings in the sound of Bow;
Sooner let earth, air, sea, to Chaos fall,
Men, monkeys, lap dogs, parrots, perish all!" 120
She said; then raging to Sir Plume repairs,
And bids her Beau demand the precious hairs:
(Sir Plume of amber snuffbox justly vain,
And the nice conduct of a clouded cane)
With earnest eyes, and round unthinking face, 125
He first the snuffbox opened, then the case,
And thus broke out—"My Lord, why, what the devil?
Z—ds! damn the lock! 'fore Gad, you must be civil!
Plague on't! 'tis past a jest—nay prithee, pox!
Give her the hair"—he spoke, and rapped his box. 130
"It grieves me much" (replied the Peer again)
"Who speaks so well should ever speak in vain.
But by this Lock, this sacred Lock I swear,
(Which never more shall join its parted hair;
Which never more its honours shall renew, 135
Clipped from the lovely head where late it grew)
That while my nostrils draw the vital air,
This hand, which won it, shall for ever wear."
He spoke, and speaking, in proud triumph spread
The long-contented honours of her head. 140
But Umbriel, hateful Gnome! forbears not so;
He breaks the Vial whence the sorrows flow.
Then see! the nymph in beauteous grief appears,
Her eyes half languishing, half drowned in tears;
On her heaved bosom hung her drooping head, 145
Which, with a sigh, she raised; and thus she said:
"For ever cursed be this detested day,
Which snatched my best, my favorite curl away!
Happy! ah ten times happy had I been,
If Hampton Court these eyes had never seen! 150

117 *Hyde Park Circus:* the Ring; see note to Canto I, line 44. 118 *in the sound of Bow:* within hearing distance of the bells of the church of St. Mary-le-Bow, which was located in the unfashionable commercial section of London. 124 *clouded cane:* mottled walking-stick.

Yet am not I the first mistaken maid,
By love of Courts to numerous ills betrayed.
Oh had I rather unadmired remained
In some lone isle, or distant Northern land;
Where the gilt Chariot never marks the way, 155
Where none learn Ombre, none e'er taste Bohea!
There kept my charms concealed from mortal eye,
Like roses, that in deserts bloom and die.
What moved my mind with youthful Lords to roam?
O had I stayed, and said my prayers at home! 160
'Twas this, the morning omens seemed to tell,
Thrice from my trembling hand the patch box fell;
The tottering China shook without a wind,
Nay, Poll sat mute, and Shock was most unkind!
A Sylph too warned me of the threats of fate, 165
In mystic visions, now believed too late!
See the poor remnants of these slighted hairs!
My hands shall rend what even thy rapine spares:
These in two sable ringlets taught to break,
Once gave new beauties to the snowy neck; 170
The sister lock now sits uncouth, alone,
And in its fellow's fate foresees its own;
Uncurled it hangs, the fatal shears demands,
And tempts once more, thy sacrilegious hands.
Oh hadst thou, cruel! been content to seize 175
Hairs less in sight, or any hairs but these!"

156 *Bohea:* a fashionable kind of tea.

CANTO V

She said: the pitying audience melt in tears.
But Fate and Jove had stopped the Baron's ears.
In vain Thalestris with reproach assails,
For who can move when fair Belinda fails?
Not half so fixed the Trojan could remain, 5
While Anna begged and Dido raged in vain.
Then grave Clarissa graceful waved her fan;

5 *The Trojan:* Aeneas, who deserted Dido, Queen of Carthage, despite the prayers of her sister Anna.

Silence ensued, and thus the nymph began:
"Say why are Beauties praised and honoured most,
The wise man's passion, and the vain man's toast? 10
Why decked with all that land and sea afford,
Why Angels called, and Angel-like adored?
Why round our coaches crowd the white-gloved Beaux,
Why bows the side-box from its inmost rows;
How vain are all these glories, all our pains, 15
Unless good sense preserve what beauty gains:
That men may say, when we the front-box grace,
'Behold the first in virtue as in face!'
Oh! if to dance all night, and dress all day,
Charmed the smallpox, or chased old age away; 20
Who would not scorn what housewife's cares produce,
Or who would learn one earthly thing of use?
To patch, nay ogle, might become a Saint,
Nor could it sure be such a sin to paint.
But since, alas! frail beauty must decay, 25
Curled or uncurled, since Locks will turn to grey;
Since painted, or not painted, all shall fade,
And she who scorns a man, must die a maid;
What then remains but well our power to use,
And keep good humour still whate'er we lose? 30
And trust me, dear! good humour can prevail,
When airs, and flights, and screams, and scolding fail.
Beauties in vain their pretty eyes may roll;
Charms strike the sight, but merit wins the soul."
So spoke the Dame, but no applause ensued; 35
Belinda frowned, Thalestris called her Prude.
"To arms, to arms!" the fierce Virago cries,
And swift as lightning to the combat flies.
All side in parties, and begin th' attack;
Fans clap, silks rustle, and tough whalebones crack; 40
Heroes' and Heroines' shouts confusedly rise,
And bass and treble voices strike the skies.
No common weapons in their hands are found,
Like Gods they fight, nor dread a mortal wound.
So when bold Homer makes the Gods engage, 45
And heavenly breasts with human passions rage;
'Gainst Pallas, Mars; Latona, Hermes arms;

And all Olympus rings with loud alarms:
Jove's thunder roars, heaven trembles all around,
Blue Neptune storms, the bellowing deeps resound: 50
Earth shakes her nodding towers, the ground gives way,
And the pale ghosts start at the flash of day!
Triumphant Umbriel on a sconce's height
Clapped his glad wings, and sat to view the fight:
Propped on their bodkin spears, the Sprites survey 55
The growing combat, or assist the fray.
While through the press enraged Thalestris flies,
And scatters death around from both her eyes,
A Beau and Witling perished in the throng,
One died in metaphor, and one in song. 60
"O cruel nymph! a living death I bear,"
Cried Dapperwit, and sunk beside his chair.
A mournful glance Sir Fopling upwards cast,
"Those eyes are made so killing"—was his last.
Thus on Mæander's flowery margin lies 65
Th' expiring Swan, and as he sings he dies.
When bold Sir Plume had drawn Clarissa down,
Chloe stepped in, and killed him with a frown;
She smiled to see the doughty hero slain,
But, at her smile, the Beau revived again. 70
Now Jove suspends his golden scales in air,
Weighs the Men's wits against the Lady's hair;
The doubtful beam long nods from side to side;
At length the wits mount up, the hairs subside.
See, fierce Belinda on the Baron flies, 75
With more than usual lightning in her eyes:
Nor feared the Chief th' unequal fight to try,
Who sought no more than on his foe to die.
But this bold Lord with manly strength endued,
She with one finger and a thumb subdued: 80
Just where the breath of life his nostrils drew,
A charge of Snuff the wily virgin threw;
The Gnomes direct, to every atom just,
The pungent grains of titillating dust.
Sudden with starting tears each eye o'erflows, 85

53 *sconce:* a wall-bracket for candles. 59 *Witling:* a young dandy or fop.

And the high dome re-echoes to his nose.
  Now meet thy fate, incensed Belinda cried,
And drew a deadly bodkin from her side.
(The same, his ancient personage to deck,
Her great great grandsire wore about his neck, 90
In three seal rings; which after, melted down,
Formed a vast buckle for his widow's gown:
Her infant grandame's whistle next it grew,
The bells she jingled, and the whistle blew;
Then in a bodkin graced her mother's hairs, 95
Which long she wore, and now Belinda wears.)
  "Boast not my fall" (he cried) "insulting foe!
Thou by some other shalt be laid as low.
Nor think, to die dejects my lofty mind:
All that I dread is leaving you behind! 100
Rather than so, ah let me still survive,
And burn in Cupid's flames—but burn alive."
  "Restore the Lock!" she cries; and all around
"Restore the Lock!" the vaulted roofs rebound.
Not fierce Othello in so loud a strain 105
Roared for the handkerchief that caused his pain.
But see how oft ambitious aims are crossed,
And chiefs contend till all the prize is lost!
The Lock, obtained with guilt, and kept with pain,
In every place is sought, but sought in vain: 110
With such a prize no mortal must be blest,
So heaven decrees! with heaven who can contest?
  Some thought it mounted to the Lunar sphere,
Since all things lost on earth are treasured there.
There Heroes' wits are kept in ponderous vases, 115
And beaux' in snuffboxes and tweezer cases.
There broken vows and deathbed alms are found,
And lovers' hearts with ends of riband bound,
The courtier's promises, and sick man's prayers,
The smiles of harlots, and the tears of heirs, 120
Cages for gnats, and chains to yoke a flea,
Dried butterflies, and tomes of casuistry.
  But trust the Muse—she saw it upward rise,
Though marked by none but quick, poetic eyes:

(So Rome's great founder to the heavens withdrew, 125
To Proculus alone confessed in view)
A sudden Star, it shot through liquid air,
And drew behind a radiant trail of hair.
Not Berenice's Locks first rose so bright,
The heavens bespangling with dishevelled light. 130
The Sylphs behold it kindling as it flies,
And pleased pursue its progress through the skies.
This the Beau monde shall from the Mall survey,
And hail with music its propitious ray.
This the blest Lover shall for Venus take, 135
And send up vows from Rosamonda's lake.
This Partridge soon shall view in cloudless skies,
When next he looks through Galileo's eyes;
And hence th' egregious wizard shall foredoom
The fate of Louis, and the fall of Rome. 140
Then cease, bright Nymph! to mourn thy ravished hair,
Which adds new glory to the shining sphere!
Not all the tresses that fair head can boast,
Shall draw such envy as the Lock you lost.
For, after all the murders of your eye, 145
When, after millions slain, yourself shall die;
When those fair suns shall set, as set they must,
And all those tresses shall be laid in dust,
This Lock, the Muse shall consecrate to fame,
And midst the stars inscribe Belinda's name. 150

126 *Proculus:* Roman senator who confirmed the translation of Romulus, the founder of Rome, to heaven. 129 *Berenice's Locks:* the hair of the Egyptian queen Berenice became a constellation. 133 *Beau monde:* the world of fashion; *Mall:* fashionable promenade in St. James' Park. 136 *Rosamonda's lake:* a pond in St. James' Park, often identified with unhappy lovers. 137 *Partridge:* an astrologer of the day. 140 *Louis:* Louis XIV of France.

ESSAY ON MAN

(*Epistle II*)

I. Know then thyself, presume not God to scan;
The proper study of Mankind is Man.
Placed on this isthmus of a middle state,

A Being darkly wise, and rudely great:
With too much knowledge for the Sceptic side, 5
With too much weakness for the Stoic's pride,
He hangs between; in doubt to act, or rest;
In doubt to deem himself a God, or Beast;
In doubt his Mind or Body to prefer;
Born but to die, and reasoning but to err; 10
Alike in ignorance, his reason such,
Whether he thinks too little, or too much:
Chaos of Thought and Passion, all confused;
Still by himself abused, or disabused;
Created half to rise, and half to fall; 15
Great lord of all things, yet a prey to all;
Sole judge of Truth, in endless Error hurled:
The glory, jest, and riddle of the world!
  Go, wondrous creature! mount where Science guides,
Go, measure earth, weigh air, and state the tides; 20
Instruct the planets in what orbs to run,
Correct old Time, and regulate the Sun;
Go, soar with Plato to th' empyreal sphere,
To the first good, first perfect, and first fair;
Or tread the mazy round his followers trod, 25
And quitting sense call imitating God;
As Eastern priests in giddy circles run,
And turn their heads to imitate the Sun.
Go, teach Eternal Wisdom how to rule—
Then drop into thyself, and be a fool! 30
  Superior beings, when of late they saw
A mortal Man unfold all Nature's law,
Admired such wisdom in an earthly shape,
And showed a NEWTON as we show an Ape.
  Could he, whose rules the rapid Comet bind, 35
Describe or fix one movement of his Mind?
Who saw its fires here rise, and there descend,
Explain his own beginning, or his end?
Alas what wonder! Man's superior part
Unchecked may rise, and climb from art to art; 40
But when his own great work is but begun,

26 *quitting sense:* leaving the sensory world.

What Reason weaves, by Passion is undone.
Trace Science then, with Modesty thy guide;
First strip off all her equipage of Pride;
Deduct what is but Vanity, or Dress, 45
Or Learning's Luxury, or Idleness;
Or tricks to show the stretch of human brain,
Mere curious pleasure, or ingenious pain;
Expunge the whole, or lop th' excrescent parts
Of all our Vices have created Arts; 50
Then see how little the remaining sum,
Which served the past, and must the times to come!
II. Two Principles in human nature reign;
Self-love, to urge, and Reason, to restrain;
Nor this a good, nor that a bad we call, 55
Each works its end, to move or govern all:
And to their proper operation still,
Ascribe all Good; to their improper, Ill.
Self-love, the spring of motion, acts the soul;
Reason's comparing balance rules the whole. 60
Man, but for that, no action could attend,
And but for this, were active to no end:
Fixed like a plant on his peculiar spot,
To draw nutrition, propagate, and rot:
Or, meteor-like, flame lawless through the void, 65
Destroying others, by himself destroyed.
Most strength the moving principle requires;
Active its task, it prompts, impels, inspires.
Sedate and quiet the comparing lies,
Form'd but to check, deliberate, and advise. 70
Self-love still stronger, as its objects nigh;
Reason's at distance, and in prospect lie:
That sees immediate good by present sense;
Reason, the future and the consequence.
Thicker than arguments, temptations throng, 75
At best more watchful this, but that more strong.
The action of the stronger to suspend,
Reason still use, to Reason still attend.
Attention, habit, and experience gains;

59 *acts:* activates.

Each strengthens Reason, and Self-love restrains. 80
Let subtle schoolmen teach these friends to fight,
More studious to divide than to unite;
And Grace and Virtue, Sense and Reason split,
With all the rash dexterity of wit.
Wits, just like Fools, at war about a name, 85
Have full as oft no meaning, or the same.
Self-love and Reason to one end aspire,
Pain their aversion, Pleasure their desire;
But greedy That, its object would devour,
This taste the honey, and not wound the flower: 90
Pleasure, or wrong or rightly understood,
Our greatest evil, or our greatest good.
  III. Modes of Self-love the Passions we may call:
'Tis real good, or seeming, moves them all:
But since not every good we can divide, 95
And Reason bids us for our own provide;
Passions, though selfish, if their means be fair,
List under Reason, and deserve her care;
Those, that imparted, court a nobler aim,
Exalt their kind, and take some Virtue's name. 100
  In lazy Apathy let Stoics boast
Their Virtue fixed; 'tis fixed as in a frost;
Contracted all, retiring to the breast;
But strength of mind is Exercise, not Rest:
The rising tempest puts in act the soul, 105
Parts it may ravage, but preserves the whole.
On life's vast ocean diversely we sail,
Reason the card, but Passion is the gale;
Nor God alone in the still calm we find,
He mounts the storm, and walks upon the wind. 110
  Passions, like Elements, though born to fight,
Yet, mixed and softened, in his work unite:
These 'tis enough to temper and employ;
But what composes Man, can Man destroy?
Suffice that Reason keep to Nature's road, 115
Subject, compound them, follow her and God.

98 *List:* enlist. 99 *Those, that imparted:* passions to which reason has given its approval. 108 *card:* compass.

Love, Hope, and Joy, fair pleasure's smiling train,
Hate, Fear, and Grief, the family of pain,
These mixed with art, and to due bounds confined,
Make and maintain the balance of the mind: 120
The lights and shades, whose well accorded strife
Gives all the strength and colour of our life.
Pleasures are ever in our hands or eyes;
And when, in act, they cease, in prospect, rise:
Present to grasp, and future still to find, 125
The whole employ of body and of mind.
All spread their charms, but charm not all alike;
On different senses different objects strike;
Hence different Passions more or less inflame,
As strong or weak, the organs of the frame; 130
And hence one MASTER PASSION in the breast,
Like Aaron's serpent, swallows up the rest.
As Man, perhaps, the moment of his breath,
Receives the lurking principle of death;
The young disease, that must subdue at length, 135
Grows with his growth, and strengthens with his strength:
So, cast and mingled with his very frame,
The Mind's disease, its RULING PASSION came;
Each vital humour which should feed the whole,
Soon flows to this, in body and in soul: 140
Whatever warms the heart, or fills the head,
As the mind opens, and its functions spread,
Imagination plies her dangerous art,
And pours it all upon the peccant part.
Nature its mother, Habit is its nurse; 145
Wit, Spirit, Faculties, but make it worse;
Reason itself but gives it edge and power;
As Heaven's blest beam turns vinegar more sour.
We, wretched subjects, though to lawful sway,
In this weak queen some favorite still obey: 150
Ah! if she lend not arms, as well as rules,
What can she more than tell us we are fools?

132 *Aaron's serpent:* when Aaron cast down his rod before Pharaoh, it turned into a serpent which consumed all the serpents into which the rods of the Egyptian magicians had been transformed. 144 *peccant:* diseased. 150 *queen:* i. e., reason.

Teach us to mourn our Nature, not to mend,
A sharp accuser, but a helpless friend!
Or from a judge turn pleader, to persuade 155
The choice we make, or justify it made;
Proud of an easy conquest all along,
She but removes weak passions for the strong:
So, when small humours gather to a gout,
The doctor fancies he has driven them out. 160
  Yes, Nature's road must ever be preferred;
Reason is here no guide, but still a guard:
'Tis hers to rectify, not overthrow,
And treat this passion more as friend than foe:
A mightier Power the strong direction sends, 165
And several Men impels to several ends:
Like varying winds, by other passions tost,
This drives them constant to a certain coast.
Let power or knowledge, gold or glory, please,
Or (oft more strong than all) the love of ease; 170
Through life 'tis followed, even at life's expense;
The merchant's toil, the sage's indolence,
The monk's humility, the hero's pride,
All, all alike, find Reason on their side.
  Th' Eternal Art educing good from ill, 175
Grafts on this Passion our best principle:
'Tis thus the Mercury of Man is fixed,
Strong grows the Virtue with his nature mixed;
The dross cements what else were too refined,
And in one interest body acts with mind. 180
  As fruits, ungrateful to the planter's care,
On savage stocks inserted, learn to bear;
The surest Virtues thus from Passions shoot,
Wild Nature's vigor working at the root.
What crops of wit and honesty appear 185
From spleen, from obstinacy, hate, or fear!
See anger, zeal and fortitude supply;
Even avarice, prudence; sloth, philosophy;
Lust, through some certain strainers well refined,
Is gentle love, and charms all womankind; 190

166 *several:* various. 175 *Eternal Art:* Providence.

Envy, to which th' ignoble mind's a slave,
Is emulation in the learned or brave;
Nor Virtue, male or female, can we name,
But what will grow on Pride, or grow on Shame.
  Thus Nature gives us (let it check our pride) 195
The virtue nearest to our vice allied:
Reason the bias turns to good from ill,
And Nero reigns a Titus, if he will.
The fiery soul abhorred in Catiline,
In Decius charms, in Curtius is divine: 200
The same ambition can destroy or save,
And makes a patriot as it makes a knave.
  IV. This light and darkness in our chaos joined,
What shall divide? The God within the mind.
  Extremes in Nature equal ends produce, 205
In Man they join to some mysterious use;
Though each by turns the other's bound invade,
As, in some well-wrought picture, light and shade,
And oft so mix, the difference is too nice
Where ends the Virtue, or begins the Vice. 210
  Fools! who from hence into the notion fall,
That Vice or Virtue there is none at all.
If white and black blend, soften, and unite
A thousand ways, is there no black or white?
Ask your own heart, and nothing is so plain; 215
'Tis to mistake them, costs the time and pain.
  V. Vice is a monster of so frightful mien,
As, to be hated, needs but to be seen;
Yet seen too oft, familiar with her face,
We first endure, then pity, then embrace. 220
But where th' Extreme of Vice, was ne'er agreed:
Ask where's the North? at York, 'tis on the Tweed;
In Scotland, at the Orcades; and there,
At Greenland, Zembla, or the Lord knows where.
No creature owns it in the first degree, 225
But thinks his neighbour further gone than he;

198 *Nero:* a Roman emperor famed for his depravity and cruelty; *Titus:* a Roman emperor famed for his benevolence. 199 *Catiline:* a Roman conspirator. 200 *Decius, Curtius:* two legendary Romans who sacrificed their lives for the good of Rome.

Even those who dwell beneath its very zone,
Or never feel the rage, or never own;
What happier natures shrink at with affright,
The hard inhabitant contends is right. 230

VI. Virtuous and vicious every Man must be,
Few in th' extreme, but all in the degree;
The rogue and fool by fits is fair and wise;
And even the best, by fits, what they despise.
'Tis but by parts we follow good or ill; 235
For, Vice or Virtue, Self directs it still;
Each individual seeks a several goal;
But HEAVEN's great view is One, and that the Whole.
That counterworks each folly and caprice;
That disappoints th' effect of every vice; 240
That, happy frailties to all ranks applied;
Shame to the virgin, to the matron pride,
Fear to the statesman, rashness to the chief,
To kings presumption, and to crowds belief:
That, Virtue's ends from Vanity can raise, 245
Which seeks no interest, no reward but praise;
And build on wants, and on defects of mind,
The joy, the peace, the glory of Mankind.

Heaven forming each on other to depend,
A master, or a servant, or a friend, 250
Bids each on other for assistance call,
Till one Man's weakness grows the strength of all.
Wants, frailties, passions, closer still ally
The common interest, or endear the tie.
To these we owe true friendship, love sincere, 255
Each home-felt joy that life inherits here;
Yet from the same we learn, in its decline,
Those joys, those loves, those interests to resign;
Taught half by Reason, half by mere decay,
To welcome death, and calmly pass away. 260

Whate'er the Passion, knowledge, fame, or pelf,
Not one will change his neighbour with himself.
The learned is happy nature to explore,
The fool is happy that he knows no more;
The rich is happy in the plenty given, 265
The poor contents him with the care of Heaven.

See the blind beggar dance, the cripple sing,
The sot a hero, lunatic a king;
The starving chemist in his golden views
Supremely blest, the poet in his Muse. 270
See some strange comfort every state attend,
And Pride bestowed on all, a common friend;
See some fit Passion every age supply,
Hope travels through, nor quits us when we die.
Behold the child, by Nature's kindly law, 275
Pleased with a rattle, tickled with a straw:
Some livelier plaything gives his youth delight,
A little louder, but as empty quite:
Scarfs, garters, gold, amuse his riper stage,
And beads and prayer books are the toys of age: 280
Pleased with this bauble still, as that before;
Till tired he sleeps, and Life's poor play is o'er.
Meanwhile Opinion gilds with varying rays
Those painted clouds that beautify our days;
Each want of happiness by hope supplied, 285
And each vacuity of sense by Pride:
These build as fast as knowledge can destroy;
In Folly's cup still laughs the bubble, joy;
One prospect lost, another still we gain;
And not a vanity is given in vain; 290
Even mean Self-love becomes, by force divine,
The scale to measure others' wants by thine.
See! and confess, one comfort still must rise,
'Tis this, Though Man's a fool, yet GOD IS WISE.

269 *chemist:* alchemist. 280 *beads:* rosaries.

MORAL ESSAY FOUR: ON RICHES

To Richard Boyle, Earl of Burlington

'Tis strange, the Miser should his Cares employ
To gain those Riches he can ne'er enjoy:
Is it less strange, the Prodigal should waste
His wealth, to purchase what he ne'er can taste?

Not for himself he sees, or hears, or eats; 5
Artists must choose his Pictures, Music, Meats:
He buys for Topham, Drawings and Designs,
For Pembroke, Statues, dirty Gods, and Coins;
Rare monkish Manuscripts for Hearne alone,
And Books for Mead, and Butterflies for Sloane. 10
Think we all these are for himself! no more
Than his fine Wife, alas! or finer Whore.
For what has Virro painted, built, and planted?
Only to show, how many Tastes he wanted.
What brought Sir Visto's ill got wealth to waste? 15
Some Dæmon whispered, "Visto! have a Taste."
Heaven visits with a Taste the wealthy fool,
And needs no Rod but Ripley with a Rule.
See! sportive fate, to punish awkward pride,
Bids Bubo build, and sends him such a Guide: 20
A standing sermon, at each year's expense,
That never Coxcomb reached Magnificence!
You show us, Rome was glorious, not profuse,
And pompous buildings once were things of Use.
Yet shall (my Lord) your just, your noble rules 25
Fill half the land with Imitating Fools;
Who random drawings from your sheets shall take,
And of one beauty many blunders make;
Load some vain Church with old Theatric state,
Turn Arcs of triumph to a Garden gate; 30
Reverse your Ornaments, and hang them all
On some patched dog-hole eked with ends of wall;
Then clap four slices of Pilaster on't,
That, laced with bits of rustic, makes a Front.

7 *Topham:* Richard Topham, a man noted for his art collection. 8 *Pembroke:* the eighth Earl of Pembroke, who had a collection of statues, pictures, and coins. 9 *Hearne:* Thomas Hearne, a leading medieval scholar. 10 *Mead, Sloan:* both were physicians of Pope's day; Mead was famous for his library, and Sloan for his collection of "natural curiosities." 13, 15 *Virro, Sir Visto:* it is not certain whether Pope had any specific member of the *nouveau riche* in mind here. 18 *Ripley:* an architect whose works Pope thought inferior. 20 *Bubo:* George Bubb, a Whig politician who later took the name Dodington and finally became Baron Melcombe. 23 *You:* the Earl of Burlington, to whom this poem is addressed, was publishing Inigo Jones' *Designs* and Palladio's *Antiquities of Rome.*

Shall call the winds through long arcades to roar, 35
Proud to catch cold at a Venetian door;
Conscious they act a true Palladian part,
And, if they starve, they starve by rules of art.
  Oft have you hinted to your brother Peer,
A certain truth, which many buy too dear: 40
Something there is more needful than Expense,
And something previous even to Taste—'tis Sense:
Good Sense, which only is the gift of Heaven,
And though no Science, fairly worth the seven:
A Light, which in yourself you must perceive; 45
Jones and Le Nôtre have it not to give.
  To build, to plant, whatever you intend,
To rear the Column, or the Arch to bend,
To swell the Terrace, or to sink the Grot;
In all, let Nature never be forgot. 50
But treat the Goddess like a modest fair,
Nor overdress, nor leave her wholly bare;
Let not each beauty everywhere be spied,
Where half the skill is decently to hide.
He gains all points, who pleasingly confounds, 55
Surprises, varies, and conceals the Bounds.
  Consult the Genius of the Place in all;
That tells the Waters or to rise, or fall;
Or helps th' ambitious Hill the heavens to scale,
Or scoops in circling theatres the Vale; 60
Calls in the Country, catches opening glades,
Joins willing woods, and varies shades from shades;
Now breaks, or now directs, th' intending Lines;
Paints as you plant, and, as you work, designs.
  Still follow Sense, of every Art the Soul, 65
Parts answering parts shall slide into a whole,
Spontaneous beauties all around advance,
Start even from Difficulty, strike from Chance;
Nature shall join you; Time shall make it grow
A Work to wonder at—perhaps a STOWE. 70

46 *Jones and Le Nôtre:* Inigo Jones was a celebrated architect and designer; Le Nôtre was a famous designer of French gardens. 70 *Stowe:* the residence of Lord Viscount Cobham, which was much admired for its beauty.

Without it, proud Versailles! thy glory falls;
And Nero's Terraces desert their walls:
The vast Parterres a thousand hands shall make,
Lo! COBHAM comes, and floats them with a Lake:
Or cut wide views through Mountains to the Plain, 75
You'll wish your hill or sheltered seat again.
Even in an ornament its place remark,
Nor in an Hermitage set Dr. Clarke.
Behold Villario's ten years' toil complete;
His Quincunx darkens, his Espaliers meet; 80
The Wood supports the Plain, the parts unite,
And strength of Shade contends with strength of Light;
A waving Glow the bloomy beds display,
Blushing in bright diversities of day,
With silver-quivering rills meandered o'er— 85
Enjoy them, you! Villario can no more:
Tired of the scene Parterres and Fountains yield,
He finds at last he better likes a Field.

Through his young Woods how pleased Sabinus strayed,
Or sat delighted in the thickening shade, 90
With annual joy the reddening shoots to greet,
Or see the stretching branches long to meet!
His Son's fine Taste an opener Vista loves,
Foe to the Dryads of his Father's groves;
One boundless Green, or flourished Carpet views, 95
With all the mournful family of Yews:
The thriving plants, ignoble broomsticks made,
Now sweep those Alleys they were born to shade.

At Timon's Villa let us pass a day,
Where all cry out, "What sums are thrown away!" 100
So proud, so grand: of that stupendous air,
Soft and Agreeable come never there.
Greatness, with Timon, dwells in such a draught

78: the bust of Dr. Samuel Clarke, one of Queen Caroline's favorites, had been placed in the Hermitage at Richmond Park; this was a great source of amusement to Queen Caroline's enemies. 79 *Villario:* Earl Tylney of Castlemaine, who owned a great mansion in Essex. 80 *Quincunx:* a group of five trees, four of them forming a square and the fifth in the center; *Espalier:* a lattice or trellis. 89 *Sabinus:* this name, like "Timon," probably refers to an imaginary person.

As brings all Brobdignag before your thought.
To compass this, his building is a Town, 105
His pond an Ocean, his parterre a Down:
Who but must laugh, the Master when he sees,
A puny insect, shivering at a breeze!
Lo, what huge heaps of littleness around!
The whole, a laboured Quarry above ground. 110
Two Cupids squirt before: a Lake behind
Improves the keenness of the Northern wind.
His Gardens next your admiration call,
On every side you look, behold the Wall!
No pleasing Intricacies intervene, 115
No artful wildness to perplex the scene;
Grove nods at grove, each Alley has a brother,
And half the platform just reflects the other.
The suffering eye inverted Nature sees,
Trees cut to Statues, Statues thick as trees; 120
With here a Fountain, never to be played;
And there a Summerhouse, that knows no shade;
Here Amphitrite sails through myrtle bowers;
There Gladiators fight, or die in flowers;
Unwatered see the drooping sea-horse mourn, 125
And swallows roost in Nilus' dusty Urn.
My Lord advances with majestic mien,
Smit with the mighty pleasure, to be seen:
But soft—by regular approach—not yet—
First through the length of yon hot Terrace sweat; 130
And when up ten steep slopes you've dragged your thighs,
Just at his Study door he'll bless your eyes.
His Study! with what Authors is it stored?
In Books, not Authors, curious is my Lord;
To all their dated Backs he turns you round: 135
These Aldus printed, those Du Sueil has bound.
Lo, some are Vellum, and the rest as good
For all his Lordship knows, but they are Wood.
For Locke or Milton 'tis in vain to look,

113, 114 *Amphitrite, Gladiators:* i. e., statues. 136 *Aldus:* Aldo Manutius, a famous printer of the Renaissance; *Du Sueil:* a French bookbinder of the eighteenth century.

These shelves admit not any modern book. 140
And now the Chapel's silver bell you hear,
That summons you to all the Pride of Prayer:
Light quirks of Music, broken and uneven,
Make the soul dance upon a Jig to Heaven.
On painted Ceilings you devoutly stare, 145
Where sprawl the Saints of Verrio or Laguerre,
On gilded clouds in fair expansion lie,
And bring all Paradise before your eye.
To rest, the Cushion and soft Dean invite,
Who never mentions Hell to ears polite. 150
But hark! the chiming Clocks to dinner call;
A hundred footsteps scrape the marble Hall:
The rich Buffet well-coloured Serpents grace,
And gaping Tritons spew to wash your face.
Is this a dinner? this a Genial room? 155
No, 'tis a Temple, and a Hecatomb.
A solemn Sacrifice, performed in state,
You drink by measure, and to minutes eat.
So quick retires each flying course, you'd swear
Sancho's dread Doctor and his Wand were there. 160
Between each Act the trembling salvers ring,
From soup to sweet wine, and God bless the King.
In plenty starving, tantalized in state,
And complaisantly helped to all I hate,
Treated, caressed, and tired, I take my leave, 165
Sick of his civil Pride from Morn to Eve;
I curse such lavish cost, and little skill,
And swear no Day was ever passed so ill.
Yet hence the Poor are clothed, the Hungry fed;
Health to himself, and to his Infants bread 170
The Laborer bears: What his hard Heart denies,
His charitable Vanity supplies.
Another age shall see the golden Ear

146 *Verrio, Laguerre:* Antonio Verrio painted the ceilings at Windsor and Hampton Court; Laguerre painted the ceiling at Blenheim Castle, and elsewhere. 153–4: here Pope is ridiculing the practice of placing statues of serpents or statues with open mouths ejecting water in such places as dining chambers. 160: a reference to an incident in *Don Quixote,* chapter 47.

Embrown the Slope, and nod on the Parterre,
Deep Harvests bury all his pride has planned, 175
And laughing Ceres reassume the land.
  Who then shall grace, or who improve the Soil?
Who plants like BATHURST, or who builds like BOYLE.
'Tis Use alone that sanctifies Expense,
And Splendour borrows all her rays from Sense. 180
  His Father's Acres who enjoys in peace,
Or makes his Neighbours glad, if he increase:
Whose cheerful Tenants bless their yearly toil,
Yet to their Lord owe more than to the soil;
Whose ample Lawns are not ashamed to feed 185
The milky heifer and deserving steed;
Whose rising Forests, not for pride or show,
But future Buildings, future Navies, grow:
Let his plantations stretch from down to down,
First shade a Country, and then raise a Town. 190
  You too proceed! make falling Arts your care,
Erect new wonders, and the old repair;
Jones and Palladio to themselves restore,
And be whate'er Vitruvius was before:
Till Kings call forth th' Ideas of your mind, 195
(Proud to accomplish what such hands designed,)
Bid Harbours open, public Ways extend,
Bid Temples, worthier of the God, ascend;
Bid the broad Arch the dangerous Flood contain,
The Mole projected break the roaring Main; 200
Back to his bounds their subject Sea command,
And roll obedient Rivers through the Land:
These Honours, Peace to happy Britain brings,
These are Imperial Works, and worthy Kings.

178 *Bathurst:* a close friend of Pope's, and one whose taste in landscaping Pope admired. 194 *Vitruvius:* a Roman who wrote a work on architecture. 200 *Mole projected:* a proposed breakwater or jetty.

WILLIAM WORDSWORTH

[1770–1850]

William Wordsworth was born in Cockermouth, Cumberland; his mother died when he was eight, his father when he was thirteen. After graduating from Cambridge (1791), Wordsworth went to France, where he became deeply interested in the French Revolution and had an affair with a Frenchwoman, Annette Vallon, who bore him an illegitimate daughter, Anne-Caroline. Returning to England, Wordsworth fell into a state of dejection which he did not escape until he and his sister Dorothy were able to settle in a cottage at Racedown in Dorsetshire (1795).

Wordsworth's meeting with Coleridge in 1795 led to their collaboration on the volume called LYRICAL BALLADS *(1798), in which Wordsworth's "We Are Seven" and "Lines Composed a Few Miles Above Tintern Abbey" first appeared. In 1800, after Wordsworth, Dorothy, and Coleridge had made a trip to Germany, Wordsworth published a second edition of* LYRICAL BALLADS. *This edition contained not only the five "Lucy Poems" and "Michael," but also the famous Preface in which Wordsworth attacked the artificial diction of the poets of the eighteenth century and announced his intention to write his own poetry in "the very language of men" and to concern himself with "incidents and situations from common life."*

In 1802 Wordsworth made a settlement with Annette Vallon and married his cousin, Mary Hutchinson. By 1810 he had written almost all of his finest poetry. He spent a large part of the remaining forty years of his life in revising THE PRELUDE, *a long narrative account of his youth which he had begun in 1799 but which was not published until 1850. In 1843 he was appointed Poet Laureate. He was buried in the churchyard at Grasmere.*

Wordsworth's complete poems may be found in THE POETICAL WORKS OF WORDSWORTH, *edited by Thomas Hutchinson and revised by Ernest de Selincourt (1950); a good selection from them is presented by Carlos Baker in* THE PRELUDE, WITH A SELECTION FROM THE

SHORTER POEMS *(1954). G. M. Harper has written a two-volume biography,* WILLIAM WORDSWORTH: HIS LIFE, WORKS, AND INFLUENCE *(1929).*

EXPOSTULATION AND REPLY

"Why, William, on that old grey stone,
Thus for the length of half a day,
Why, William, sit you thus alone,
And dream your time away?

"Where are your books?—that light bequeathed 5
To Beings else forlorn and blind!
Up! Up! and drink the spirit breathed
From dead men to their kind.

"You look round on your Mother Earth,
As if she for no purpose bore you; 10
As if you were her first-born birth,
And none had lived before you!"

One morning thus, by Esthwaite lake,
When life was sweet, I knew not why,
To me my good friend Matthew spake, 15
And thus I made reply:

"The eye—it cannot choose but see;
We cannot bid the ear be still;
Our bodies feel, where'er they be,
Against or with our will. 20

"Nor less I deem that there are Powers
Which of themselves our minds impress;
That we can feed this mind of ours
In a wise passiveness.

"Think you, 'mid all this mighty sum 25
Of things for ever speaking,
That nothing of itself will come,
But we must still be seeking?

"—Then ask not wherefore, here, alone,
Conversing as I may,
I sit upon this old grey stone,
And dream my time away." 30

THE TABLES TURNED

An Evening Scene on the Same Subject

Up! up! my Friend, and quit your books;
Or surely you'll grow double:
Up! up! my Friend, and clear your looks;
Why all this toil and trouble?

The sun, above the mountain's head, 5
A freshening lustre mellow
Through all the long green fields has spread,
His first sweet evening yellow.

Books! 't is a dull and endless strife:
Come, hear the woodland linnet, 10
How sweet his music! on my life,
There's more of wisdom in it.

And hark! how blithe the throstle sings!
He, too, is no mean preacher:
Come forth into the light of things, 15
Let Nature be your Teacher.

She has a world of ready wealth,
Our minds and hearts to bless—
Spontaneous wisdom breathed by health,
Truth breathed by cheerfulness. 20

One impulse from a vernal wood
May teach you more of man,
Of moral evil and of good,
Than all the sages can.

Sweet is the lore which Nature brings; 25
Our meddling intellect
Mis-shapes the beauteous forms of things:—
We murder to dissect.

Enough of Science and of Art;
Close up those barren leaves; 30
Come forth, and bring with you a heart
That watches and receives.

TINTERN ABBEY

Five years have past; five summers, with the length
Of five long winters! and again I hear
These waters, rolling from their mountain-springs
With a soft inland murmur.—Once again
Do I behold these steep and lofty cliffs, 5
That on a wild secluded scene impress
Thoughts of more deep seclusion; and connect
The landscape with the quiet of the sky.
The day is come when I again repose
Here, under this dark sycamore, and view 10
These plots of cottage-ground, these orchard-tufts,
Which at this season, with their unripe fruits,
Are clad in one green hue, and lose themselves
'Mid groves and copses. Once again I see
These hedge-rows, hardly hedge-rows, little lines 15
Of sportive wood run wild: these pastoral farms,
Green to the very door; and wreaths of smoke
Sent up, in silence, from among the trees!
With some uncertain notice, as might seem
Of vagrant dwellers in the houseless woods, 20
Or of some Hermit's cave, where by his fire
The Hermit sits alone.

These beauteous forms,
Through a long absence, have not been to me
As is a landscape to blind man's eye:
But oft, in lonely rooms, and 'mid the din 25
Of towns and cities, I have owed to them
In hours of weariness, sensations sweet,
Felt in the blood, and felt along the heart;
And passing even into my purer mind,
With tranquil restoration:—feelings too 30

Of unremembered pleasure: such, perhaps,
As have no slight or trivial influence
On that best portion of a good man's life,
His little, nameless, unremembered, acts
Of kindness and of love. Nor less, I trust, 35
To them I may have owed another gift,
Of aspect more sublime; that blessed mood,
In which the burthen of the mystery,
In which the heavy and the weary weight
Of all this unintelligble world, 40
Is lightened:—that serene and blessed mood,
In which the affections gently lead us on,—
Until, the breath of this corporeal frame
And even the motion of our human blood
Almost suspended, we are laid asleep 45
In body, and become a living soul:
While with an eye made quiet by the power
Of harmony, and the deep power of joy,
We see into the life of things.

If this
Be but a vain belief, yet, oh! how oft— 50
In darkness and amid the many shapes
Of joyless daylight; when the fretful stir
Unprofitable, and the fever of the world,
Have hung upon the beatings of my heart—
How oft, in spirit, have I turned to thee, 55
O sylvan Wye! thou wanderer thro' the woods,
How often has my spirit turned to thee!
And now, with gleams of half extinguished thought,
With many recognitions dim and faint,
And somewhat of a sad perplexity, 60
The picture of the mind revives again:
While here I stand, not only with the sense
Of present pleasure, but with pleasing thoughts
That in this moment there is life and food
For future years. And so I dare to hope, 65
Though changed, no doubt, from what I was when first

56 *Wye:* river flowing between England and Wales.

I came among these hills; when like a roe
I bounded o'er the mountains, by the sides
Of the deep rivers, and the lonely streams,
Wherever nature led: more like a man 70
Flying from something that he dreads, than one
Who sought the thing he loved. For nature then
(The coarser pleasures of my boyish days,
And their glad animal movements all gone by)
To me was all in all.—I cannot paint 75
What then I was. The sounding cataract
Haunted me like a passion: the tall rock,
The mountain, and the deep and gloomy wood,
Their colours and their forms, were then to me
An appetite; a feeling and a love, 80
That had no need of a remoter charm,
By thought supplied, nor any interest
Unborrowed from the eye.—That time is past,
And all its aching joys are now no more,
And all its dizzy raptures. Not for this 85
Faint I, nor mourn nor murmur; other gifts
Have followed; for such loss, I would believe,
Abundant recompense. For I have learned
To look on nature, not as in the hour
Of thoughtless youth; but hearing oftentimes 90
The still, sad music of humanity,
Nor harsh nor grating, though of ample power
To chasten and subdue. And I have felt
A presence that disturbs me with the joy
Of elevated thoughts; a sense sublime 95
Of something far more deeply interfused,
Whose dwelling is the light of setting suns,
And the round ocean and the living air,
And the blue sky, and in the mind of man;
A motion and a spirit, that impels 100
All thinking things, all objects of all thought,
And rolls through all things. Therefore am I still
A lover of the meadows and the woods,
And mountains; and of all that we behold
From this green earth; of all the mighty world 105
Of eye, and ear,—both what they half create,

And what perceive; well pleased to recognise
In nature and the language of the sense,
The anchor of my purest thoughts, the nurse,
The guide, the guardian of my heart, and soul 110
Of all my moral being.

Nor perchance,
If I were not thus taught, should I the more
Suffer my genial spirits to decay:
For thou art with me here upon the banks
Of this fair river; thou my dearest Friend, 115
My dear, dear Friend; and in thy voice I catch
The language of my former heart, and read
My former pleasures in the shooting lights
Of thy wild eyes. Oh! yet a little while
May I behold in thee what I was once, 120
My dear, dear Sister! and this prayer I make,
Knowing that Nature never did betray
The heart that loved her; 'tis her privilege,
Through all the years of this our life, to lead
From joy to joy: for she can so inform 125
The mind that is within us, so impress
With quietness and beauty, and so feed
With lofty thoughts, that neither evil tongues,
Rash judgments, nor the sneers of selfish men,
Nor greetings where no kindness is, nor all 130
The dreary intercourse of daily life,
Shall e'er prevail against us, or disturb
Our cheerful faith that all which we behold
Is full of blessings. Therefore let the moon
Shine on thee in thy solitary walk; 135
And let the misty mountain-winds be free
To blow against thee: and, in after years,
When these wild ecstasies shall be matured
Into a sober pleasure; when thy mind
Shall be a mansion for all lovely forms, 140
Thy memory be as a dwelling-place
For all sweet sounds and harmonies; oh! then,
If solitude, or fear, or pain, or grief,
Should be thy portion, with what healing thoughts

Of tender joy wilt thou remember me, 145
And these my exhortations! Nor, perchance—
If I should be where I no more can hear
Thy voice, nor catch from thy wild eyes these gleams
Of past existence—wilt thou then forget
That on the banks of this delightful stream 150
We stood together; and that I, so long
A worshipper of Nature, hither came
Unwearied in that service: rather say
With warmer love—oh! with far deeper zeal
Of holier love. Nor wilt thou then forget, 155
That after many wanderings, many years
Of absence, these steep woods and lofty cliffs,
And this green pastoral landscape, were to me
More dear, both for themselves and for thy sake!

LUCY GRAY

OR, SOLITUDE

Oft I had heard of Lucy Gray:
And, when I crossed the wild,
I chanced to see at break of day
The solitary child.

No mate, no comrade Lucy knew; 5
She dwelt on a wide moor,
—The sweetest thing that ever grew
Beside a human door!

You yet may spy the fawn at play,
The hare upon the green; 10
But the sweet face of Lucy Gray
Will never more be seen.

"To-night will be a stormy night—
You to the town must go;
And take a lantern, Child, to light 15
Your mother through the snow."

"That, Father! will I gladly do:
'T is scarcely afternoon—
The minster-clock has just struck two,
And yonder is the moon!" 20

At this the Father raised his hook,
And snapped a faggot-band;
He plied his work;—and Lucy took
The lantern in her hand.

Not blither is the mountain roe: 25
With many a wanton stroke
Her feet disperse the powdery snow,
That rises up like smoke.

The storm came on before its time:
She wandered up and down; 30
And many a hill did Lucy climb:
But never reached the town.

The wretched parents all that night
Went shouting far and wide;
But there was neither sound nor sight 35
To serve them for a guide.

At day-break on a hill they stood
That overlooked the moor;
And thence they saw the bridge of wood,
A furlong from their door. 40

They wept—and, turning homeward, cried,
"In heaven we all shall meet;"
—When in the snow the mother spied
The print of Lucy's feet.

Then downwards from the steep hill's edge 45
They tracked the footmarks small;
And through the broken hawthorne hedge,
And by the long stone-wall;

And then an open field they crossed;
The marks were still the same; 50
They tracked them on, nor ever lost;
And to the bridge they came.

They followed from the snowy bank
Those footmarks, one by one,
Into the middle of the plank; 55
And further there were none!

—Yet some maintain that to this day
She is a living child;
That you may see sweet Lucy Gray
Upon the lonesome wild. 60

O'er rough and smooth she trips along,
And never looks behind;
And sings a solitary song
That whistles in the wind.

STRANGE FITS OF PASSION HAVE I KNOWN

Strange fits of passion have I known:
And I will dare to tell,
But in the Lover's ear alone,
What once to me befell.

When she I loved looked every day 5
Fresh as a rose in June,
I to her cottage bent my way,
Beneath an evening-moon.

Upon the moon I fixed my eye,
All over the wide lea; 10
With quickening pace my horse drew nigh
Those paths so dear to me.

And now we reached the orchard-plot;
And, as we climbed the hill,
The sinking moon to Lucy's cot 15
Came near, and nearer still.

In one of those sweet dreams I slept,
Kind Nature's gentlest boon!
And all the while my eyes I kept
On the descending moon. 20

My horse moved on; hoof after hoof
He raised, and never stopped:
When down behind the cottage roof,
At once, the bright moon dropped.

What fond and wayward thoughts will slide 25
Into a Lover's head!
"O mercy!" to myself I cried,
"If Lucy should be dead!"

SHE DWELT AMONG THE UNTRODDEN WAYS

She dwelt among the untrodden ways
  Beside the springs of Dove,
A maid whom there were none to praise
  And very few to love:

A violet by a mossy stone 5
  Half hidden from the eye!
—Fair as a star, when only one
  Is shining in the sky.

She lived unknown, and few could know
  When Lucy ceased to be; 10
But she is in her grave, and, oh,
  The difference to me!

THREE YEARS SHE GREW IN SUN AND SHOWER

Three years she grew in sun and shower,
Then Nature said, "A lovelier flower
On earth was never sown;
This Child I to myself will take;
She shall be mine, and I will make 5
A Lady of my own.

"Myself will to my darling be
Both law and impulse: and with me
The Girl, in rock and plain,

In earth and heaven, in glade and bower, 10
Shall feel an overseeing power
To kindle or restrain.

"She shall be sportive as the fawn
That wild with glee across the lawn,
Or up the mountain springs; 15
And hers shall be the breathing balm,
And hers the silence and the calm
Of mute insensate things.

"The floating clouds their state shall lend
To her; for her the willow bend; 20
Nor shall she fail to see
Even in the motions of the Storm
Grace that shall mould the Maiden's form
By silent sympathy.

"The stars of midnight shall be dear 25
To her; and she shall lean her ear
In many a secret place
Where rivulets dance their wayward round,
And beauty born of murmuring sound
Shall pass into her face. 30

"And vital feelings of delight
Shall rear her form to stately height,
Her virgin bosom swell;
Such thoughts to Lucy I will give
While she and I together live 35
Here in this happy dell."

Thus Nature spake—The work was done—
How soon my Lucy's race was run!
She died, and left to me
This heath, this calm, and quiet scene;
The memory of what has been,
And never more will be.

I TRAVELLED AMONG UNKNOWN MEN

I travelled among unknown men,
  In lands beyond the sea;
Nor, England! did I know till then
  What love I bore to thee.

'Tis past, that melancholy dream! 5
  Nor will I quit thy shore
A second time; for still I seem
  To love thee more and more.

Among thy mountains did I feel
  The joy of my desire; 10
And she I cherished turned her wheel
  Beside an English fire.

Thy mornings showed, thy nights concealed
  The bowers where Lucy played;
And thine too is the last green field 15
  That Lucy's eyes surveyed.

A SLUMBER DID MY SPIRIT SEAL

A slumber did my spirit seal;
  I had no human fears;
She seemed a thing that could not feel
  The touch of earthly years.

No motion has she now, no force; 5
  She neither hears nor sees;
Rolled round in earth's diurnal course,
  With rocks, and stones, and trees.

SHE WAS A PHANTOM OF DELIGHT

She was a Phantom of delight
When first she gleamed upon my sight;
A lovely Apparition, sent
To be a moment's ornament;
Her eyes as stars of Twilight fair; 5
Like Twilight's, too, her dusky hair;
But all things else about her drawn
From May-time and the cheerful Dawn;
A dancing Shape, an Image gay,
To haunt, to startle, and way-lay. 10

I saw her upon nearer view,
A Spirit, yet a Woman too!
Her household motions light and free,
And steps of virgin-liberty;
A countenance in which did meet 15
Sweet records, promises as sweet;
A Creature not too bright or good
For human nature's daily food;
For transient sorrows, simple wiles,
Praise, blame, love, kisses, tears, and smiles. 20

And now I see with eyes serene
The very pulse of the machine;
A Being breathing thoughtful breath,
A Traveller between life and death;
The reason firm, the temperate will, 25
Endurance, foresight, strength, and skill;
A perfect Woman, nobly planned,
To warn, to comfort, and command;
And yet a Spirit still, and bright
With something of angelic light. 30

22 *machine:* i.e., the "bodily frame."

MY HEART LEAPS UP

My heart leaps up when I behold
  A rainbow in the sky:
So was it when my life began;
So is it now I am a man;
So be it when I shall grow old, 5
  Or let me die!
The Child is father of the Man;
And I could wish my days to be
Bound each to each by natural piety.

THE SOLITARY REAPER

Behold her, single in the field,
  Yon solitary Highland lass!
Reaping and singing by herself;
  Stop here, or gently pass!
Alone she cuts and binds the grain, 5
And sings a melancholy strain;
O listen! for the Vale profound
Is overflowing with the sound.

No Nightingale did ever chaunt
  More welcome notes to weary bands 10
Of travelers in some shady haunt,
  Among Arabian sands:
A voice so thrilling ne'er was heard
In spring-time from the Cuckoo-bird,
Breaking the silence of the seas 15
Among the farthest Hebrides.

Will no one tell me what she sings?—
  Perhaps the plaintive numbers flow
For old, unhappy, far-off things,
  And battles long ago: 20
Or is it some more humble lay,
Familiar matter of to-day?

Some natural sorrow, loss, or pain,
That has been, and may be again?

Whate'er the theme, the Maiden sang 25
  As if her song could have no ending;
I saw her singing at her work,
  And o'er the sickle bending;—
I listened, motionless and still;
And, as I mounted up the hill, 30
The music in my heart I bore,
Long after it was heard no more.

RESOLUTION AND INDEPENDENCE

I

There was a roaring in the wind all night;
The rain came heavily and fell in floods;
But now the sun is rising calm and bright;
The birds are singing in the distant woods;
Over his own sweet voice the Stock-dove broods; 5
The Jay makes answer as the Magpie chatters;
And all the air is filled with pleasant noise of waters.

II

All things that love the sun are out of doors;
The sky rejoices in the morning's birth;
The grass is bright with rain-drops;—on the moors 10
The hare is running races in her mirth;
And with her feet she from the plashy earth
Raises a mist; that, glittering in the sun,
Runs with her all the way, wherever she doth run.

III

I was a Traveller then upon the moor; 15
I saw the hare that raced about with joy;
I heard the woods and distant waters roar;
Or heard them not, as happy as a boy:
The pleasant season did my heart employ:
My old remembrances went from me wholly; 20
And all the ways of men, so vain and melancholy.

IV

But, as it sometimes chanceth, from the might
Of joy in minds that can no further go,
As high as we have mounted in delight
In our dejection do we sink as low; 25
To me that morning did it happen so;
And fears and fancies thick upon me came;
Dim sadness—and blind thoughts, I knew not, nor
could name.

V

I heard the sky-lark warbling in the sky;
And I bethought me of the playful hare: 30
Even such a happy Child of earth am I;
Even as these blissful creatures do I fare;
Far from the world I walk, and from all care;
But there may come another day to me—
Solitude, pain of heart, distress, and poverty. 35

VI

My whole life I have lived in pleasant thought,
As if life's business were a summer mood;
As if all needful things would come unsought
To genial faith, still rich in genial good;
But how can He expect that others should 40
Build for him, sow for him, and at his call
Love him, who for himself will take no heed at all?

VII

I thought of Chatterton, the marvellous Boy,
The sleepless Soul that perished in his pride;
Of Him who walked in glory and in joy
Following his plough, along the mountain-side: 45
By our own spirits are we deified:
We Poets in our youth begin in gladness;
But thereof come in the end despondency and madness.

43 *Chatterton:* Thomas Chatterton, English poet, died in 1770 at age of 18.
45 *Him:* Robert Burns, 1759–1796.

VIII

Now, whether it were by peculiar grace, 50
A leading from above, a something given,
Yet it befell that, in this lonely place,
When I with these untoward thoughts had striven,
Beside a pool bare to the eye of heaven
I saw a Man before me unawares: 55
The oldest man he seemed that ever wore grey hairs.

IX

As a huge stone is sometimes seen to lie
Couched on the bald top of an eminence;
Wonder to all who do the same espy,
By what means it could thither come, and whence; 60
So that it seems a thing endued with sense:
Like a sea-beast crawled forth, that on a shelf
Of rock or sand reposeth, there to sun itself;

X

Such seemed this Man, not all alive nor dead,
Nor all asleep—in his extreme old age: 65
His body was bent double, feet and head
Coming together in life's pilgrimage;
As if some dire constraint of pain, or rage
Of sickness felt by him in times long past,
A more than human weight upon his frame had cast. 70

XI

Himself he propped, limbs, body, and pale face,
Upon a long grey staff of shaven wood:
And, still as I drew near with gentle pace,
Upon the margin of that moorish flood
Motionless as a cloud the old Man stood, 7!
That heareth not the loud winds when they call;
And moveth all together, if it move at all.

XII

At length, himself unsettling, he the pond
Stirred with his staff, and fixedly did look

Upon the muddy water, which he conned, 80
As if he had been reading in a book:
And now a stranger's privilege I took;
And, drawing to his side, to him did say,
"This morning gives us promise of a glorious day."

XIII

A gentle answer did the old Man make, 85
In courteous speech which forth he slowly drew:
And him with further words I thus bespake,
"What occupation do you there pursue?
This is a lonesome place for one like you."
Ere he replied, a flash of mild surprise 90
Broke from the sable orbs of his yet-vivid eyes.

XIV

His words came feebly, from a feeble chest,
But each in solemn order followed each,
With something of a lofty utterance drest—
Choice word and measured phrase, above the reach 95
Of ordinary men; a stately speech;
Such as grave Livers do in Scotland use,
Religious men, who give to God and man their dues.

XV

He told, that to these waters he had come
To gather leeches, being old and poor: 100
Employment hazardous and wearisome!
And he had many hardships to endure:
From pond to pond he roamed, from moor to moor;
Housing, with God's good help, by choice or chance;
And in this way he gained an honest maintenance. 105

XVI

The old Man still stood talking by my side;
But now his voice to me was like a stream
Scarce heard; nor word from word could I divide;

80 *conned:* studied. 100 *leeches:* blood-sucking worms, once used by physicians to bleed their patients.

And the whole body of the Man did seem
Like one whom I had met with in a dream; 110
Or like a man from some far region sent,
To give me human strength, by apt admonishment.

XVII

My former thoughts returned: the fear that kills;
And hope that is unwilling to be fed;
Cold, pain, and labor, and all fleshly ills; 115
And mighty Poets in their misery dead.
—Perplexed, and longing to be comforted,
My question eagerly did I renew,
"How is it that you live, and what is it you do?"

XVIII

He with a smile did then his words repeat; 120
And said that, gathering leeches, far and wide
He travelled; stirring thus about his feet
The waters of the pools where they abide.
"Once I could meet with them on every side;
But they have dwindled long by slow decay; 125
Yet still I persevere, and find them where I may."

XIX

While he was talking thus, the lonely place,
The old Man's shape, and speech—all troubled me:
In my mind's eye I seemed to see him pace
About the weary moors continually, 130
Wandering about alone and silently.
While I these thoughts within myself pursued,
He, having made a pause, the same discourse renewed.

XX

And soon with this he other matter blended,
Cheerfully uttered, with demeanor kind, 135
But stately in the main; and, when he ended,
I could have laughed myself to scorn to find
In that decrepit Man so firm a mind.
"God," said I, "be my help and stay secure;
I'll think of the Leech-gatherer on the lonely moor!" 140

THERE WAS A BOY

There was a Boy: ye knew him well, ye cliffs
And islands of Winander!—many a time
At evening, when the earliest stars began
To move along the edges of the hills,
Rising or setting, would he stand alone 5
Beneath the trees or by the glimmering lake,
And there, with fingers interwoven, both hands
Pressed closely palm to palm, and to his mouth
Uplifted, he, as through an instrument,
Blew mimic hootings to the silent owls, 10
That they might answer him; and they would shout
Across the watery vale, and shout again,
Responsive to his call, with quivering peals,
And long halloos and screams, and echoes loud,
Redoubled and redoubled, concourse wild 15
Of jocund din; and, when a lengthened pause
Of silence came and baffled his best skill,
Then sometimes, in that silence while he hung
Listening, a gentle shock of mild surprise
Has carried far into his heart the voice 20
Of mountain torrents; or the visible scene
Would enter unawares into his mind,
With all its solemn imagery, its rocks,
Its woods, and that uncertain heaven, received
Into the bosom of the steady lake. 25

This Boy was taken from his mates, and died
In childhood, ere he was full twelve years old.
Fair is the spot, most beautiful the vale
Where he was born; the grassy churchyard hangs
Upon a slope above the village school, 30
And through that churchyard when my way has led
On summer evenings, I believe that there
A long half hour together I have stood
Mute, looking at the grave in which he lies!

FROM *The Prelude* (v, 364–397)

IT IS A BEAUTEOUS EVENING, CALM AND FREE

It is a beauteous evening, calm and free;
The holy time is quiet as a Nun
Breathless with adoration; the broad sun
Is sinking down in its tranquility;
The gentleness of heaven broods o'er the Sea:
Listen! the mighty Being is awake,
And doth with his eternal motion make
A sound like thunder—everlastingly.
Dear Child! dear Girl! that walkest with me here,
If thou appear untouched by solemn thought,
Thy nature is not therefore less divine:
Thou liest in Abraham's bosom all the year,
And worship'st at the Temple's inner shrine,
God being with thee when we know it not.

THE WORLD IS TOO MUCH WITH US; LATE AND SOON

The world is too much with us; late and soon,
Getting and spending, we lay waste our powers:
Little we see in Nature that is ours;
We have given our hearts away, a sordid boon!
The Sea that bares her bosom to the moon;
The winds that will be howling at all hours,
And are up-gathered now like sleeping flowers;
For this, for everything, we are out of tune;
It moves us not.—Great God! I'd rather be
A Pagan suckled in a creed outworn;
So might I, standing on this pleasant lea,
Have glimpses that would make me less forlorn;
Have sight of Proteus rising from the sea;
Or hear old Triton blow his wreathèd horn.

13 *Proteus:* a sea-god who, when seized, would assume different shapes.
14 *Triton:* a sea-god, son of Poseidon.

COMPOSED UPON WESTMINSTER BRIDGE

September 3, 1802

Earth has not anything to show more fair:
Dull would he be of soul who could pass by
A sight so touching in its majesty:
This City now doth, like a garment, wear
The beauty of the morning; silent, bare, 5
Ships, towers, domes, theaters, and temples lie
Open unto the fields, and to the sky;
All bright and glittering in the smokeless air.
Never did sun more beautifully steep
In his first splendor, valley, rock, or hill; 10
Ne'er saw I, never felt, a calm so deep!
The river glideth at his own sweet will:
Dear God! the very houses seem asleep;
And all that mighty heart is lying still!

LONDON, 1802

Milton! thou shouldst be living at this hour:
England hath need of thee; she is a fen
Of stagnant waters: altar, sword, and pen,
Fireside, the heroic wealth of hall and bower,
Have forfeited their ancient English dower 5
Of inward happiness. We are selfish men;
Oh! raise us up, return to us again;
And give us manners, virtue, freedom, power.
Thy soul was like a Star, and dwelt apart:
Thou hadst a voice whose sound was like the sea: 10
Pure as the naked heavens, majestic, free,
So didst thou travel on life's common way,
In cheerful godliness; and yet thy heart
The lowliest duties on herself did lay.

JOHN KEATS

[*1795–1821*]

John Keats was the son of the chief hostler at a London livery stable. In his boyhood he attended a private school at Enfield, where a young schoolmaster, Charles Cowden Clarke, helped develop his interest in literature. Both of Keats' parents died by the time he was fifteen; at sixteen, he was apprenticed by his guardian to a London apothecary-surgeon. Finding the medical profession distasteful, he maintained his friendship with Clarke and read widely in Clarke's library. His sonnet "On First Looking into Chapman's Homer" (1816) indicates his enthusiastic response to this reading.

In 1816, through Clarke, Keats was introduced to Leigh Hunt, and through Hunt he met Shelley, Lamb, Hazlitt, and the artists Haydon and Severn. Having decided to devote his life to poetry, he published some early poems in a volume called POEMS *(1817), and undertook the writing of the "poetic romance"* ENDYMION. *Published in 1818,* ENDYMION *was severely criticized by the most influential reviewers of the day.*

After a walking tour to Scotland, Keats met and fell in love with Fanny Brawne, to whom he later addressed the sonnets "To Fanny" and "Bright Star." In the next two years, he produced all of his greatest poems—"La Belle Dame Sans Merci," "Ode on a Grecian Urn," "Ode to a Nightingale," "To Autumn," "The Eve of St. Agnes," and others. Dying of tuberculosis, a disease which had taken both his mother and his brother Thomas, Keats sailed to Italy with his friend Joseph Severn in the fall of 1820, and died in Rome in February, 1821. His body was buried in the Protestant Cemetery at Rome.

Good editions of Keats' complete poems are H. W. Garrod's THE POETICAL WORKS OF JOHN KEATS *(1939) and C. DeWitt Thorpe's* COMPLETE POEMS AND SELECTED LETTERS *(1935). Sidney Colvin's* JOHN

KEATS: HIS LIFE AND POETRY, HIS FRIENDS, CRITICS, AND AFTER-FAME *(1917) and Amy Lowell's two-volume* JOHN KEATS *(1925) are the major biographies.*

LINES ON THE MERMAID TAVERN

Souls of Poets dead and gone,
What Elysium have ye known,
Happy field or mossy cavern,
Choicer than the Mermaid Tavern?
Have ye tippled drink more fine 5
Than mine host's Canary wine?
Or are fruits of Paradise
Sweeter than those dainty pies
Of venison? O generous food!
Drest as though bold Robin Hood 10
Would, with his maid Marian,
Sup and bowse from horn and can.

I have heard that on a day
Mine host's sign-board flew away,
Nobody knew whither, till 15
An astrologer's old quill
To a sheepskin gave the story,
Said he saw you in your glory,
Underneath a new-old sign
Sipping beverage divine, 20
And pledging with contented smack
The Mermaid in the Zodiac.

Souls of Poets dead and gone,
What Elysium have ye known,
Happy field or mossy cavern, 25
Choicer than the Mermaid Tavern?

Lines on the Mermaid Tavern: the Mermaid Tavern is the tavern in London believed to have been frequented by Shakespeare, Jonson, and their friends.
12 *bowse:* drink. Related to the word "booze."

THE DEVON MAID

Where be ye going, you Devon maid?
  And what have ye there in the basket?
Ye tight little fairy, just fresh from the dairy,
  Will ye give me some cream if I ask it?

I love your Meads, and I love your flowers, 5
  And I love your junkets mainly,
But 'hind the door I love kissing more,
  O look not so disdainly.

I love your hills and I love your dales,
  And I love your flocks a-bleating— 10
But O, on the heather to lie together,
  With both our hearts a-beating!

I'll put your basket all safe in a nook;
  Your shawl I'll hang on the willow;
And we will sigh in the daisy's eye, 15
  And kiss on a grass green pillow.

LA BELLE DAME SANS MERCI

Ah, what can ail thee, wretched wight,
  Alone and palely loitering;
The sedge is withered from the lake,
  And no birds sing.

Ah, what can ail thee, wretched wight, 5
  So haggard and so woe-begone?
The squirrel's granary is full,
  And the harvest's done.

I see a lily on thy brow
  With anguish moist and fever dew, 10
And on thy cheek a fading rose
  Fast withereth too.

La Belle Dame Sans Merci: "The beautiful lady without mercy." 1 *wight:* creature. [Keats' second version of this poem is reprinted here.]

I met a lady in the meads,
  Full beautiful, a faery's child:
Her hair was long, her foot was light, 15
  And her eyes were wild.

I set her on my pacing steed,
  And nothing else saw all day long;
For sideways would she lean, and sing
  A faery's song. 20

I made a garland for her head,
  And bracelets too, and fragrant zone;
She looked at me as she did love,
  And made sweet moan.

She found me roots of relish sweet, 25
  And honey wild, and manna dew,
And sure in language strange she said,
  I love thee true.

She took me to her elfin grot,
  And there she gazed and sighèd deep, 30
And there I shut her wild sad eyes—
  So kissed to sleep.

And there we slumbered on the moss,
  And there I dreamed, ah woe betide
The latest dream I ever dreamed 35
  On the cold hill side.

I saw pale kings, and princes too,
  Pale warriors, death-pale were they all;
Who cried—"La belle Dame sans merci
  Hath thee in thrall!" 40

I saw their starved lips in the gloom,
  With horrid warning gapèd wide,
And I awoke, and found me here
  On the cold hill side.

And this is why I sojourn here, 45
  Alone and palely loitering,
Though the sedge is withered from the lake,
  And no birds sing.

ODE TO A NIGHTINGALE

I

My heart aches, and a drowsy numbness pains
My sense, as though of hemlock I had drunk,
Or emptied some dull opiate to the drains
One minute past, and Lethe-wards had sunk:
'Tis not through envy of thy happy lot, 5
But being too happy in thine happiness,—
That thou, light-wingèd Dryad of the trees,
In some melodious plot
Of beechen green, and shadows numberless,
Singest of summer in full-throated ease. 10

II

O, for a draught of vintage! that hath been
Cool'd a long age in the deep-delvèd earth,
Tasting of Flora and the country green,
Dance, and Provençal song, and sunburnt mirth!
O for a beaker full of the warm South, 15
Full of the true, the blushful Hippocrene,
With beaded bubbles winking at the brim,
And purple-stainèd mouth;
That I might drink, and leave the world unseen,
And with thee fade away into the forest dim: 20

III

Fade far away, dissolve, and quite forget
What thou among the leaves hast never known,
The weariness, the fever, and the fret
Here, where men sit and hear each other groan;
Where palsy shakes a few, sad, last gray hairs, 25
Where youth grows pale, and spectre-thin, and dies;

2 *hemlock:* a poison. 4 *Lethe-wards:* Lethe was the river of forgetfulness in the Greek underworld. 13 *Flora:* Roman goddess of flowers. 16 *Hippocrene:* a fountain on Mount Helicon, whose waters were believed by the ancient Greeks to impart poetic inspiration.

Where but to think is to be full of sorrow
And leaden-eyed despairs,
Where Beauty cannot keep her lustrous eyes,
Or new Love pine at them beyond tomorrow. 30

IV

Away! away! for I will fly to thee,
Not charioted by Bacchus and his pards,
But on the viewless wings of Poesy,
Though the dull brain perplexes and retards:
Already with thee! tender is the night, 35
And haply the Queen-Moon is on her throne,
Clustered around by all her starry fays;
But here there is no light,
Save what from heaven is with the breezes blown
Through verdurous glooms and winding mossy ways. 40

V

I cannot see what flowers are at my feet,
Nor what soft incense hangs upon the boughs,
But, in embalmèd darkness, guess each sweet
Wherewith the seasonable month endows
The grass, the thicket, and the fruit-tree wild; 45
White hawthorn, and the pastoral eglantine;
Fast fading violets covered up in leaves;
And mid-May's eldest child,
The coming musk-rose, full of dewy wine,
The murmurous haunt of flies on summer eves. 50

VI

Darkling I listen; and for many a time
I have been half in love with easeful Death,
Called him soft names in many a musèd rhyme,
To take into the air my quiet breath;
Now more than ever seems it rich to die, 55
To cease upon the midnight with no pain,

32 *pards:* leopards, which supposedly drew the chariot of the wine-god Bacchus. 33 *viewless:* invisible. 43 *embalmèd:* sweet-smelling.

While thou art pouring forth thy soul abroad
In such an ecstasy!
Still wouldst thou sing, and I have ears in vain—
To thy high requiem become a sod. 60

VII

Thou wast not born for death, immortal Bird!
No hungry generations tread thee down;
The voice I hear this passing night was heard
In ancient days by emperor and clown:
Perhaps the self-same song that found a path 65
Through the sad heart of Ruth, when, sick for home,
She stood in tears amid the alien corn;
The same that oft-times hath
Charmed magic casements, opening on the foam
Of perilous seas, in faery lands forlorn. 70

VIII

Forlorn! the very word is like a bell
To toll me back from thee to my sole self!
Adieu! the fancy cannot cheat so well
As she is famed to do, deceiving elf.
Adieu! adieu! thy plaintive anthem fades 75
Past the near meadows, over the still stream,
Up the hill-side; and now 'tis buried deep
In the next valley-glades:
Was it a vision, or a waking dream?
Fled is that music:—Do I wake or sleep? 80

ODE ON A GRECIAN URN

1

Thou still unravished bride of quietness,
Thou foster-child of silence and slow time,
Sylvan historian, who canst thus express
A flowery tale more sweetly than our rhyme:
What leaf-fringed legend haunts about thy shape 5
Of deities or mortals, or of both,

In Tempe or the dales of Arcady?
What men or gods are these? what maidens loth?
What mad pursuit? What struggle to escape?
What pipes and timbrels? What wild ecstasy? 10

II

Heard melodies are sweet, but those unheard
Are sweeter; therefore, ye soft pipes, play on;
Not to the sensual ear, but, more endeared,
Pipe to the spirit ditties of no tone:
Fair youth, beneath the trees, thou canst not leave 15
Thy song, nor ever can those trees be bare;
Bold Lover, never, never canst thou kiss,
Though winning near the goal—yet, do not grieve;
She cannot fade, though thou hast not thy bliss,
For ever wilt thou love, and she be fair! 20

III

Ah, happy, happy boughs! that cannot shed
Your leaves, nor ever bid the Spring adieu;
And, happy melodist, unwearièd,
For ever piping songs for ever new;
More happy love! more happy, happy love! 25
For ever warm and still to be enjoyed,
For ever panting, and for ever young;
All breathing human passion far above,
That leaves a heart high-sorrowful and cloyed,
A burning forehead, and a parching tongue. 30

IV

Who are these coming to the sacrifice?
To what green altar, O mysterious priest,
Lead'st thou that heifer lowing at the skies,
And all her silken flanks with garlands drest?
What little town by river or sea shore, 35
Or mountain-built with peaceful citadel,
Is emptied of this folk, this pious morn?
And, little town, thy streets for evermore
Will silent be; and not a soul to tell
Why thou art desolate, can e'er return. 40

7 *Tempe:* a beautiful valley in Greece; *Arcady:* Arcadia, an ancient pastoral district in Greece, believed to be a carefree paradise.

ode - hymn of praise

V

O Attic shape! Fair attitude! with brede
Of marble men and maidens overwrought,
With forest branches and the trodden weed;
Thou, silent form, dost tease us out of thought
As doth eternity: Cold Pastoral! 45
When old age shall this generation waste,
Thou shalt remain, in midst of other woe
Than ours, a friend to man, to whom thou say'st,
"Beauty is truth, truth beauty—that is all
Ye know on earth, and all ye need to know." 50

41 *Attic:* Athenian—Greek; *brede:* embroidery.

ODE ON MELANCHOLY

I

No, no, go not to Lethe, neither twist
Wolf's-bane, tight-rooted, for its poisonous wine;
Nor suffer thy pale forehead to be kissed
By nightshade, ruby grape of Proserpine;
Make not your rosary of yew-berries, 5
Nor let the beetle, nor the death-moth be
Your mournful Psyche, nor the downy owl
A partner in your sorrow's mysteries;
For shade to shade will come too drowsily,
And drown the wakeful anguish of the soul. 10

II

But when the melancholy fit shall fall
Sudden from heaven like a weeping cloud,
That fosters the droop-headed flowers all,

1 *Lethe:* river of forgetfulness in the Greek underworld. 2 *Wolf's-bane:* poisonous plant. 4 *nightshade:* poisonous plant; *Proserpine:* queen of the Roman underworld. 5 *yew-berries:* poisonous berries of the yew tree, which was often associated with mourning. 6 *beetle:* an Egyptian symbol of the soul's resurrection after death; *death-moth:* the "death's-head moth," so called because the markings on its back resemble a human skull. 7 *Psyche:* 1) goddess beloved by Cupid, 2) the soul, often symbolized by a butterfly. 9 *shade:* ghost in classical underworld.

And hides the green hill in an April shroud;
Then glut thy sorrow on a morning rose, 15
Or on the rainbow of the salt sand-wave,
Or on the wealth of globèd peonies;
Or if thy mistress some rich anger shows,
Emprison her soft hand, and let her rave,
And feed deep, deep upon her peerless eyes. 20

III

She dwells with Beauty—Beauty that must die;
And Joy, whose hand is ever at his lips
Bidding adieu; and aching Pleasure nigh,
Turning to poison while the bee-mouth sips:
Ay, in the very temple of Delight 25
Veiled Melancholy has her sovran shrine,
Though seen of none save him whose strenuous tongue
Can burst Joy's grape against his palate fine:
His soul shall taste the sadness of her might,
And be among her cloudy trophies hung. 30

TO AUTUMN

I

Season of mists and mellow fruitfulness,
Close bosom-friend of the maturing sun:
Conspiring with him how to load and bless
With fruit the vines that round the thatch-eves run;
To bend with apples the mossed cottage-trees, 5
And fill all fruit with ripeness to the core;
To swell the gourd, and plump the hazel shells
With a sweet kernel; to set budding more,
And still more, later flowers for the bees,
Until they think warm days will never cease, 10
For Summer has o'er-brimmed their clammy cells.

II

Who hath not seen thee oft amid thy store?
Sometimes whoever seeks abroad may find
Thee sitting careless on a granary floor,
Thy hair soft-lifted by the winnowing wind; 15
Or on a half-reaped furrow sound asleep,

Drowsed with the fume of poppies, while thy hook
Spares the next swath and all its twinèd flowers:
And sometimes like a gleaner thou dost keep
Steady thy laden head across a brook; 20
Or by a cider-press, with patient look,
Thou watchest the last oozings hours by hours.

III

Where are the songs of Spring? Ay, where are they?
Think not of them, thou hast thy music too,—
While barrèd clouds bloom the soft-dying day, 25
And touch the stubble-plains with rosy hue;
Then in a wailful choir the small gnats mourn
Among the river sallows, borne aloft
Or sinking as the light wind lives or dies;
And full-grown lambs loud bleat from hilly bourn; 30
Hedge-crickets sing; and now with treble soft
The red-breast whistles from a garden-croft;
And gathering swallows twitter in the skies.

28 *sallows:* willow-trees. 30 *bourn:* region.

THE EVE OF ST. AGNES

I

St. Agnes' Eve—Ah, bitter chill it was!
The owl, for all his feathers, was a-cold;
The hare limped trembling through the frozen grass,
And silent was the flock in woolly fold:
Numb were the Beadsman's fingers while he told 5
His rosary, and while his frosted breath,
Like pious incense from a censer old,
Seemed taking flight for heaven, without a death,
Past the sweet Virgin's picture, while his prayer he saith.

The Eve of St. Agnes: on this night (January 20), according to medieval superstition, a young girl could, by following a certain ritual, discover the identity of her future husband. 5 *Beadsman:* a man paid to pray for the souls of his patrons.

II

His prayer he saith, this patient, holy man; 10
Then takes his lamp, and riseth from his knees,
And back returneth, meager, barefoot, wan,
Along the chapel aisle by slow degrees:
The sculptured dead, on each side, seem to freeze,
Imprisoned in black, purgatorial rails: 15
Knights, ladies, praying in dumb orat'ries,
He passeth by, and his weak spirit fails
To think how they may ache in icy hoods and mails.

III

Northward he turneth through a little door,
And scarce three steps, ere Music's golden tongue 20
Flattered to tears this aged man and poor;
But no—already had his death-bell rung:
The joys of all his life were said and sung;
His was harsh penance on St. Agnes' Eve:
Another way he went, and soon among 25
Rough ashes sat he for his soul's reprieve,
And all night kept awake, for sinners' sake to grieve.

IV

That ancient Beadsman heard the prelude soft;
And so it chanced, for many a door was wide,
From hurry to and fro. Soon, up aloft, 30
The silver, snarling trumpets 'gan to chide:
The level chambers, ready with their pride,
Were glowing to receive a thousand guests:
The carvèd angels, ever eager-eyed,
Stared, where upon their heads the cornice rests, 35
With hair blown back and wings put crosswise on their breasts.

V

At length burst in the argent revelry,
With plume, tiara, and all rich array,
Numerous as shadows haunting faerily

16 *orat'ries:* small chapels. 37 *argent:* silver.

The brain new-stuffed, in youth, with triumphs gay 40
Of old romance. These let us wish away,
And turn, sole-thoughted, to one Lady there,
Whose heart had brooded, all that wintry day,
On love, and winged St. Agnes' saintly care,
As she had heard old dames full many times declare. 45

VI

They told her how, upon St. Agnes' Eve,
Young virgins might have visions of delight,
And soft adorings from their loves receive
Upon the honeyed middle of the night,
If ceremonies due they did aright; 50
As, supperless to bed they must retire,
And couch supine their beauties, lily white;
Nor look behind, nor sideways, but require
Of Heaven with upward eyes for all that they desire.

VII

Full of this whim was thoughtful Madeline: 55
The music, yearning like a god in pain,
She scarcely heard: her maiden eyes divine,
Fixed on the floor, saw many a sweeping train
Pass by—she heeded not at all: in vain
Came many a tiptoe, amorous cavalier, 60
And back retired; not cooled by high disdain,
But she saw not: her heart was otherwhere:
She sighed for Agnes' dreams, the sweetest of the year.

VIII

She danced along with vague, regardless eyes,
Anxious her lips, her breathing quick and short: 65
The hallowed hour was near at hand: she sighs
Amid the timbrels, and the thronged resort
Of whisperers in anger, or in sport;
'Mid looks of love, defiance, hate, and scorn,
Hoodwinked with faery fancy; all amort, 70

70 *amort:* death-like.

Save to St. Agnes and her lambs unshorn,
And all the bliss to be before tomorrow morn.

IX

So, purposing each moment to retire,
She lingered still. Meantime, across the moors,
Had come young Porphyro, with heart on fire 75
For Madeline. Beside the portal doors,
Buttressed from moonlight, stands he, and implores
All saints to give him sight of Madeline,
But for one moment in the tedious hours,
That he might gaze and worship all unseen; 80
Perchance speak, kneel, touch, kiss—in sooth such things have
been.

X

He ventures in: let no buzzed whisper tell:
All eyes be muffled, or a hundred swords
Will storm his heart, Love's fev'rous citadel:
For him, those chambers held barbarian hordes, 85
Hyena foemen, and hot-blooded lords,
Whose very dogs would execrations howl
Against his lineage: not one breast affords
Him any mercy, in that mansion foul,
Save one old beldame, weak in body and in soul. 90

XI

Ah, happy chance! the aged creature came,
Shuffling along with ivory-headed wand,
To where he stood, hid from the torch's flame,
Behind a broad hall-pillar, far beyond
The sound of merriment and chorus bland: 95
He startled her; but soon she knew his face,
And grasped his fingers in her palsied hand,
Saying, "Mercy, Porphyro! hie thee from this place:
They are all here tonight, the whole blood-thirsty race!"

71 *lambs unshorn:* it was the practice to sacrifice two unshorn lambs to St. Agnes; their wool was then sheared and spun by nuns.

XII

"Get hence! get hence! there's dwarfish Hildebrand: 100
He had a fever late, and in the fit
He cursèd thee and thine, both house and land:
Then there's that old Lord Maurice, not a whit
More tame for his gray hairs—Alas me! flit!
Flit like a ghost away."—"Ah, Gossip dear, 105
We're safe enough; here in this arm-chair sit,
And tell me how—" "Good saints! not here, not here!
Follow me, child, or else these stones will be thy bier."

XIII

He followed through a lowly archèd way,
Brushing the cobwebs with his lofty plume; 110
And as she muttered "Well-a—well-a-day!"
He found him in a little moonlight room,
Pale, latticed, chill, and silent as a tomb.
"Now tell me where is Madeline," said he,
"O tell me, Angela, by the holy loom 115
Which none but secret sisterhood may see,
When they St. Agnes' wool are weaving piously."

XIV

"St. Agnes! Ah! it is St. Agnes' Eve—
Yet men will murder upon holy days.
Thou must hold water in a witch's sieve, 120
And be liege-lord of all the Elves and Fays
To venture so: it fills me with amaze
To see thee, Porphyro!—St. Agnes' Eve!
God's help! my lady fair the conjurer plays
This very night: good angels her deceive! 125
But let me laugh awhile,—I've mickle time to grieve."

XV

Feebly she laugheth in the languid moon,
While Porphyro upon her face doth look,
Like puzzled urchin on an aged crone
Who keepeth closed a wondrous riddle-book, 130

126 *mickle:* much.

As spectacled she sits in chimney nook.
But soon his eyes grew brilliant, when she told
His lady's purpose; and he scarce could brook
Tears, at the thought of those enchantments cold,
And Madeline asleep in lap of legends old. 135

XVI

Sudden a thought came like a full-blown rose,
Flushing his brow, and in his painèd heart
Made purple riot: then doth he propose
A stratagem, that makes the beldame start:
"A cruel man and impious thou art: 140
Sweet lady, let her pray, and sleep, and dream
Alone with her good angels, far apart
From wicked men like thee. Go, go!—I deem
Thou canst not surely be the same that thou didst seem."

XVII

"I will not harm her, by all saints I swear," 145
Quoth Porphyro: "O may I ne'er find grace
When my weak voice shall whisper its last prayer,
If one of her soft ringlets I displace,
Or look with ruffian passion in her face:
Good Angela, believe me by these tears; 150
Or I will, even in a moment's space,
Awake, with horrid shout, my foemen's ears,
And beard them, though they be more fanged than wolves
and bears."

XVIII

"Ah! why wilt thou affright a feeble soul?
A poor, weak, palsy-stricken, churchyard thing, 155
Whose passing-bell may ere the midnight toll;
Whose prayers for thee, each morn and evening,
Were never missed."—Thus plaining, doth she bring
A gentler speech from burning Porphyro;
So woful, and of such deep sorrowing, 160
That Angela gives promise she will do
Whatever he shall wish, betide her weal or woe.

162 *weal:* happiness.

XIX

Which was, to lead him, in close secrecy,
Even to Madeline's chamber, and there hide
Him in a closet, of such privacy 165
That he might see her beauty unespied,
And win perhaps that night a peerless bride,
While legioned fairies paced the coverlet,
And pale enchantment held her sleepy-eyed.
Never on such a night have lovers met, 170
Since Merlin paid his demon all the monstrous debt.

XX

"It shall be as thou wishest," said the Dame:
"All cates and dainties shall be storèd there
Quickly on this feast-night: by the tambour frame
Her own lute thou wilt see: no time to spare, 175
For I am slow and feeble, and scarce dare
On such a catering trust my dizzy head.
Wait here, my child, with patience; kneel in prayer
The while. Ah! thou must needs the lady wed,
Or may I never leave my grave among the dead." 180

XXI

So saying she hobbled off with busy fear.
The lover's endless minutes slowly passed;
The dame returned, and whispered in his ear
To follow her; with aged eyes aghast
From fright of dim espial. Safe at last 185
Through many a dusky gallery, they gain
The maiden's chamber, silken, hushed and chaste;
Where Porphyro took covert, pleased amain.
His poor guide hurried back with agues in her brain.

XXII

Her faltering hand upon the balustrade, 190
Old Angela was feeling for the stair,

171: Merlin, the sorcerer of Arthurian legend, was forced to pay the Devil for his gift of magical powers. 173 *cates:* delicacies. 174 *tambour frame:* embroidery frame. 188 *amain:* exceedingly.

When Madeline, St. Agnes' charmèd maid,
Rose, like a missioned spirit, unaware:
With silver taper's light, and pious care,
She turned, and down the aged gossip led 195
To a safe level matting. Now prepare,
Young Porphyro, for gazing on that bed;
She comes, she comes again, like ring-dove frayed and fled.

XXIII

Out went the taper as she hurried in;
Its little smoke, in pallid moonshine, died: 200
She closed the door, she panted, all akin
To spirits of the air, and visions wide:
No uttered syllable, or, woe betide!
But to her heart, her heart was voluble,
Paining with eloquence her balmy side; 205
As though a tongueless nightingale should swell
Her throat in vain, and die, heart-stifled, in her dell.

XXIV

A casement high and triple-arched there was,
All garlanded with carven imag'ries
Of fruits, and flowers, and bunches of knot-grass, 210
And diamonded with panes of quaint device,
Innumerable of stains and splendid dyes,
As are the tiger-moth's deep-damasked wings;
And in the midst, 'mid thousand heraldries,
And twilight saints, and dim emblazonings, 215
A shielded scutcheon blushed with blood of queens and kings.

XXV

Full on this casement shone the wintry moon,
And threw warm gules on Madeline's fair breast,
As down she knelt for heaven's grace and boon;
Rose-bloom, fell on her hands, together prest, 220
And on her silver cross soft amethyst,

198 *frayed:* frightened. 214 *heraldries:* emblems of lineage. 216 *scutcheon:* badge. 218 *gules:* red marks—a term of heraldry. 221 *amethyst:* violet.

And on her hair a glory, like a saint:
She seemed a splendid angel, newly drest,
Save wings, for heaven:—Porphyro grew faint:
She knelt, so pure a thing, so free from mortal taint. 225

XXVI

Anon his heart revives: her vespers done,
Of all its wreathèd pearls her hair she frees;
Unclasps her warmèd jewels one by one;
Loosens her fragrant bodice; by degrees
Her rich attire creeps rustling to her knees: 230
Half-hidden, like a mermaid in sea-weed,
Pensive awhile she dreams awake, and sees
In fancy, fair St. Agnes in her bed,
But dares not look behind, or all the charm is fled.

XXVII

Soon, trembling in her soft and chilly nest, 235
In sort of wakeful swoon, perplexed she lay,
Until the poppied warmth of sleep oppressed
Her soothèd limbs, and soul fatigued away;
Flown, like a thought, until the morrow-day;
Blissfully havened both from joy and pain; 240
Clasped like a missal where swart Paynims pray;
Blinded alike from sunshine and from rain,
As though a rose should shut, and be a bud again.

XXVIII

Stolen to this paradise, and so entranced,
Porphyro gazed upon her empty dress, 245
And listened to her breathing, if it chanced
To wake into a slumberous tenderness;
Which when he heard, that minute did he bless,
And breathed himself: then from the closet crept,
Noiseless as fear in a wide wilderness, 250
And over the hushed carpet, silent, stept,
And 'tween the curtains peeped, where, lo!—how fast she slept.

241: Shut up as tightly as a Christian prayer-book in a pagan temple.

XXIX

Then by the bed-side, where the faded moon
Made a dim, silver twilight, soft he set
A table, and, half anguished, threw thereon 255
A cloth of woven crimson, gold, and jet—
O for some drowsy Morphean amulet!
The boisterous, midnight, festive clarion,
The kettle-drum, and far-heard clarinet,
Affray his ears, though but in dying tone:— 260
The hall-door shuts again, and all the noise is gone.

XXX

And still she slept an azure-lidded sleep,
In blanchèd linen, smooth, and lavendered,
While he from forth the closet brought a heap
Of candied apple, quince, and plum, and gourd; 265
With jellies soother than the creamy curd,
And lucent syrops, tinct with cinnamon;
Manna and dates, in argosy transferred
From Fez; and spicèd dainties, every one,
From silken Samarcand to cedared Lebanon. 270

XXXI

These delicates he heaped with glowing hand
On golden dishes and in baskets bright
Of wreathèd silver: sumptuous they stand
In the retirèd quiet of the night,
Filling the chilly room with perfume light.— 275
"And now, my love, my seraph fair, awake!
Thou art my heaven, and I thine eremite:
Open thine eyes, for meek St. Agnes' sake,
Or I shall drowse beside thee, so my soul doth ache."

XXXII

Thus whispering, his warm, unnervèd arm 280
Sank in her pillow. Shaded was her dream

257 *Morphean amulet:* trance-producing charm. Morpheus, the god of dreams, was the son of Sleep. 266 *soother:* smoother. 276 *seraph:* angel. 277 *eremite:* hermit.

By the dusk curtains:—'twas a midnight charm
Impossible to melt as icèd stream:
The lustrous salvers in the moonlight gleam;
Broad golden fringe upon the carpet lies: 285
It seemed he never, never could redeem
From such a steadfast spell his lady's eyes;
So mused awhile, entoiled in woofèd phantasies.

XXXIII

Awakening up, he took her hollow lute,—
Tumultuous,—and, in chords that tenderest be, 290
He play'd an ancient ditty, long since mute,
In Provence called, "La belle dame sans mercy:"
Close to her ear touching the melody;—
Wherewith disturbed, she uttered a soft moan:
He ceased—she panted quick—and suddenly 295
Her blue affrayèd eyes wide open shone:
Upon his knees he sank, pale as smooth-sculptured stone.

XXXIV

Her eyes were open, but she still beheld,
Now wide awake, the vision of her sleep:
There was a painful change, that nigh expelled 300
The blisses of her dream so pure and deep
At which fair Madeline began to weep,
And moan forth witless words with many a sigh;
While still her gaze on Porphyro would keep;
Who knelt, with joinèd hands and piteous eye, 305
Fearing to move or speak, she looked so dreamingly.

XXXV

"Ah, Porphyro!" said she, "but even now
Thy voice was at sweet tremble in mine ear,
Made tuneable with every sweetest vow;
And those sad eyes were spiritual and clear: 310
How changed thou art! how pallid, chill, and drear!
Give me that voice again, my Porphyro,
Those looks immortal, those complainings dear!

288 *woofèd:* woven.

Oh leave me not in this eternal woe,
For if thou diest, my love, I know not where to go." 315

XXXVI

Beyond a mortal man impassioned far
At these voluptuous accents, he arose,
Ethereal, flushed, and like a throbbing star
Seen mid the sapphire heaven's deep repose;
Into her dream he melted, as the rose 320
Blendeth its odor with the violet,—
Solution sweet: meantime the frostwind blows
Like Love's alarum pattering the sharp sleet
Against the window-panes; St. Agnes' moon hath set.

XXXVII

'Tis dark: quick pattereth the flaw-blown sleet. 325
"This is no dream, my bride, my Madeline!"
'Tis dark: the icèd gusts still rave and beat:
"No dream, alas! alas! and woe is mine!
Porphyro will leave me here to fade and pine.
Cruel! what traitor could thee hither bring? 330
I curse not, for my heart is lost in thine,
Though thou forsakest a deceivèd thing;—
A dove forlorn and lost with sick unprunèd wing."

XXXVIII

"My Madeline! sweet dreamer! lovely bride!
Say, may I be for aye thy vassal blest? 335
Thy beauty's shield, heart-shaped and vermeil-dyed?
Ah, silver shrine, here will I take my rest
After so many hours of toil and quest,
A famished pilgrim,—saved by miracle.
Though I have found, I will not rob thy nest, 340
Saving of thy sweet self; if thou think'st well
To trust, fair Madeline, to no rude infidel.

325 *flaw:* gust. 336 *vermeil:* scarlet.

XXXIX

"Hark! 'tis an elfin-storm from faery land,
Of haggard seeming, but a boon indeed:
Arise—arise! the morning is at hand;— 345
The bloated wassailers will never heed;—
Let us away, my love, with happy speed;
There are no ears to hear, or eyes to see,—
Drowned all in Rhenish and the sleepy mead:
Awake! arise! my love, and fearless be, 350
For o'er the southern moors I have a home for thee."

XL

She hurried at his words, beset with fears,
For there were sleeping dragons all around,
At glaring watch, perhaps, with ready spears—
Down the wide stairs a darkling way they found.— 355
In all the house was heard no human sound.
A chain-drooped lamp was flickering by each door;
The arras, rich with horseman, hawk, and hound,
Fluttered in the besieging wind's uproar;
And the long carpets rose along the gusty floor. 360

XLI

They glide, like phantoms, into the wide hall;
Like phantoms, to the iron porch, they glide;
Where lay the porter in uneasy sprawl,
With a huge empty flagon by his side:
The wakeful bloodhound rose, and shook his hide, 365
But his sagacious eye an inmate owns:
By one and one, the bolts full easy slide:—
The chains lie silent on the footworn stones;—
The key turns, and the door upon its hinges groans.

XLII

And they are gone: aye, ages long ago 370
These lovers fled away into the storm.
That night the Baron dreamt of many a woe,

344 *haggard seeming:* wild appearance. 349 *Rhenish:* wine; *mead:* a liquor. 358 *arras:* hanging tapestry.

And all his warrior-guests, with shade and form
Of witch, and demon, and large coffin-worm,
Were long be-nightmared. Angela the old 375
Died palsy-twitched, with meager face deform;
The Beadsman after thousand avès told,
For aye unsought-for slept among his ashes cold.

ON FIRST LOOKING INTO CHAPMAN'S HOMER

Much have I travelled in the realms of gold,
And many goodly states and kingdoms seen;
Round many western islands have I been
Which bards in fealty to Apollo hold.
Oft of one wide expanse had I been told 5
That deep-browed Homer ruled as his demesne:
Yet did I never breathe its pure serene
Till I heard Chapman speak out loud and bold.
Then felt I like some watcher of the skies
When a new planet swims into his ken; 10
Or like stout Cortez when with eagle eyes
He stared at the Pacific—and all his men
Looked at each other with a wild surmise—
Silent, upon a peak in Darien.

Chapman: George Chapman was the Elizabethan translator of Homer. 1 *realms of gold:* classical literature. 3 *western islands:* the literature of the European nations since classical times. 4: Which poets hold in allegiance to the god of poetry. 6 *demesne:* domain. 11: Balboa, not Cortez, was the first European to look upon the Pacific Ocean. It is believed that Keats made this error because he had been so impressed by Titian's painting of Cortez. 14 *Darien:* Panama.

WHEN I HAVE FEARS THAT I MAY CEASE TO BE

When I have fears that I may cease to be
Before my pen has gleaned my teeming brain,
Before high-pilèd books, in charactery,

3 *charactery:* writing.

Hold like rich garners the full ripened grain;
When I behold, upon the night's starred face, 5
Huge cloudy symbols of a high romance,
And think that I may never live to trace
Their shadows, with the magic hand of chance;
And when I feel, fair creature of an hour,
That I shall never look upon thee more, 10
Never have relish in the faery power
Of unreflecting love;—then on the shore
Of the wide world I stand alone, and think
Till Love and Fame to nothingness do sink.

TO ONE WHO HAS BEEN LONG IN CITY PENT

To one who has been long in city pent
'Tis very sweet to look into the fair
And open face of heaven,—to breathe a prayer
Full in the smile of the blue firmament.
Who is more happy, when, with heart's content, 5
Fatigued he sinks into some pleasant lair
Of wavy grass, and reads a debonair
And gentle tale of love and languishment?
Returning home at evening, with an ear
Catching the notes of Philomel,—an eye 10
Watching the sailing cloudlet's bright career,
He mourns that day so soon has glided by,
E'en like the passage of an angel's tear
That falls through the clear ether silently.

10 *Philomel:* the nightingale.

BRIGHT STAR! WOULD I WERE STEADFAST AS THOU ART

Bright star! would I were steadfast as thou art—
Not in lone splendour hung aloft the night,
And watching, with eternal lids apart,

Like Nature's patient sleepless Eremite,
The moving waters at their priestlike task 5
Of pure ablution round earth's human shores,
Or gazing on the new soft-fallen mask
Of snow upon the mountains and the moors—
No—yet still steadfast, still unchangeable,
Pillowed upon my fair love's ripening breast, 10
To feel for ever its soft fall and swell,
Awake for ever in a sweet unrest,
Still, still to hear her tender-taken breath,
And so live ever—or else swoon to death.

4 *Eremite:* hermit.

TO FANNY

I cry your mercy—pity—love!—ay, love!
Merciful love that tantalizes not,
One-thoughted, never-wandering, guileless love,
Unmasked, and being seen—without a blot!
O! let me have thee whole,—all—all—be mine! 5
That shape, that fairness, that sweet minor zest
Of love, your kiss,—those hands, those eyes divine,
That warm, white, lucent, million-pleasured breast,—
Yourself—your soul—in pity give me all,
Withhold no atom's atom or I die, 10
Or living on, perhaps, your wretched thrall,
Forget, in the midst of idle misery,
Life's purposes,—the palate of my mind
Losing its gust, and my ambition blind!

ROBERT BROWNING

[1812–1889]

universal characteristics without judgment

*Robert Browning, the son of a clerk in the Bank of England, was born in Camberwell, a suburb of London. Though he attended the University of London for less than a year, he read widely throughout his boyhood in his father's remarkably well-stocked library; and in some of his long early poems—*PARACELSUS *(1835) and* SORDELLO *(1840), especially—he made extensive use of his out-of-the-way learning.*

Browning tried to achieve fame through writing plays for the great actor-manager W. C. Macready, but his dramas were not successful, and with the exception of PIPPA PASSES *(1842), they are little read today. His practice in playwriting, however, led him to the poetic form in which he wrote what is now considered his finest poetry—the "dramatic monologue."* DRAMATIC ROMANCES AND LYRICS *(1845) contained many of Browning's most famous poems: "How They Brought the Good News from Ghent to Aix," "Soliloquy of the Spanish Cloister," "My Last Duchess," "The Bishop Orders His Tomb at St. Praxed's Church," "The Lost Leader," and others.*

In 1844, the invalid poetess Elizabeth Barrett published a volume of poetry which contained a favorable reference to Browning; Browning visited her at her home, and, in spite of her despotic father, managed to elope with her to Italy (1846), where they spent most of their time until Elizabeth's death (1861). Browning's most important publications during this period were the volumes CHRISTMAS EVE AND EASTER-DAY *(1850) and* MEN AND WOMEN *(1855), which contained, among other poems, "Fra Lippo Lippi," "'Childe Roland to the Dark Tower Came,'" and "The Statue and the Bust." In 1864 appeared* DRAMATIS PERSONAE, *and in 1868–69 was published Browning's masterpiece,* THE RING AND THE BOOK*—a long poem in which he tells through dramatic monologues the story of an old Roman murder case as seen through the eyes of various participants and onlookers.*

world a testing ground for man's soul

A comprehensive edition of Browning's poetry is Augustine Birrell's THE COMPLETE POETICAL WORKS OF ROBERT BROWNING *(1915); a good selection is to be found in Horace Gregory's* SELECTED POETRY *(1956). W. C. DeVane's* A BROWNING HANDBOOK *(1935, 1955) gives helpful information about the poems. Browning's chief biographers are Ernest Dowden* (THE LIFE OF ROBERT BROWNING, *1917) and Betty Miller* (ROBERT BROWNING, A PORTRAIT, *1953).*

PORPHYRIA'S LOVER

The rain set early in to-night,
  The sullen wind was soon awake,
It tore the elm-tops down for spite,
  And did its worst to vex the lake:
  I listened with heart fit to break. 5
When glided in Porphyria; straight
  She shut the cold out and the storm,
And kneeled and made the cheerless grate
  Blaze up, and all the cottage warm;
  Which done, she rose, and from her form 10
Withdrew the dripping cloak and shawl,
  And laid her soiled gloves by, untied
Her hat and let the damp hair fall,
  And, last, she sat down by my side
  And called me. When no voice replied, 15
She put my arm about her waist,
  And made her smooth white shoulder bare,
And all her yellow hair displaced,
  And, stooping, made my cheek lie there,
  And spread, o'er all, her yellow hair, 20
Murmuring how she loved me—she
  Too weak, for all her heart's endeavor,
To set its struggling passion free
  From pride, and vainer ties dissever,
  And give herself to me forever. 25
But passion sometimes would prevail,
  Nor could to-night's gay feast restrain
A sudden thought of one so pale
  For love of her, and all in vain:

So, she was come through wind and rain. 30
Be sure I looked up at her eyes
  Happy and proud; at last I knew
Porphyria worshipped me; surprise
  Made my heart swell, and still it grew
  While I debated what to do. 35
That moment she was mine, mine, fair,
  Perfectly pure and good: I found
A thing to do, and all her hair
  In one long yellow string I wound
  Three times her little throat around, 40
And strangled her. No pain felt she;
  I am quite sure she felt no pain.
As a shut bud that holds a bee,
  I warily oped her lids: again
  Laughed the blue eyes without a stain. 45
And I untightened next the tress
  About her neck; her cheek once more
Blushed bright beneath my burning kiss:
  I propped her head up as before,
  Only, this time my shoulder bore 50
Her head, which droops upon it still:
  The smiling rosy little head,
So glad it has its utmost will,
  That all it scorned at once is fled,
  And I, its love, am gained instead! 55
Porphyria's love: she guessed not how
  Her darling one wish would be heard.
And thus we sit together now,
  And all night long we have not stirred,
  And yet God has not said a word! 60

SOLILOQUY OF THE SPANISH CLOISTER

I

Gr-r-r—there go, my heart's abhorrence!
  Water your damned flower-pots, do!
If hate killed men, Brother Lawrence,

God's blood, would not mine kill you!
What? your myrtle-bush wants trimming? 5
Oh, that rose has prior claims—
Needs its leaden vase filled brimming?
Hell dry you up with its flames!

II

At the meal we sit together:
Salve tibi! I must hear 10
Wise talk of the kind of weather,
Sort of season, time of year:
Not a plenteous cork-crop: scarcely
Dare we hope oak-galls, I doubt:
What's the Latin name for "parsley"? 15
What's the Greek name for Swine's Snout?

III

Whew! We'll have our platter burnished,
Laid with care on our own shelf!
With a fire-new spoon we're furnished,
And a goblet for ourself, 20
Rinsed like something sacrificial
Ere 'tis fit to touch our chaps—
Marked with L. for our initial!
(He-he! There his lily snaps!)

IV

Saint, forsooth! While brown Dolores 25
Squats outside the Convent bank
With Sanchicha, telling stories,
Steeping tresses in the tank,
Blue-black, lustrous, thick like horsehairs,
—Can't I see his dead eye glow, 30
Bright as 'twere a Barbary corsair's?
(That is, if he'd let it show!)

V

When he finishes refection,
Knife and fork he never lays

10 *Salve tibi:* Hail to thee. 31 *Barbary corsair:* pirate of the Barbary coast.
33 *refection:* a meal.

Cross-wise, to my recollection, 35
  As do I, in Jesu's praise.
I the Trinity illustrate,
  Drinking watered orange-pulp—
In three sips the Arian frustrate;
  While he drains his at one gulp. 40

VI

Oh, those melons? If he's able
  We're to have a feast! so nice!
One goes to the Abbot's table,
  All of us get each a slice.
How go on your flowers? None double 45
  Not one fruit-sort can you spy?
Strange!—And I, too, at such trouble,
  Keep them close-nipped on the sly!

VII

There's a great text in Galatians,
  Once you trip on it, entails 50
Twenty-nine distinct damnations,
  One sure, if another fails:
If I trip him just a-dying,
  Sure of heaven as sure can be,
Spin him round and send him flying 55
  Off to hell, a Manichee?

VIII

Or, my scrofulous French novel
  On gray paper with blunt type!
Simply glance at it, you grovel
  Hand and foot in Belial's gripe: 60
If I double down its pages
  At the woeful sixteenth print,

39 *the Arian:* a follower of Arius, whose anti-Trinitarian views were branded heretical by the Council of Nicea in 325 A. D. 49 *text in Galatians:* Galatians 3:10–11, which refers to Deuteronomy 28:16–44, where the twenty-nine damnations are listed. 56 *Manichee:* the sort of heretic that Brother Lawrence would become if the speaker were able to "trip him" on the text from Galatians.

When he gathers his greengages,
  Ope a sieve and slip it in't?

IX

Or, there's Satan!—one might venture 65
  Pledge one's soul to him, yet leave
Such a flaw in the indenture
  As he'd miss till, past retrieve,
Blasted lay that rose-acacia
  We're so proud of! *Hy, Zy, Hine.* 70
'St, there's Vespers! *Plena gratiâ*
  Ave, Virgo! Gr-r-r—you swine!

63 *greengages:* plums. 64 *sieve:* basket. 70 *Hy, Zy, Hine:* apparently, the sound of the vesper bells. 71–2 *Plena gratiâ/ Ave, Virgo:* Hail, Virgin, full of grace—the beginning of a prayer.

MY LAST DUCHESS

Ferrara
That's my last Duchess painted on the wall,
Looking as if she were alive. I call
That piece a wonder now: Frà Pandolf's hands
Worked busily a day, and there she stands.
Will't please you sit and look at her? I said 5
"Frà Pandolf" by design, for never read
Strangers like you that pictured countenance,
The depth and passion of its earnest glance,
But to myself they turned (since none puts by
The curtain I have drawn for you, but I) 10
And seemed as they would ask me, if they durst,
How such a glance came there; so, not the first
Are you to turn and ask thus. Sir 'twas not
Her husband's presence only, called that spot
Of joy into the Duchess' cheek: perhaps 15
Frà Pandolf chanced to say "Her mantle laps

Ferrara: a city in Italy noted for its artistic refinements during the Renaissance. 3 *Frà Pandolf:* Brother Pandolf, an imaginary painter.

Over my lady's wrist too much," or "Paint
Must never hope to reproduce the faint
Half-flush that dies along her throat:" such stuff
Was courtesy, she thought, and cause enough 20
For calling up that spot of joy. She had
A heart—how shall I say?—too soon made glad,
Too easily impressed; she liked whate'er
She looked on, and her looks went everywhere.
Sir, 'twas all one! My favor at her breast, 25
The drooping of the daylight in the West,
The bough of cherries some officious fool
Broke in the orchard for her, the white mule
She rode with round the terrace—all and each
Would draw from her alike the approving speech, 30
Or blush, at least. She thanked men,—good! but thanked
Somehow—I know not how—as if she ranked
My gift of a nine-hundred-years-old name
With anybody's gift. Who'd stoop to blame
This sort of trifling? Even had you skill 35
In speech—(which I have not)—to make your will
Quite clear to such an one, and say, "Just this
Or that in you disgusts me; here you miss,
Or there exceed the mark"—and if she let
Herself be lessoned so, nor plainly set 40
Her wits to yours, forsooth, and made excuse,
—E'en then would be some stooping; and I choose
Never to stoop. Oh sir, she smiled, no doubt,
Whene'er I passed her; but who passed without
Much the same smile? This grew; I gave commands; 45
Then all smiles stopped together. There she stands
As if alive. Will't please you rise? We'll meet
The company below, then. I repeat,
The Count your master's known munificence
Is ample warrant that no just pretence 50
Of mine for dowry will be disallowed;
Though his fair daughter's self, as I avowed
At starting, is my object. Nay, we'll go
Together down, sir. Notice Neptune, though,

50 *pretense:* claim. 54 *Neptune:* Roman god of the sea.

Taming a sea-horse, thought a rarity, 55
Which Claus of Innsbruck cast in bronze for me!

56 *Claus of Innsbruck:* Claus is an imaginary sculptor; Innsbruck, a city in Austria, was famous for its statues.

JOHANNES AGRICOLA IN MEDITATION

There's heaven above, and night by night
I look right through its gorgeous roof;
No suns and moons though e'er so bright
Avail to stop me; splendour-proof
I keep the broods of stars aloof: 5
For I intend to get to God,
For 'tis to God I speed so fast,
For in God's breast, my own abode,
Those shoals of dazzling glory, passed,
I lay my spirit down at last. 10
I lie where I have always lain,
God smiles as he has always smiled;
Ere suns and moons could wax and wane,
Ere stars were thundergirt, or piled
The heavens, God thought on me his child; 15
Ordained a life for me, arrayed
Its circumstances, every one
To the minutest; ay, God said
This head this hand should rest upon
Thus, ere he fashioned star or sun. 20
And having thus created me,
Thus rooted me, he bade me grow,
Guiltless for ever, like a tree
That buds and blooms, nor seeks to know
The law by which it prospers so: 25

Johannes Agricola in Meditation: Johannes Agricola, a German contemporary of Martin Luther, was the founder of Antinomianism, a doctrine which holds that Christians are no longer accountable to the Ten Commandments and that man is saved by faith alone, regardless of his moral behavior. Some scholars believe that the poem is a satire on Calvinism, which has certain affinities with Antinomianism.

But sure that thought and word and deed
  All go to swell his love for me,
Me, made because that love had need
  Of something irreversibly
  Pledged solely its content to be. 30
Yes, yes, a tree which must ascend,
  No poison-gourd foredoomed to stoop!
I have God's warrant, could I blend
  All hideous sins, as in a cup,
  To drink the mingled venoms up; 35
Secure my nature will convert
  The draught to blossoming gladness fast:
While sweet dews turn to the gourd's hurt,
  And bloat, and while they bloat it, blast,
  As from the first its lot was cast. 40
For as I lie, smiled on, full-fed
  By unexhausted power to bless,
I gaze below on hell's fierce bed,
  And those its waves of flame oppress,
  Swarming in ghastly wretchedness; 45
Whose life on earth aspired to be
  One altar-smoke, so pure!—to win
If not love like God's love for me,
  At least to keep his anger in;
  And all their striving turned to sin. 50
Priest, doctor, hermit, monk grown white
  With prayer, the broken-hearted nun,
The martyr, the wan acolyte,
  The incense-swinging child,—undone
  Before God fashioned star or sun! 55
God, whom I praise; how could I praise,
  If such as I might understand,
Make out and reckon on his ways,
  And bargain for his love, and stand,
  Paying a price, at his right hand? 60

53 *acolyte:* a religious attendant or helper.

THE BISHOP ORDERS HIS TOMB AT SAINT PRAXED'S CHURCH

Rome, 15—

Vanity, saith the preacher, vanity!
Draw round my bed: is Anselm keeping back?
Nephews—sons mine . . . ah God, I know not! Well—
She, men would have to be your mother once,
Old Gandolf envied me, so fair she was! 5
What's done is done, and she is dead beside,
Dead long ago, and I am Bishop since,
And as she died so must we die ourselves,
And thence ye may perceive the world's a dream.
Life, how and what is it? As here I lie 10
In this state-chamber, dying by degrees,
Hours and long hours in the dead night, I ask
"Do I live, am I dead?" Peace, peace seems all.
Saint Praxed's ever was the church for peace;
And so, about this tomb of mine. I fought 15
With tooth and nail to save my niche, ye know:
—Old Gandolf cozened me, despite my care;
Shrewd was that snatch from out the corner South
He graced his carrion with, God curse the same!
Yet still my niche is not so cramped but thence 20
One sees the pulpit o' the epistle-side,
And somewhat of the choir, those silent seats,
And up into the aery dome where live
The angels, and a sunbeam's sure to lurk:
And I shall fill my slab of basalt there, 25
And 'neath my tabernacle take my rest,
With those nine columns round me, two and two,
The odd one at my feet where Anselm stands:
Peach-blossom marble, all, the rare, the ripe
As fresh-poured red wine of a mighty pulse. 30
—Old Gandolf with his paltry onion-stone,
Put me where I may look at him! True peach,
Rosy and flawless: how I earned the prize!

31 *onion-stone:* a poor grade of marble.

Draw close: that conflagration of my church
—What then? So much was saved if aught were missed! 35
My sons, ye would not be my death? Go dig
The white-grape vineyard where the oil-press stood,
Drop water gently till the surface sink,
And if ye find . . . Ah, God, I know not, I! . . .
Bedded in store of rotten fig-leaves soft, 40
And corded up in a tight olive-frail,
Some lump, ah God, of *lapis lazuli,*
Big as a Jew's head cut off at the nape,
Blue as a vein o'er the Madonna's breast. . . .
Sons, all have I bequeathed you, villas, all, 45
That brave Frascati villa with its bath,
So, let the blue lump poise between my knees,
Like God the Father's globe on both his hands
Ye worship in the Jesu Church so gay,
For Gandolf shall not choose but see and burst! 50
Swift as a weaver's shuttle fleet our years:
Man goeth to the grave, and where is he?
Did I say basalt for my slab, sons? Black—
'Twas ever antique-black I meant! How else
Shall ye contrast my frieze to come beneath? 55
The bas-relief in bronze ye promised me,
Those Pans and Nymphs ye wot of, and perchance
Some tripod, thyrsus, with a vase or so,
The Saviour at his sermon on the mount,
Saint Praxed in a glory, and one Pan 60
Ready to twitch the Nymph's last garment off,
And Moses with the tables . . . but I know
Ye mark me not! What do they whisper thee,
Child of my bowels, Anselm? Ah, ye hope
To revel down my villas while I gasp 65
Bricked o'er with beggar's mouldy travertine
Which Gandolf from his tomb-top chuckles at!
Nay, boys, ye love me—all of jasper, then!

41 *olive-frail:* olive-basket. 42 *lapis lazuli:* semi-precious blue stone. 46 *Frascati:* suburb of Rome. 49 *Jesu Church:* Jesuit Church in Rome. 58 *thyrsus:* staff carried in festivals honoring the god of wine. 62 *tables:* tablets inscribed with the Ten Commandments.

'Tis jasper ye stand pledged to, lest I grieve.
My bath must needs be left behind, alas! 70
One block, pure green as a pistachio-nut,
There's plenty jasper somewhere in the world—
And have I not Saint Praxed's ear to pray
Horses for ye, and brown Greek manuscripts,
And mistresses with great smooth marbly limbs? 75
—That's if ye carve my epitaph aright,
Choice Latin, picked phrase, Tully's every word,
No gaudy ware like Gandolf's second line—
Tully, my masters? Ulpian serves his need!
And then how I shall lie through centuries, 80
And hear the blessed mutter of the mass,
And see God made and eaten all day long,
And feel the steady candle-flame, and taste
Good strong thick stupefying incense-smoke!
For as I lie here, hours of the dead night, 85
Dying in state and by such slow degrees,
I fold my arms as if they clasped a crook,
And stretch my feet forth straight as stone can point,
And let the bedclothes, for a mortcloth, drop
Into great laps and folds of sculptor's-work: 90
And as yon tapers dwindle, and strange thoughts
Grow, with a certain humming in my ears,
About the life before I lived this life,
And this life too, popes, cardinals and priests,
Saint Praxed at his sermon on the mount, 95
Your tall pale mother with her talking eyes,
And new-found agate urns as fresh as day,
And marble's language, Latin pure, discreet,
—Aha, ELUCESCEBAT quoth our friend?
No Tully, said I, Ulpian at the best! 100
Evil and brief hath been my pilgrimage.
All *lapis*, all, sons! Else I give the Pope
My villas! Will ye ever eat my heart?

77 *Tully:* Cicero, Roman orator; his full name was Marcus Tullius Cicero. 79 *Ulpian:* a Roman jurist whose Latin represented a decline from the classical purity of Cicero. 99 *elucescebat:* "He was illustrious." The purer form would be *elucebat.*

Ever your eyes were as a lizard's quick,
They glitter like your mother's for my soul, 105
Or ye would heighten my impoverished frieze,
Piece out its starved design, and fill my vase
With grapes, and add a vizor and a Term,
And to the tripod ye would tie a lynx
That in his struggle throws the thyrsus down, 110
To comfort me on my entablature
Whereon I am to lie till I must ask
"Do I live, am I dead?" There, leave me, there!
For ye have stabbed me with ingratitude
To death—ye wish it—God, ye wish it! Stone— 115
Gritstone, a-crumble! Clammy squares which sweat
As if the corpse they keep were oozing through—
And no more *lapis* to delight the world!
Well go! I bless ye. Fewer tapers there,
But in a row: and, going, turn your backs 120
—Ay, like departing altar-ministrants,
And leave me in my church, the church for peace,
That I may watch at leisure if he leers—
Old Gandolf, at me, from his onion-stone,
As still he envied me, so fair she was! 125

108 *Term:* bust on a pedestal. 111 *entablature:* platform on columns. 116 *Gritstone:* coarse sandstone.

THE LOST LEADER

I

Just for a handful of silver he left us,
  Just for a riband to stick in his coat—
Found the one gift of which fortune bereft us,
  Lost all the others she lets us devote;
They, with the gold to give, doled him out silver, 5
  So much was theirs who so little allowed:
How all our copper had gone for his service!
  Rags—were they purple, his heart had been proud!

The Lost Leader: Browning admitted that when he wrote this poem he was thinking of Wordsworth, who had changed from a liberal to a conservative and had become Poet Laureate.

We that had loved him so, followed him, honored him,
  Lived in his mild and magnificent eye, 10
Learned his great language, caught his clear accents,
  Made him our pattern to live and to die!
Shakespeare was of us, Milton was for us,
  Burns, Shelley, were with us,—they watch from their graves!
He alone breaks from the van and the freemen, 15
  He alone sinks to the rear and the slaves!

II

We shall march prospering,—not thro' his presence;
  Songs may inspirit us,—not from his lyre;
Deeds will be done,—while he boasts his quiescence,
  Still bidding crouch whom the rest bade aspire: 20
Blot out his name, then, record one lost soul more,
  One task more declined, one more footpath untrod,
One more devil's-triumph and sorrow for angels,
  One wrong more to man, one more insult to God!
Life's night begins: let him never come back to us! 25
  There would be doubt, hesitation and pain,
Forced praise on our part—the glimmer of twilight,
  Never glad confident morning again!
Best fight on well, for we taught him—strike gallantly,
  Menace our heart ere we master his own; 30
Then let him receive the new knowledge and wait us,
  Pardoned in heaven, the first by the throne!

MEETING AT NIGHT

I

The gray sea and the long black land;
And the yellow half-moon large and low;
And the startled little waves that leap
In fiery ringlets from their sleep,
As I gain the cove with pushing prow, 5
And quench its speed i' the slushy sand.

II

Then a mile of warm sea-scented beach;
Three fields to cross till a farm appears;

A tap at the pane, the quick sharp scratch
And blue spurt of a lighted match, 10
And a voice less loud, thro' its joys and fears,
Than the two hearts beating each to each!

PARTING AT MORNING

Round the cape of a sudden came the sea,
And the sun looked over the mountain's rim:
And straight was a path of gold for him,
And the need of a world of men for me.

3 *him:* the sun.

MEMORABILIA

I

Ah, did you once see Shelley plain,
  And did he stop and speak to you
And did you speak to him again?
  How strange it seems and new!

II

But you were living before that, 5
  And also you are living after;
And the memory I started at—
  My starting moves your laughter.

III

I crossed a moor, with a name of its own
  And a certain use in the world no doubt, 10
Yet a hand's-breadth of it shines alone
  'Mid the blank miles round about:

IV

For there I picked up on the heather
  And there I put inside my breast
A moulted feather, an eagle-feather! 15
  Well, I forget the rest.

CHILDE ROLAND TO THE DARK TOWER CAME

I

My first thought was, he lied in every word,
That hoary cripple, with malicious eye
Askance to watch the working of his lie
On mine, and mouth scarce able to afford
Suppression of the glee, that pursed and scored 5
Its edge, at one more victim gained thereby.

II

What else should he be set for, with his staff?
What, save to waylay with his lies, ensnare
All travelers who might find him posted there,
And ask the road? I guessed what skull-like laugh 10
Would break, what crutch 'gin write my epitaph
For pastime in the dusty thoroughfare,

III

If at his counsel I should turn aside
Into that ominous tract which, all agree,
Hides the Dark Tower. Yet acquiescingly 15
I did turn as he pointed: neither pride
Nor hope rekindling at the end descried,
So much as gladness that some end might be.

IV

For, what with my whole world-wide wandering,
What with my search drawn out through years, my hope 20
Dwindled into a ghost not fit to cope
With that obstreperous joy success would bring,
I hardly tried now to rebuke the spring
My heart made, finding failure in its scope.

The title comes from Edgar's lines in *King Lear* (III, iv, 171–173):
Childe Rowland to the dark tower came,
His word was still,—Fie, foh, and fum,
I smell the blood of a British man.
Childe is a youth of noble birth. In an older version of the story, Roland, the son of King Arthur, sets out to rescue his sisters who are being held prisoners in a castle (the dark tower). In Browning's story, Roland is simply a knight who succeeds in reaching his goal, the dark tower, by refusing to give up or turn aside, as the knights Cuthbert and Giles had done. The significance of the story is its allegorical intent.

V

As when a sick man very near to death 25
Seems dead indeed, and feels begin and end
The tears, and takes the farewell of each friend,
And hears one bid the other go, draw breath
Freelier outside, ("since all is o'er," he saith,
"And the blow fallen no grieving can amend;") 30

VI

While some discuss if near the other graves
Be room enough for this, and when a day
Suits best for carrying the corpse away,
With care about the banners, scarves and staves:
And still the man hears all, and only craves 35
He may not shame such tender love and stay.

VII

Thus, I had so long suffered in this quest,
Heard failure prophesied so oft, been writ
So many times among "The Band"—to wit,
The knights who to the Dark Tower's search addressed 40
Their steps—that just to fail as they, seemed best,
And all the doubt was now—should I be fit?

VIII

So, quiet as despair, I turned from him,
That hateful cripple, out of his highway
Into the path he pointed. All the day 45
Had been a dreary one at best, and dim
Was settling to its close, yet shot one grim
Red leer to see the plain catch its estray.

IX

For mark! no sooner was I fairly found
Pledged to the plain, after a pace or two, 50
Than, pausing to throw backward a last view
O'er the safe road, 'twas gone; grey plain all round:
Nothing but plain to the horizon's bound.
I might go on; nought else remained to do.

34 *staves:* staffs. 48 *estray:* strayed animals, i. e., Roland.

X

So, on I went. I think I never saw 55
Such starved ignoble nature; nothing throve:
For flowers—as well expect a cedar grove!
But cockle, spurge, according to their law
Might propagate their kind, with none to awe,
You'd think; a burr had been a treasure-trove. 60

XI

No! penury, inertness and grimace,
In some strange sort, were the land's portion. 'See
Or shut your eyes,' said Nature peevishly,
'It nothing skills: I cannot help my case:
'Tis the Last Judgment's fire must cure this place, 65
Calcine its clods and set my prisoners free.'

XII

If there pushed any ragged thistle-stalk
Above its mates, the head was chopped; the bents
Were jealous else. What made those holes and rents
In the dock's harsh swarth leaves, bruised as to baulk 70
All hope of greenness? 't is a brute must walk
Pashing their life out, with a brute's intents.

XIII

As for the grass, it grew as scant as hair
In leprosy; thin dry blades pricked the mud
Which underneath looked kneaded up with blood. 75
One stiff blind horse, his every bone a-stare,
Stood stupified, however he came there:
Thrust out past service from the devil's stud!

XIV

Alive? he might be dead for aught I know
With that red gaunt and colloped neck a-strain, 80
And shut eyes underneath the rusty mane;
Seldom went such grotesqueness with such woe;
I never saw a brute I hated so;
He must be wicked to deserve such pain.

66 *Calcine:* powderize. 68 *bents:* coarse grass. 70 *dock's:* broad-leaf weed's. 72 *pashing:* smashing. 80 *colloped:* ridged with ropelike muscles.

XV

I shut my eyes and turned them on my heart. 85
As a man calls for wine before he fights,
I asked one draught of earlier, happier sights,
Ere fitly I could hope to play my part.
Think first, fight afterwards—the soldier's art:
One taste of the old time sets all to rights. 90

XVI

Not it! I fancied Cuthbert's reddening face
Beneath its garniture of curly gold,
Dear fellow, till I almost felt him fold
An arm in mine to fix me to the place,
That way he used. Alas, one night's disgrace! 95
Out went my heart's new fire and left it cold.

XVII

Giles then, the soul of honor—there he stands
Frank as ten years ago when knighted first.
What honest man should dare (he said) he durst.
Good—but the scene shifts—faugh! what hangman hands 100
Pin to his breast a parchment? His own bands
Read it. Poor traitor, spit upon and curst!

XVIII

Better this present than a past like that;
Back therefore to my darkening path again!
No sound, no sight as far as eye could strain. 105
Will the night send a howlet or a bat?
I asked: when something on the dismal flat
Came to arrest my thoughts and change their train.

XIX

A sudden little river crossed my path
As unexpected as a serpent comes. 110
No sluggish tide congenial to the glooms;
This, as it frothed by, might have been a bath
For the fiend's glowing hoof—to see the wrath
Of its black eddy bespate with flakes and spumes.

92 *garniture:* embellishment. 106 *howlet:* owl.

XX

So petty yet so spiteful! All along, 115
Low scrubby alders kneeled down over it;
Drenched willows flung them headlong in a fit
Of mute despair, a suicidal throng:
The river which had done them all the wrong,
Whate'er that was, rolled by, deterred no whit. 120

XXI

Which, while I forded,—good saints, how I feared
To set my foot upon a dead man's cheek,
Each step, or feel the spear I thrust to seek
For hollows, tangled in his hair or beard!
—It may have been a water-rat I speared, 125
But, ugh! it sounded like a baby's shriek.

XXII

Glad was I when I reached the other bank.
Now for a better country. Vain presage!
Who were the strugglers, what war did they wage,
Whose savage trample thus could pad the dank 130
Soil to a plash? Toads in a poisoned tank,
Or wild cats in a red-hot iron cage—

XXIII

The fight must so have seemed in that fell cirque.
What penned them there, with all the plain to choose?
No foot-print leading to that horrid mews, 135
None out of it. Mad brewage set to work
Their brains, no doubt, like galley-slaves the Turk
Pits for his pastime, Christians against Jews.

XXIV

And more than that—a furlong on—why, there!
What bad use was that engine for, that wheel, 140
Or brake, not wheel—that harrow fit to reel
Men's bodies out like silk? with all the air

114 *bespate:* spattered. 130 *pad:* trample. 135 *mews:* den, cave.
141–2: some instrument of physical torture is suggested by the lines, perhaps the rack.

Of Tophet's tool, on earth left unaware,
  Or brought to sharpen its rusty teeth of steel.

XXV

Then came a bit of stubbed ground, once a wood, 145
  Next a marsh, it would seem, and now mere earth
  Desperate and done with; (so a fool finds mirth,
Makes a thing and then mars it, till his mood
Changes and off he goes!) within a rood—
  Bog, clay and rubble, sand and stark black dearth. 150

XXVI

Now blotches rankling, coloured gay and grim,
  Now patches where some leanness of the soil's
  Broke into moss or substances like boils;
Then came some palsied oak, a cleft in him
Like a distorted mouth that splits its rim 155
  Gaping at death, and dies while it recoils.

XXVII

And just as far as ever from the end!
  Nought in the distance but the evening, nought
  To point my footstep further! At the thought,
A great black bird, Apollyon's bosom-friend, 160
Sailed past, nor beat his wide wing dragon-penned
  That brushed my cap—perchance the guide I sought.

XXVIII

For, looking up, aware I somehow grew,
  'Spite of the dusk, the plain had given place
  All round to mountains—with such name to grace 165
Mere ugly heights and heaps now stolen in view.
How thus they had surprised me,—solve it, you!
  How to get from them was no clearer case.

XXIX

Yet half I seemed to recognise some trick
  Of mischief happened to me, God knows when— 170

143 *Tophet:* hell. 144 *rood:* unit of measurement: sometimes a square measure of about one-fourth acre; sometimes a linear measurement of a rod. 160 *Apollyon's:* the devil's. 161 *dragon-penned:* dragon-feathered.

In a bad dream perhaps. Here ended, then,
Progress this way. When, in the very nick
Of giving up, one time more, came a click
As when a trap shuts—you're inside the den!

XXX

Burningly it came on me all at once, 175
This was the place! those two hills on the right,
Crouched like two bulls locked horn in horn in fight;
While to the left, a tall scalped mountain . . . Dunce,
Dotard, a-dozing at the very nonce,
After a life spent training for the sight! 180

XXXI

What in the midst lay but the Tower itself?
The round squat turret, blind as the fool's heart,
Built of brown stone, without a counterpart
In the whole world. The tempest's mocking elf
Points to the shipman thus the unseen shelf 185
He strikes on, only when the timbers start.

XXXII

Not see? because of night perhaps?—why, day
Came back again for that! before it left,
The dying sunset kindled through a cleft:
The hills, like giants at a hunting, lay, 190
Chin upon hand, to see the game at bay,—
"Now stab and end the creature—to the heft!"

XXXIII

Not hear? when noise was everywhere! it tolled
Increasing like a bell. Names in my ears,
Of all the lost adventurers my peers,— 195
How such a one was strong, and such was bold,
And such was fortunate, yet each of old
Lost, lost! one moment knelled the woe of years.

XXXIV

There they stood, ranged along the hillsides, met
To view the last of me, a living frame 200
For one more picture! in a sheet of flame

I saw them and I knew them all. And yet
Dauntless the slug-horn to my lips I set
And blew. *"Childe Roland to the Dark Tower came."*

202 *slug-horn:* trumpet.

RABBI BEN EZRA

I

Grow old along with me!
The best is yet to be,
The last of life, for which the first was made:
Our times are in His hand
Who saith "A whole I planned, 5
Youth shows but half; trust God: see all, nor be afraid!"

II

Not that, amassing flowers,
Youth sighed, "Which rose make ours,
Which lily leave and then as best recall?"
Not that, admiring stars, 10
It yearned "Nor Jove, nor Mars;
Mine be some figured flame which blends, transcends them all!"

III

Not for such hopes and fears
Annulling youth's brief years,
Do I remonstrate: folly wide the mark! 15
Rather I prize the doubt
Low kinds exist without,
Finished and finite clods, untroubled by a spark.

IV

Poor vaunt of life indeed,
Were man but formed to feed 20
On joy, to solely seek and find and feast:
Such feasting ended, then

Rabbi Ben Ezra: Ibn Ezra was a medieval Jewish philosopher of the late 12th century.

As sure an end to men;
Irks care the crop-full bird? Frets doubt the maw-crammed beast?

V

Rejoice we are allied 25
To That which doth provide
And not partake, effect and not receive!
A spark disturbs our clod;
Nearer we hold of God
Who gives, than of His tribes that take, I must believe. 30

VI

Then, welcome each rebuff
That turns earth's smoothness rough,
Each sting that bids nor sit nor stand but go!
Be our joys three-parts pain!
Strive, and hold cheap the strain; 35
Learn, nor account the pang; dare, never grudge the throe!

VII

For thence,—a paradox
Which comforts while it mocks,—
Shall life succeed in that it seems to fail:
What I aspired to be, 40
And was not, comforts me:
A brute I might have been, but would not sink i' the scale.

VIII

What is he but a brute
Whose flesh has soul to suit,
Whose spirit works lest arms and legs want play? 45
To man, propose this test—
Thy body at its best,
How far can that project thy soul on its lone way?

IX

Yet gifts should prove their use:
I own the Past profuse 50
Of power each side, perfection every turn:
Eyes, ears took in their dole,

Brain treasured up the whole;
Should not the heart beat once "How good to live and learn"?

X

Not once beat "Praise be Thine! 55
I see the whole design,
I, who saw power, see now love perfect too:
Perfect I call Thy plan:
Thanks that I was a man!
Maker, remake, complete,—I trust what Thou shalt do!" 60

XI

For pleasant is this flesh;
Our soul, in its rose-mesh
Pulled ever to the earth, still yearns for rest;
Would we some prize might hold
To match those manifold 65
Possessions of the brute,—gain most, as we did best!

XII

Let us not always say,
"Spite of this flesh today
I strove, made head, gained ground upon the whole!"
As the bird wings and sings, 70
Let us cry, "All good things
Are ours, nor soul helps flesh more, now, than flesh helps soul!"

XIII

Therefore I summon age
To grant youth's heritage,
Life's struggle having so far reached its term: 75
Thence shall I pass, approved
A man, for aye removed
From the developed brute; a God though in the germ.

XIV

And I shall thereupon
Take rest, ere I be gone 80
Once more on my adventure brave and new:
Fearless and unperplexed,

When I wage battle next,
What weapons to select, what armor to indue.

XV

Youth ended, I shall try 85
My gain or loss thereby;
Leave the fire ashes, what survives is gold:
And I shall weigh the same,
Give life its praise or blame:
Young, all lay in dispute; I shall know, being old. 90

XVI

For note, when evening shuts,
A certain moment cuts
The deed off, calls the glory from the gray:
A whisper from the west
Shoots—"Add this to the rest, 95
Take it and try its worth: here dies another day."

XVII

So, still within this life,
Though lifted o'er its strife,
Let me discern, compare, pronounce at last,
"This rage was right i' the main, 100
That acquiescence vain:
The Future I may face now I have proved the Past."

XVIII

For more is not reserved
To man, with soul just nerved
To act tomorrow what he learns today: 105
Here, work enough to watch
The Master work, and catch
Hints of the proper craft, tricks of the tool's true play.

XIX

As it was better, youth
Should strive, through acts uncouth, 110
Toward making, than repose on aught found made:
So, better, age, exempt

From strife, should know, than tempt
Further. Thou waitedst age: wait death nor be afraid!

XX

Enough now, if the Right 115
And Good and Infinite
Be named here, as thou callest thy hand thine own,
With knowledge absolute,
Subject to no dispute
From fools that crowded youth, nor let thee feel alone. 120

XXI

Be there, for once and all,
Severed great minds from small,
Announced to each his station in the Past!
Was I, the world arraigned,
Were they, my soul disdained, 125
Right? Let age speak the truth and give us peace at last!

XXII

Now, who shall arbitrate?
Ten men love what I hate,
Shun what I follow, slight what I receive;
Ten, who in ears and eyes 130
Match me: we all surmise,
They this thing, and I that: whom shall my soul believe?

XXIII

Not on the vulgar mass
Called "work" must sentence pass,
Things done, that took the eye and had the price; 135
O'er which, from level stand,
The low world laid its hand,
Found straightway to its mind, could value in a trice:

XXIV

But all, the world's coarse thumb
And finger failed to plumb, 140
So passed in making up the main account;
All instincts immature,

All purposes unsure,
That weighed not as his work, yet swelled the man's amount:

XXV

Thoughts hardly to be packed 145
Into a narrow act,
Fancies that broke through language and escaped;
All I could never be,
All, men ignored in me,
This, I was worth to God, whose wheel the pitcher shaped. 150

XXVI

Ay, note that Potter's wheel,
That metaphor! and feel
Why time spins fast, why passive lies our clay,—
Thou, to whom fools propound,
When the wine makes its round, 155
'Since life fleets, all is change; the Past gone, seize to-day!'

XXVII

Fool! All that is, at all,
Lasts ever, past recall;
Earth changes, but thy soul and God stand sure:
What entered into thee, 160
That was, is, and shall be:
Time's wheel runs back or stops: Potter and clay endure.

XXVIII

He fixed thee mid this dance
Of plastic circumstance,
This Present, thou, forsooth, wouldst fain arrest: 165
Machinery just meant
To give thy soul its bent,
Try thee and turn thee forth, sufficiently impressed.

XXIX

What though the earlier grooves
Which ran the laughing loves 170

151 *Potter's wheel:* "O Lord, thou art our father; we are the clay and thou our potter; and we all are the work of thy hand." *Isaiah* 64:8.

Around thy base, no longer pause and press?
What though, about thy rim,
Skull-things in order grim
Grow out, in graver mood, obey the sterner stress?

XXX

Look not thou down but up! 175
To uses of a cup,
The festal board, lamp's flash and trumpet's peal,
The new wine's foaming flow,
The Master's lips aglow!
Thou, heaven's consummate cup, what need'st thou with
earth's wheel? 180

XXXI

But I need, now as then,
Thee, God, who mouldest men;
And since, not even while the whirl was worst,
Did I,—to the wheel of life
With shapes and colours rife, 185
Bound dizzily,—mistake my end, to slake Thy thirst:

XXXII

So, take and use Thy work:
Amend what flaws may lurk,
What strain o' the stuff, what warpings past the aim!
My times be in Thy hand! 190
Perfect the cup as planned!
Let age approve of youth, and death complete the same!

PROSPICE

Fear death?—to feel the fog in my throat,
The mist in my face,
When the snows begin, and the blasts denote
I am nearing the place,
The power of the night, the press of the storm, 5
The post of the foe;

Prospice: look forward.

Where he stands, the Arch Fear in a visible form,
Yet the strong man must go:
For the journey is done and the summit attained,
And the barriers fall, 10
Though a battle's to fight ere the guerdon be gained,
The reward of it all.
I was ever a fighter, so—one fight more,
The best and the last!
I would hate that death bandaged my eyes, and forbore, 15
And bade me creep past.
No! let me taste the whole of it, fare like my peers
The heroes of old,
Bear the brunt, in a minute pay glad life's arrears
Of pain, darkness and cold. 20
For sudden the worst turns the best to the brave,
The black minute's at end,
And the elements' rage, the fiend-voices that rave,
Shall dwindle, shall blend,
Shall change, shall become first a peace out of pain, 25
Then a light, then thy breast,
O thou soul of my soul! I shall clasp thee again,
And with God be the rest!

11 *guerdon:* reward.

EMILY DICKINSON

[1830–1886]

Emily Dickinson was born in Amherst, Massachusetts. Her father, Edward Dickinson, was a prominent lawyer in Amherst, and served two terms in Congress. At seventeen, Emily attended a female seminary; at twenty-three, she visited her father in Washington, D. C. On her return from the trip to Washington, she met in Philadelphia the Reverend Charles Wadsworth, a married man of forty; she was deeply attracted to him—though they actually met only three times.

From the age of twenty-six, Emily secluded herself in the family mansion, where she carried on a lengthy correspondence with friends, became increasingly eccentric, and wrote more than a thousand poems—of which only four were published during her lifetime. At Emily's death, her sister Lavinia discovered the poems and called upon her friends Mabel Loomis Todd and Thomas Wentworth Higginson to help her prepare them for publication. POEMS OF EMILY DICKINSON *appeared in 1890, and attracted so much interest that* POEMS OF EMILY DICKINSON—SECOND SERIES *was brought out in 1891, and a* THIRD SERIES *in 1896.*

In 1914, Martha Dickinson Bianchi, a niece of Emily's, published THE SINGLE HOUND, *a new selection of Emily's verse; and in 1924, three books—Mme. Bianchi's* LIFE AND LETTERS OF EMILY DICKINSON, *Conrad Aiken's* SELECTED POEMS OF EMILY DICKINSON, *and a so-called* COMPLETE POEMS—*made her poetry suddenly famous. In the following years there appeared several new editions of her poetry and numerous biographies, each offering a solution to the mystery of Emily's seclusion from the world. At least three men were identified as the lover who broke Emily's heart and drove her to isolate herself in her parents' home. In 1939, however, George F. Whicher's* THIS WAS A POET: A CRITICAL BIOGRAPHY OF EMILY DICKINSON *established the facts of her attachment to and correspondence with Reverend Wadsworth, and the mystery was solved.*

The only edition of Emily Dickinson's poems which can lay

claim to "completeness" is Thomas H. Johnson's three-volume THE POEMS OF EMILY DICKINSON *(1955). Besides Whicher's biography, there are Richard Chase's* EMILY DICKINSON *(1951) and Thomas H. Johnson's* EMILY DICKINSON: AN INTERPRETIVE BIOGRAPHY *(1955).*

SUCCESS IS COUNTED SWEETEST

Success is counted sweetest
By those who ne'er succeed.
To comprehend a nectar
Requires sorest need.

Not one of all the purple host 5
Who took the flag to-day
Can tell the definition,
So clear, of victory,

As he, defeated, dying,
On whose forbidden ear 10
The distant strains of triumph
Break, agonized and clear.

A WOUNDED DEER LEAPS HIGHEST

A wounded deer leaps highest,
I've heard the hunter tell;
'Tis but the ecstasy of death,
And then the brake is still.

The smitten rock that gushes, 5
The trampled steel that springs:
A cheek is always redder
Just where the hectic stings!

Mirth is the mail of anguish,
In which it caution arm, 10
Lest anybody spy the blood
And "You're hurt!" exclaim!

4 *brake:* underbrush. 8 *hectic:* fever.

THE HEART ASKS PLEASURE FIRST

The heart asks pleasure first,
And then, excuse from pain;
And then, those little anodynes
That deaden suffering;

And then, to go to sleep; 5
And then, if it should be
The will of its Inquisitor,
The liberty to die.

A PRECIOUS, MOULDERING PLEASURE 'TIS

A precious, mouldering pleasure 'tis
To meet an antique book,
In just the dress his century wore;
A privilege, I think,

His venerable hand to take, 5
And warming in our own,
A passage back, or two, to make
To times when he was young.

His quaint opinions to inspect,
His knowledge to unfold 10
On what concerns our mutual mind,
The literature of old;

What interested scholars most,
What competitions ran
When Plato was a certainty, 15
And Sophocles a man;

When Sappho was a living girl,
And Beatrice wore
The gown that Dante deified.
Facts, centuries before, 20

15 *Plato:* the great Greek philosopher. 16 *Sophocles:* Greek playwright. 17 *Sappho:* Greek poetess. 18, 19 *Beatrice, Dante:* Beatrice was the woman Dante immortalized in his *Divine Comedy*.

He traverses familiar,
As one should come to town
And tell you all your dreams were true:
He lived where dreams were born.

His presence is enchantment, 25
You beg him not to go;
Old volumes shake their vellum heads
And tantalize, just so.

THE SOUL SELECTS HER OWN SOCIETY

The soul selects her own society,
Then shuts the door;
On her divine majority
Obtrude no more.

Unmoved, she notes the chariot's pausing 5
At her low gate;
Unmoved, an emperor is kneeling
Upon her mat.

I've known her from an ample nation
Choose one; 10
Then close the valves of her attention
Like stone.

PAIN HAS AN ELEMENT OF BLANK

Pain has an element of blank;
It cannot recollect
When it began, or if there were
A day when it was not.

It has no future but itself, 5
Its infinite realms contain
Its past, enlightened to perceive
New periods of pain.

emotionally excited by nature

I TASTE A LIQUOR NEVER BREWED

I taste a liquor never brewed,
From tankards scooped in pearl;
Not all the vats upon the Rhine
Yield such an alcohol!

Inebriate of air am I, 5
And debauchee of dew,
Reeling, through endless summer days,
From inns of molten blue.

When landlords turn the drunken bee
Out of the foxglove's door, 10
When butterflies renounce their drams,
I shall but drink the more!

Till seraphs swing their snowy hats,
And saints to windows run,
To see the little tippler 15
Leaning against the sun!

13 *seraphs:* angels.

SURGEONS MUST BE VERY CAREFUL

Surgeons must be very careful
When they take the knife!
Underneath their fine incisions
Stirs the culprit,—Life!

a train compared to a horse

I LIKE TO SEE IT LAP THE MILES

I like to see it lap the miles,
And lick the valleys up,
And stop to feed itself at tanks;
And then, prodigious, step

Around a pile of mountains, 5
And, supercilious, peer
In shanties by the sides of roads;
And then a quarry pare

To fit its sides, and crawl between,
Complaining all the while 10
In horrid, hooting stanza;
Then chase itself down hill

And neigh like Boanerges;
Then, punctual as a star,
Stop—docile and omnipotent— 15
At its own stable door.

13 *Boanerges:* a loud person.

IS HEAVEN A PHYSICIAN?

Is heaven a physician?
They say that He can heal;
But medicine posthumous
Is unavailable.

Is Heaven an exchequer? 5
They speak of what we owe;
But that negotiation
I'm not a party to.

if you can't have faith, have knowledge

FAITH IS A FINE INVENTION

Faith is a fine invention
For gentlemen who see;
But microscopes are prudent
In an emergency!

REMORSE IS MEMORY AWAKE

Remorse is memory awake,
Her companies astir,—
A presence of departed acts
At window and at door.

Its past set down before the soul, 5
And lighted with a match,
Perusal to facilitate
Of its condensed despatch.

memory examines the past

Remorse is cureless,—the disease
Not even God can heal; 10
For 'tis His institution,—
The complement of hell.

I MANY TIMES THOUGHT PEACE HAD COME

I many times thought peace had come,
When peace was far away;
As wrecked men deem they sight the land
At centre of the sea,

And struggle slacker, but to prove, 5
As hopelessly as I,
How many the fictitious shores
Before the harbor lie.

SUPERIORITY TO FATE

Superiority to fate
  Is difficult to learn.
'Tis not conferred by any,
  But possible to earn

A pittance at a time, 5
  Until, to her surprise,
The soul with strict economy
  Subsists till Paradise.

IT'S SUCH A LITTLE THING TO WEEP

It's such a little thing to weep,
  So short a thing to sigh;
And yet by trades the size of these
  We men and women die!

MY LIFE CLOSED TWICE BEFORE ITS CLOSE

My life closed twice before its close;
  It yet remains to see
If Immortality unveil
  A third event to me,

So huge, so hopeless to conceive, 5
  As these that twice befell.
Parting is all we know of heaven,
  And all we need of hell.

I FELT A CLEAVAGE IN MY MIND

I felt a cleavage in my mind
  As if my brain had split;
I tried to match it, seam by seam,
  But could not make them fit.

The thought behind I strove to join 5
  Unto the thought before,
But sequence ravelled out of reach
  Like balls upon a floor.

I MEASURE EVERY GRIEF I MEET

I measure every grief I meet
With analytic eyes;
I wonder if it weighs like mine,
Or has an easier size.

I wonder if they bore it long, 5
Or did it just begin?
I could not tell the date of mine,
It feels so old a pain.

I wonder if it hurts to live,
And if they have to try, 10
And whether, could they choose between,
They would not rather die.

I wonder if when years have piled—
Some thousands—on the cause
Of early hurt, if such a lapse 15
Could give them any pause;

Or would they go on aching still
Through centuries above,
Enlightened to a larger pain
By contrast with the love. 20

THE BRAIN IS WIDER THAN THE SKY

The brain is wider than the sky,
For, put them side by side,
The one the other will include
With ease, and you beside.

The brain is deeper than the sea, 5
For, hold them, blue to blue,
The one the other will absorb,
As sponges, buckets do.

The brain is just the weight of God,
  For, lift them, pound for pound, 10
And they will differ, if they do,
  As syllable from sound.

A BIRD CAME DOWN THE WALK

A bird came down the walk:
He did not know I saw;
He bit an angle-worm in halves
And ate the fellow, raw.

And then he drank a dew 5
From a convenient grass,
And then hopped sidewise to the wall
To let a beetle pass.

He glanced with rapid eyes
That hurried all abroad,— 10
They looked like frightened beads, I thought
He stirred his velvet head

Like one in danger; cautious,
I offered him a crumb,
And he unrolled his feathers 15
And rowed him softer home

Than oars divide the ocean,
Too silver for a seam,
Or butterflies, off banks of noon,
Leap, plashless, as they swim. 20

A NARROW FELLOW IN THE GRASS

A narrow fellow in the grass
Occasionally rides;
You may have met him,—did you not?
His notice sudden is.

The grass divides as with a comb, 5
A spotted shaft is seen;
And then it closes at your feet
And opens further on.

He likes a boggy acre,
A floor too cool for corn. 10
Yet when a child, and barefoot,
I more than once, at morn,

Have passed, I thought, a whip-lash
Unbraiding in the sun,—
When, stooping to secure it, 15
It wrinkled, and was gone.

Several of nature's people
I know, and they know me;
I feel for them a transport
Of cordiality; 20

But never met this fellow,
Attended or alone,
Without a tighter breathing,
And zero at the bone.

I DIED FOR BEAUTY

I died for beauty, but was scarce
Adjusted in the tomb,
When one who died for truth was lain
In an adjoining room.

He questioned softly why I failed? 5
"For beauty," I replied.
"And I for truth,—the two are one;
We brethren are," he said.

And so, as kinsmen met a night,
We talked between the rooms, 10
Until the moss had reached our lips,
And covered up our names.

I NEVER SAW A MOOR

I never saw a moor,
I never saw the sea;
Yet know I how the heather looks,
And what a wave must be.

I never spoke with God, 5
Nor visited in heaven;
Yet certain am I of the spot
As if the chart were given.

THE LAST NIGHT THAT SHE LIVED

The last night that she lived,
It was a common night,
Except the dying; this to us
Made nature different.

We noticed smallest things,— 5
Things overlooked before,
By this great light upon our minds
Italicized, as 'twere.

That others could exist
While she must finish quite, 10
A jealousy for her arose
So nearly infinite.

We waited while she passed;
It was a narrow time,
Too jostled were our souls to speak, 15
At length the notice came.

She mentioned, and forgot;
Then lightly as a reed
Bent to the water, shivered scarce,
Consented, and was dead. 20

And we, we placed the hair,
And drew the head erect;
And then an awful leisure was,
Our faith to regulate.

THE BUSTLE IN A HOUSE

The bustle in a house
The morning after death
Is solemnest of industries
Enacted upon earth,—

The sweeping up of heart, 5
And putting love away
We shall not want to use again
Until eternity.

BECAUSE I COULD NOT STOP FOR DEATH

Because I could not stop for Death,
He kindly stopped for me;
The carriage held but just ourselves
And Immortality.

We slowly drove, he knew no haste, 5
And I had put away
My labor, and my leisure too,
For his civility.

We passed the school where children played
At wrestling in a ring; 10
We passed the fields of gazing grain,
We passed the setting sun.

We paused before a house that seemed
A swelling of the ground;
The roof was scarcely visible, 15
The cornice but a mound.

Since then 'tis centuries; but each
Feels shorter than the day
I first surmised the horses' heads
Were toward eternity.

IMMORTAL IS AN AMPLE WORD

Immortal is an ample word
When what we need is by,
But when it leaves us for a time,
'Tis a necessity.

Of heaven above the firmest proof 5
We fundamental know,
Except for its marauding hand,
It had been heaven below.

I FELT A FUNERAL IN MY BRAIN

I felt a funeral in my brain,
And mourners, to and fro,
Kept treading, treading, till it seemed
That sense was breaking through.

And when they all were seated, 5
A service like a drum
Kept beating, beating, till I thought
My mind was going numb.

And then I heard them lift a box,
And creak across my soul 10
With those same boots of lead, again.
Then space began to toll

As all the heavens were a bell,
And Being but an ear,
And I and silence some strange race, 15
Wrecked, solitary, here.

I HEARD A FLY BUZZ WHEN I DIED

I heard a fly buzz when I died;
The stillness round my form
Was like the stillness in the air
Between the heaves of storm.

The eyes beside had wrung them dry, 5
And breaths were gathering sure
For that last onset, when the king
Be witnessed in his power.

I willed my keepsakes, signed away
What portion of me I 10
Could make assignable,—and then
There interposed a fly,

With blue, uncertain, stumbling buzz,
Between the light and me;
And then the windows failed, and then 15
I could not see to see.

AFTER GREAT PAIN A FORMAL FEELING COMES

After great pain a formal feeling comes—
The nerves sit ceremonious like tombs;
The stiff Heart questions—was it He that bore?
And yesterday—or centuries before?

The feet mechanical 5
Go round a wooden way
Of ground or air or Ought, regardless grown,
A quartz contentment like a stone.

This is the hour of lead
Remembered if outlived, 10
As freezing persons recollect the snow—
First chill, then stupor, then the letting go.

FOREVER IS COMPOSED OF NOWS

Forever is composed of Nows—
'Tis not a different time,
Except for infiniteness
And latitude of home.

From this, experienced here, 5
Remove the dates to these,
Let months dissolve in further months,
And years exhale in years.

Without certificate or pause
Or celebrated days, 10
As infinite our years would be
As Anno Domini's.

YOU'LL FIND IT WHEN YOU COME TO DIE

You'll find it when you come to die
The easier to let go,
For recollecting such as went
You could not spare, you know.

And though their places somewhat filled— 5
As did their marble names
With moss—they never grew so full
You chose the newer times.

And when this world sets further back,
As dying say it does, 10
The former love distincter grows
And supersedes the fresh.

And thought of them so fair invites,
It looks too tawdry grace
To stay behind with just the toys 15
We bought to ease their place.

I TOOK ONE DRAUGHT OF LIFE

I took one draught of life,
I'll tell you what I paid,
Precisely an existence—
The market price, they said.

They weighed me, dust by dust, 5
They balanced film with film,
Then handed me my being's worth—
A single dram of Heaven.

MY LIFE HAD STOOD A LOADED GUN

My life had stood a loaded gun
In corners, till a day
The owner passed—identified,
And carried me away.

And now we roam the sov'reign woods, 5
And now we hunt the doe—
And every time I speak for him
The mountains straight reply.

And do I smile, such cordial light
Upon the valley glow— 10
It is as a Vesuvian face
Had let its pleasure through.

And when at night, our good day done,
I guard my master's head,
'Tis better than the eider duck's 15
Deep pillow to have shared.

To foe of his I'm deadly foe,
None stir the second time
On whom I lay a yellow eye
Or an emphatic thumb. 20

RENUNCIATION

Though I than he may longer live,
He longer must than I,
For I have but the art to kill—
Without the power to die.

RENUNCIATION

Renunciation
Is a piercing virtue,
The letting go
A presence for an expectation—
Not now. 5

The putting out of eyes
Just sunrise,
Lest Day Day's great progenitor
Out-show.

Renunciation is the choosing 10
Against itself,
Itself to justify
Unto itself;
When larger function
Make that appear 15
Smaller, that sated vision
Here.

A. E. HOUSMAN

[1859-1936]

A(lfred) E(dward) Housman, the son of a solicitor, was born near Bromsgrove, Worcestershire. While attending Bromsgrove School he won a scholarship to Oxford, where he began brilliantly, but ended by failing his first attempt to pass his fourth-year examinations and having to retake them. In 1882 he took a job with the Government Patent Office which required only six hours of his time each day; he spent the remainder of his time studying at the British Museum and, through his contributions to learned journals, became known as a superlative classical scholar.

Though he had written poetry in his boyhood, Housman wrote very little while he was at Oxford; it was not until he was thirty-five that he wrote the poems which made up his first volume, A SHROPSHIRE LAD *(1896). These poems, which represent more than a third of Housman's total work, included "Loveliest of Trees," "When I Was One-and-Twenty," "Oh When I Was in Love with You," "To an Athlete Dying Young," "Is My Team Ploughing," and "Terence, This is Stupid Stuff." Critical reaction was favorable, but it was not until the First World War that the poems gained their great popularity.*

In 1911 Housman became a professor of Latin in Trinity College, Cambridge, and held this position until his death. In 1922 he published LAST POEMS*—so titled, Housman said, because he did not expect to write much more poetry.* LAST POEMS *included, among others, "The Chestnut Casts His Flambeaux," "The Culprit," "The Night is Freezing Fast," and "Epitaph on an Army of Mercenaries." In his last years Housman was offered many honors, including the Order of Merit, but he declined them all. In 1936, after Housman's death, his brother Laurence published* MORE POEMS, *a collection of hitherto-unpublished lyrics and fragments.*

All of Housman's verse is to be found in THE COLLECTED POEMS OF A. E. HOUSMAN *(1940). The chief accounts of his life are Laurence*

Housman's MY BROTHER, A. E. HOUSMAN *(1938) and Percy Withers'* A BURIED LIFE: PERSONAL RECOLLECTIONS OF A. E. HOUSMAN *(1940)*.

LOVELIEST OF TREES

Loveliest of trees, the cherry now
Is hung with bloom along the bough,
And stands about the woodland ride
Wearing white for Eastertide.

Now, of my threescore years and ten, 5
Twenty will not come again,
And take from seventy springs a score,
It only leaves me fifty more.

And since to look at things in bloom
Fifty springs are little room, 10
About the woodlands I will go
To see the cherry hung with snow.

ON MOONLIT HEATH

On moonlit heath and lonesome bank
The sheep beside me graze;
And yon the gallows used to clank
Fast by the four cross ways.

A careless shepherd once would keep 5
The flocks by moonlight there,
And high amongst the glimmering sheep
The dead man stood on air.

They hang us now in Shrewsbury jail:
The whistles blow forlorn, 10
And trains all night groan on the rail
To men that die at morn.

5–6: "Hanging in chains was called keeping sheep by moonlight" (Housman's note).

There sleeps in Shrewsbury jail to-night,
  Or wakes, as may betide,
A better lad, if things went right, 15
  Than most that sleep outside.

And naked to the hangman's noose
  The morning clocks will ring
A neck God made for other use
  Than strangling in a string. 20

And sharp the link of life will snap,
  And dead on air will stand
Heels that held up as straight a chap
  As treads upon the land.

So here I'll watch the night and wait 25
  To see the morning shine,
When he will hear the stroke of eight
    And not the stroke of nine;

And wish my friend as sound a sleep
  As lads' I did not know, 30
That shepherded the moonlit sheep
  A hundred years ago.

WHEN I WATCH THE LIVING MEET

When I watch the living meet,
  And the moving pageant file
Warm and breathing through the street
  Where I lodge a little while,

If the heats of hate and lust 5
  In the house of flesh are strong,
Let me mind the house of dust
  Where my sojourn shall be long.

In the nation that is not
  Nothing stands that stood before; 10
There revenges are forgot,
  And the hater hates no more;

Lovers lying two and two
  Ask not whom they sleep beside,
And the bridegroom all night through 15
  Never turns him to the bride.

WHEN I WAS ONE-AND-TWENTY

When I was one-and-twenty
  I heard a wise man say,
'Give crowns and pounds and guineas
  But not your heart away;
Give pearls away and rubies 5
  But keep your fancy free.'
But I was one-and-twenty,
  No use to talk to me.

When I was one-and-twenty
  I heard him say again, 10
'The heart out of the bosom
  Was never given in vain;
'Tis paid with sighs a plenty
  And sold for endless rue.'
And I am two-and-twenty, 15
  And oh, 'tis true, 'tis true.

OH, WHEN I WAS IN LOVE WITH YOU

Oh, when I was in love with you,
  Then I was clean and brave,
And miles around the wonder grew
  How well did I behave.

And now the fancy passes by, 5
  And nothing will remain,
And miles around they'll say that I
  Am quite myself again.

TO AN ATHLETE DYING YOUNG

The time you won your town the race
We chaired you through the market-place;
Man and boy stood cheering by,
And home we brought you shoulder-high.

To-day, the road all runners come, 5
Shoulder-high we bring you home,
And set you at your threshold down,
Townsman of a stiller town.

Smart lad, to slip betimes away
From fields where glory does not stay 10
And early though the laurel grows
It withers quicker than the rose.

Eyes the shady night has shut
Cannot see the record cut,
And silence sounds no worse than cheers 15
After earth has stopped the ears:

Now you will not swell the rout
Of lads that wore their honours out,
Runners whom renown outran
And the name died before the man. 20

So set, before its echoes fade,
The fleet foot on the sill of shade,
And hold to the low lintel up
The still-defended challenge-cup.

And round that early-laurelled head 25
Will flock to gaze the strengthless dead,
And find unwithered on its curls
The garland briefer than a girl's.

IS MY TEAM PLOUGHING

'Is my team ploughing,
  That I was used to drive
And hear the harness jingle
  When I was man alive?'

Ay, the horses trample, 5
  The harness jingles now;
No change though you lie under
  The land you used to plough.

'Is football playing
  Along the river shore, 10
With lads to chase the leather,
  Now I stand up no more?'

Ay, the ball is flying,
  The lads play heart and soul;
The goal stands up, the keeper 15
  Stands up to keep the goal.

'Is my girl happy,
  That I thought hard to leave,
And has she tired of weeping
  As she lies down at eve?' 20

Ay, she lies down lightly,
  She lies not down to weep:
Your girl is well contented.
  Be still, my lad, and sleep.

'Is my friend hearty, 25
  Now I am thin and pine,
And has he found to sleep in
  A better bed than mine?'

Yes, lad, I lie easy,
  I lie as lads would choose; 30
I cheer a dead man's sweetheart,
  Never ask me whose.

OTHERS, I AM NOT THE FIRST

Others, I am not the first,
Have willed more mischief than they durst:
If in the breathless night I too
Shiver now, 'tis nothing new.

More than I, if truth were told, 5
Have stood and sweated hot and cold,
And through their reins in ice and fire
Fear contended with desire.

Agued once like me were they,
But I like them shall win my way 10
Lastly to the bed of mould
Where there's neither heat nor cold.

But from my grave across my brow
Plays no wind of healing now,
And fire and ice within me fight 15
Beneath the suffocating night.

WHITE IN THE MOON

White in the moon the long road lies,
The moon stands blank above;
White in the moon the long road lies
That leads me from my love.

Still hangs the hedge without a gust, 5
Still, still the shadows stay:
My feet upon the moonlit dust
Pursue the ceaseless way.

The world is round, so travellers tell,
And straight though reach the track, 10
Trudge on, trudge on, 'twill all be well,
The way will guide one back.

But ere the circle homeward hies
  Far, far must it remove:
White in the moon the long road lies 15
  That leads me from my love.

INTO MY HEART

Into my heart an air that kills
  From yon far country blows:
What are those blue remembered hills,
  What spires, what farms are those?

That is the land of lost content, 5
  I see it shining plain,
The happy highways where I went
  And cannot come again.

BE STILL, MY SOUL, BE STILL

Be still, my soul, be still; the arms you bear are brittle,
  Earth and high heaven are fixt of old and founded strong.
Think rather,—call to thought, if now you grieve a little,
  The days when we had rest, O soul, for they were long.

Men loved unkindness then, but lightless in the quarry 5
  I slept and saw not; tears fell down, I did not mourn;
Sweat ran and blood sprang out and I was never sorry:
  Then it was well with me, in days ere I was born.

Now, and I muse for why and never find the reason,
  I pace the earth, and drink the air, and feel the sun. 10
Be still, be still, my soul; it is but for a season:
  Let us endure an hour and see injustice done.

Ay, look: high heaven and earth ail from the prime foundation;
  All thoughts to rive the heart are here, and all are vain:
Horror and scorn and hate and fear and indignation— 15
  Oh why did I awake? when shall I sleep again?

THE TRUE LOVER

The lad came to the door at night,
  When lovers crown their vows,
And whistled soft and out of sight
  In shadow of the boughs.

'I shall not vex you with my face 5
  Henceforth, my love, for aye;
So take me in your arms a space
  Before the east is grey.

'When I from hence away am past
  I shall not find a bride, 10
And you shall be the first and last
  I ever lay beside.'

She heard and went and knew not why;
  Her heart to his she laid;
Light was the air beneath the sky 15
  But dark under the shade.

'Oh do you breathe, lad, that your breast
  Seems not to rise and fall,
And here upon my bosom prest
  There beats no heart at all?' 20

'Oh loud, my girl, it once would knock,
  You should have felt it then;
But since for you I stopped the clock
  It never goes again.'

'Oh lad, what is it, lad, that drips 25
  Wet from your neck on mine?
What is it falling on my lips,
  My lad, that tastes of brine?'

'Oh like enough 'tis blood, my dear,
  For when the knife has slit 30
The throat across from ear to ear
  'Twill bleed because of it.'

Under the stars the air was light
  But dark below the boughs,
The still air of the speechless night, 35
  When lovers crown their vows.

YOU SMILE UPON YOUR FRIEND TO-DAY

You smile upon your friend to-day,
  To-day his ills are over;
You hearken to the lover's say,
  And happy is the lover.

'Tis late to hearken, late to smile, 5
  But better late than never:
I shall have lived a little while
  Before I die for ever.

TERENCE, THIS IS STUPID STUFF

'Terence, this is stupid stuff:
You eat your victuals fast enough;
There can't be much amiss, 'tis clear,
To see the rate you drink your beer.
But oh, good Lord, the verse you make, 5
It gives a chap the belly-ache.
The cow, the old cow, she is dead;
It sleeps well, the horned head:
We poor lads, 'tis our turn now
To hear such tunes as killed the cow. 10
Pretty friendship 'tis to rhyme
Your friends to death before their time
Moping melancholy mad:
Come, pipe a tune to dance to, lad.'

Why, if 'tis dancing you would be, 15
There's brisker pipes than poetry.
Say, for what were hop-yards meant,

Or why was Burton built on Trent?
Oh many a peer of England brews
Livelier liquor than the Muse, 20
And malt does more than Milton can
To justify God's ways to man.
Ale, man, ale's the stuff to drink
For fellows whom it hurts to think:
Look into the pewter pot 25
To see the world as the world's not.
And faith, 'tis pleasant till 'tis past:
The mischief is that 'twill not last.
Oh I have been to Ludlow fair
And left my necktie God knows where, 30
And carried half-way home, or near,
Pints and quarts of Ludlow beer:
Then the world seemed none so bad,
And I myself a sterling lad;
And down in lovely muck I've lain, 35
Happy till I woke again.
Then I saw the morning sky:
Heigho, the tale was all a lie;
The world, it was the old world yet,
I was I, my things were wet, 40
And nothing now remained to do
But begin the game anew.

Therefore, since the world has still
Much good, but much less good than ill,
And while the sun and moon endure 45
Luck's a chance, but trouble's sure,
I'd face it as a wise man would,
And train for ill and not for good.
'Tis true, the stuff I bring for sale
Is not so brisk a brew as ale: 50
Out of a stem that scored the hand
I wrung it in a weary land.
But take it: if the smack is sour,

18 *Burton built on Trent:* Burton-upon-Trent, an English city famous for its breweries. 22 *To justify God's ways to man:* Milton, in writing *Paradise Lost,* stated his intention as being to "assert Eternal Providence,/And justify the ways of God to man" (*Paradise Lost,* I, 25–6). 25 *pewter pot:* ale-mug.

The better for the embittered hour;
It should do good to heart and head 55
When your soul is in my soul's stead;
And I will friend you, if I may,
In the dark and cloudy day.

There was a king reigned in the East:
There, when kings will sit to feast, 60
They get their fill before they think
With poisoned meat and poisoned drink.
He gathered all that springs to birth
From the many-venomed earth;
First a little, thence to more 65
He sampled all her killing store;
And easy, smiling, seasoned sound,
Sate the king when healths went round.
They put arsenic in his meat
And stared aghast to watch him eat; 70
They poured strychnine in his cup
And shook to see him drink it up:
They shook, they stared as white's their shirt:
Them it was their poison hurt.
—I tell the tale that I heard told. 75
Mithridates, he died old.

THE CHESTNUT CASTS HIS FLAMBEAUX

The chestnut casts his flambeaux, and the flowers
Stream from the hawthorn on the wind away,
The doors clap to, the pane is blind with showers.
Pass me the can, lad; there's an end of May.

There's one spoilt spring to scant our mortal lot, 5
One season ruined of our little store.
May will be fine next year as like as not:
Oh ay, but then we shall be twenty-four.

We for a certainty are not the first
Have sat in taverns while the tempest hurled 10

1 *flambeaux:* literally, "lighted torch." 4 *can:* ale-can.

Their hopeful plans to emptiness, and cursed
  Whatever brute and blackguard made the world.

It is in truth iniquity on high
  To cheat our sentenced souls of aught they crave,
And mar the merriment as you and I 15
  Fare on our long fool's-errand to the grave.

Iniquity it is; but pass the can.
  My lad, no pair of kings our mothers bore;
Our only portion is the estate of man:
  We want the moon, but we shall get no more. 20

If here today the cloud of thunder lours
  Tomorrow it will hie on far behests;
The flesh will grieve on other bones than ours
  Soon, and the soul will mourn in other breasts.

The troubles of our proud and angry dust 25
  Are from eternity, and shall not fail.
Bear them we can, and if we can we must.
  Shoulder the sky, my lad, and drink your ale.

COULD MAN BE DRUNK FOR EVER

Could man be drunk for ever
  With liquor, love, or fights,
Lief should I rouse at morning
  And lief lie down of nights.

But men at whiles are sober 5
  And think by fits and starts,
And if they think, they fasten
  Their hands upon their hearts.

THE CULPRIT

The night my father got me
  His mind was not on me;
He did not plague his fancy

To muse if I should be
The son you see. 5

The day my mother bore me
She was a fool and glad,
For all the pain I cost her,
That she had borne the lad
That borne she had. 10

My mother and my father
Out of the light they lie;
The warrant would not find them,
And here 'tis only I
Shall hang so high. 15

Oh let not man remember
The soul that God forgot,
But fetch the county kerchief
And noose me in the knot,
And I will rot. 20

For so the game is ended
That should not have begun.
My father and my mother
They had a likely son,
And I have none. 25

13 *warrant:* legal summons. 18 *county kerchief:* blindfold.

EIGHT O'CLOCK

He stood, and heard the steeple
Sprinkle the quarters on the morning town.
One, two, three, four, to market-place and people
It tossed them down.

Strapped, noosed, nighing his hour, 5
He stood and counted them and cursed his luck;
And then the clock collected in the tower
Its strength, and struck.

THE NIGHT IS FREEZING FAST

The night is freezing fast,
  To-morrow comes December;
    And winterfalls of old
Are with me from the past;
  And chiefly I remember 5
    How Dick would hate the cold.

Fall, winter, fall; for he,
  Prompt hand and headpiece clever,
    Has woven a winter robe,
And made of earth and sea 10
  His overcoat for ever,
    And wears the turning globe.

IN THE MORNING, IN THE MORNING

In the morning, in the morning,
  In the happy field of hay,
Oh they looked at one another
  By the light of day.

In the blue and silver morning 5
  On the haycock as they lay,
Oh they looked at one another
  And they looked away.

WHEN FIRST MY WAY

When first my way to fair I took
  Few pence in purse had I,
And long I used to stand and look
  At things I could not buy.

Now times are altered: if I care 5
  To buy a thing, I can;

The pence are here and here's the fair,
  But where's the lost young man?

—To think that two and two are four
  And neither five nor three 10
The heart of man has long been sore
  And long 'tis like to be.

EPITAPH ON AN ARMY OF MERCENARIES

These, in the day when heaven was falling,
  The hour when earth's foundations fled,
Followed their mercenary calling
  And took their wages and are dead.

Their shoulders held the sky suspended; 5
  They stood, and earth's foundations stay;
What God abandoned, these defended,
  And saved the sum of things for pay.

Mercenaries: hired soldiers.

OH STAY AT HOME, MY LAD

Oh stay at home, my lad, and plough
  The land and not the sea,
And leave the soldiers at their drill,
And all about the idle hill
  Shepherd your sheep with me. 5

Oh stay with company and mirth
  And daylight and the air;
Too full already is the grave
Of fellows that were good and brave
  And died because they were. 10

GOOD CREATURES, DO YOU LOVE YOUR LIVES

Good creatures, do you love your lives
  And have you ears for sense?
Here is a knife like other knives,
  That cost me eighteen pence.

I need but stick it in my heart 5
  And down will come the sky,
And earth's foundations will depart
  And all you folk will die.

TO STAND UP STRAIGHT

To stand up straight and tread the turning mill,
To lie flat and know nothing and be still,
Are the two trades of man; and which is worse
I know not, but I know that both are ill.

I DID NOT LOSE MY HEART IN SUMMER'S EVEN

I did not lose my heart in summer's even,
  When roses to the moonrise burst apart:
When plumes were under heel and lead was flying,
  In blood and smoke and flame I lost my heart.

I lost it to a soldier and a foeman, 5
  A chap that did not kill me, but he tried;
That took the sabre straight and took it striking,
  And laughed and kissed his hand to me and died.

MY DREAMS ARE OF A FIELD AFAR

My dreams are of a field afar
  And blood and smoke and shot.
There in their graves my comrades are,
  In my grave I am not.

I too was taught the trade of man   5
  And spelt the lesson plain;
But they, when I forgot and ran,
  Remembered and remain.

PARTA QUIES

Good-night; ensured release,
Imperishable peace,
    Have these for yours,
While sea abides, and land,
And earth's foundations stand,   5
    And heaven endures.

When earth's foundations flee,
Nor sky nor land nor sea
    At all is found,
Content you, let them burn: 10
It is not your concern;
    Sleep on, sleep sound.

Parta Quies: quiet is born.

WILLIAM BUTLER YEATS

[*1865–1939*]

William Butler Yeats was born in Sandymount, Ireland, the son of an Irish artist. He spent his boyhood and youth in Ireland and England, attending schools in both countries. He began writing poems in his boyhood; MOSADA: A POEM (*1886*) *was published when he was twenty-one. In London in the later 1880's he met William Morris, W. E. Henley, Oscar Wilde, and Arthur Symons; somewhat later he came under the influence of the French Symbolists, notably Mallarmé and Villiers de L'Isle Adam. His earlier volumes of poetry and plays—*THE WANDERINGS OF OISIN (*1889*), THE COUNTESS KATHLEEN AND VARIOUS LYRICS (*1892*), THE WIND AMONG THE REEDS (*1899*), *and* THE SHADOWY WATERS (*1900*)*—make considerable use of Irish subject-matter, but they show clearly the influence of the Pre-Raphaelites and the Symbolists.*

About 1900, Yeats, Lady Gregory and others founded the Abbey Theatre in Dublin, and Yeats wrote many plays for this group. From this time on, his poems were to exhibit a much less "romantic" attitude, a greater use of realistic detail, and—interestingly—an increasing preoccupation with occult and philosophical matters. The change from his earlier manner became steadily more apparent in THE GREEN HELMET (*1910*), RESPONSIBILITIES (*1914*), THE WILD SWANS AT COOLE (*1919*), *and* MICHAEL ROBARTES AND THE DANCER (*1921*).

In 1917 Yeats married Georgie Lees; and in 1923 he received the Nobel Prize for literature. Though he tended to hold himself aloof from the Irish struggle for independence, its events supplied the subject for some of his finest poetry; and he served as a senator of the Irish Free State from 1922 to 1928. His later volumes of poetry include THE TOWER (*1928*), THE WINDING STAIR AND OTHER POEMS (*1933*), A FULL MOON IN MARCH (*1935*), *and* LAST POEMS (*1936–39*). *With each volume his stature as a poet grew, and during the last ten years of his life, he was generally acclaimed as the greatest living English poet.*

the opposite sides of the personality and attempt to balance these characteristics to keep wheel turning.

Yeats' verse is published in two volumes, THE COLLECTED POEMS *(1950) and* THE COLLECTED PLAYS *(1952). His autobiographical writings appear in a volume called* AUTOBIOGRAPHIES *(1926); the authorized biography is Joseph Hone's* W. B. YEATS *(1943). Richard Ellmann's* YEATS: THE MAN AND THE MASK *(1948) is an important critical study, and James Hall and Martin Steinman's* THE PERMANENCE OF YEATS *(1950) is an excellent collection of critical essays on Yeats.*

age of enlightenment and the age of the fool and finally again age of darkness

THE BALLAD OF MOLL MAGEE

Come round me, little childer;
There, don't fling stones at me
Because I mutter as I go;
But pity Moll Magee.

My man was a poor fisher 5
With shore lines in the say;
My work was saltin' herrings
The whole of the long day.

And sometimes from the saltin' shed
I scarce could drag my feet, 10
Under the blessed moonlight,
Along the pebbly street.

I'd always been but weakly,
And my baby was just born;
A neighbour minded her by day, 15
I minded her till morn.

I lay upon my baby;
Ye little childer dear,
I looked on my cold baby
When the morn grew frosty and clear. 20

A weary woman sleeps so hard!
My man grew red and pale,
And gave me money, and bade me go
To my own place, Kinsale.

1 *childer:* children. 6 *say:* sea.

He drove me out and shut the door, 25
And gave his curse to me;
I went away in silence,
No neighbour could I see.

The windows and the doors were shut,
One star shone faint and green, 30
The little straws were turnin' round
Across the bare boreen.

I went away in silence:
Beyond old Martin's byre
I saw a kindly neighbor 35
Blowin' her morning fire.

She drew from me my story—
My money's all used up,
And still, with pityin', scornin' eye,
She gives me bite and sup. 40

She says my man will surely come,
And fetch me home agin;
But always, as I'm movin' round,
Without doors or within,

Pilin' the wood or pilin' the turf, 45
Or goin' to the well,
I'm thinkin' of my baby
And keenin' to mysel'.

And sometimes I am sure she knows
When, openin' wide His door, 50
God lights the stars, His candles,
And looks upon the poor.

So now, ye little childer,
Ye won't fling stones at me;
But gather with your shinin' looks 55
And pity Moll Magee.

32 *boreen:* narrow lane or byroad. 34 *byre:* cow house. 48 *keenin':* weeping.

THE BALLAD OF FATHER GILLIGAN

The old priest Peter Gilligan
Was weary night and day;
For half his flock were in their beds,
Or under green sods lay.

Once, while he nodded on a chair, 5
At the moth-hour of eve,
Another poor man sent for him,
And he began to grieve.

'I have no rest, nor joy, nor peace,
For people die and die'; 10
And after cried he, 'God forgive!
My body spake, not I!'

He knelt, and leaning on the chair
He prayed and fell asleep;
And the moth-hour went from the fields, 15
And stars began to peep.

They slowly into millions grew,
And leaves shook in the wind;
And God covered the world with shade,
And whispered to mankind. 20

Upon the time of sparrow-chirp
When moths came once more,
The old priest Peter Gilligan
Stood upright on the floor.

'Mavrone, mavrone! the man has died 25
While I slept on the chair';
He roused his horse out of its sleep,
And rode with little care.

He rode now as he never rode,
By rocky lane and fen; 30
The sick man's wife opened the door:
'Father! you come again!'

'And is the poor man dead?' he cried.
'He died an hour ago.'
The old priest Peter Gilligan 35
In grief swayed to and fro.

'When you were gone, he turned and died
As merry as a bird.'
The old priest Peter Gilligan
He knelt him at that word. 40

'He Who hath made the night of stars
For souls who tire and bleed,
Sent one of His great angels down
To help me in my need.

He Who is wrapped in purple robes, 45
With planets in His care,
Had pity on the least of things
Asleep upon a chair.'

WHEN YOU ARE OLD

When you are old and grey and full of sleep,
And nodding by the fire, take down this book,
And slowly read, and dream of the soft look
Your eyes had once, and of their shadows deep;

How many loved your moments of glad grace, 5
And loved your beauty with love false or true,
But one man loved the pilgrim soul in you,
And loved the sorrows of your changing face;

And bending down beside the glowing bars,
Murmur, a little sadly, how Love fled 10
And paced upon the mountains overhead
And hid his face amid a crowd of stars.

RECONCILIATION

Some may have blamed you that you took away
The verses that could move them on the day
When, the ears being deafened, the sight of the eyes blind
With lightning, you went from me, and I could find
Nothing to make a song about but kings, 5
Helmets, and swords, and half-forgotten things
That were like memories of you—but now
We'll out, for the world lives as long ago;
And while we're in our laughing, weeping fit,
Hurl helmets, crowns, and swords into the pit. 10
But, dear, cling close to me; since you were gone,
My barren thoughts have chilled me to the bone.

A DRINKING SONG

Wine comes in at the mouth
And love comes in at the eye;
That's all we shall know for truth
Before we grow old and die.
I lift the glass to my mouth, 5
I look at you, and I sigh.

THE COMING OF WISDOM WITH TIME

Though leaves are many, the root is one;
Through all the lying days of my youth
I swayed my leaves and flowers in the sun;
Now I may wither into the truth.

TO A FRIEND WHOSE WORK HAS COME TO NOTHING

Now all the truth is out,
Be secret and take defeat
From any brazen throat,
For how can you compete,
Being honour bred, with one 5
Who, were it proved he lies,
Were neither shamed in his own
Nor in his neighbours' eyes?
Bred to a harder thing
Than Triumph, turn away 10
And like a laughing string
Whereon mad fingers play
Amid a place of stone,
Be secret and exult,
Because of all things known 15
That is most difficult.

A COAT

I made my song a coat
Covered with embroideries
Out of old mythologies
From heel to throat;
But the fools caught it, 5
Wore it in the world's eyes
As though they'd wrought it.
Song, let them take it,
For there's more enterprise
In walking naked. 10

AN IRISH AIRMAN FORESEES HIS DEATH

I know that I shall meet my fate
Somewhere among the clouds above;
Those that I fight I do not hate,

Those that I guard I do not love;
My country is Kiltartan Cross, 5
My countrymen Kiltartan's poor,
No likely end could bring them loss
Or leave them happier than before.
Nor law, nor duty bade me fight,
Nor public men, nor cheering crowds, 10
A lonely impulse of delight
Drove to this tumult in the clouds;
I balanced all, brought all to mind,
The years to come seemed waste of breath,
A waste of breath the years behind 15
In balance with this life, this death.

TO A YOUNG GIRL

My dear, my dear, I know
More than another
What makes your heart beat so;
Not even your own mother
Can know it as I know, 5
Who broke my heart for her
When the wild thought,
That she denies
And has forgot,
Set all her blood astir 10
And glittered in her eyes.

THE SCHOLARS

Bald heads forgetful of their sins,
Old, learned, respectable bald heads
Edit and annotate the lines
That young men, tossing on their beds,
Rhymed out in love's despair 5
To flatter beauty's ignorant ear.

All shuffle there; all cough in ink;
All wear the carpet with their shoes;

All think what other people think;
All know the man their neighbour knows. 10
Lord, what would they say
Did their Catullus walk that way?

12 *Catullus:* Roman lyric poet, best known for his love poems.

ON WOMAN

May God be praised for woman
That gives up all her mind,
A man may find in no man
A friendship of her kind
That covers all he has brought 5
As with her flesh and bone,
Nor quarrels with a thought
Because it is not her own.

Though pedantry denies,
It's plain the Bible means 10
That Solomon grew wise
While talking with his queens,
Yet never could, although
They say he counted grass,
Count all the praises due 15
When Sheba was his lass,
When she the iron wrought, or
When from the smithy fire
It shuddered in the water:
Harshness of their desire 20
That made them stretch and yawn,
Pleasure that comes with sleep,
Shudder that made them one.
What else He give or keep
God grant me—no, not here, 25
For I am not so bold
To hope a thing so dear
Now I am growing old,
But when, if the tale's true,
The Pestle of the moon 30

That pounds up all anew
Brings me to birth again—
To find what once I had
And know what once I have known,
Until I am driven mad, 35
Sleep driven from my bed,
By tenderness and care,
Pity, an aching head,
Gnashing of teeth, despair;
And all because of someone 40
Perverse creature of chance,
And live like Solomon
That Sheba led a dance.

A DEEP-SWORN VOW

Others because you did not keep
That deep-sworn vow have been friends of mine;
Yet always when I look death in the face,
When I clamber to the heights of sleep,
Or when I grow excited with wine, 5
Suddenly I meet your face.

ON BEING ASKED FOR A WAR POEM

I think it better that in times like these
A poet's mouth be silent, for in truth
We have no gift to set a statesman right;
He has had enough of meddling who can please
A young girl in the indolence of her youth, 5
Or an old man upon a winter's night.

THE LEADERS OF THE CROWD

They must to keep their certainty accuse
All that are different of a base intent;
Pull down established honour; hawk for news

Whatever their loose phantasy invent
And murmur it with bated breath, as though 5
The abounding gutter had been Helicon
Or calumny a song. How can they know
Truth flourishes where the student's lamp has shone,
And there alone, that have no solitude?
So the crowd come they care not what may come. 10
They have loud music, hope every day renewed
And heartier loves; that lamp is from the tomb.

6 *Helicon:* i. e., a spring on Mt. Helicon, the mountain sacred to the Muses.

THE SECOND COMING

Turning and turning in the widening gyre
The falcon cannot hear the falconer;
Things fall apart; the centre cannot hold;
Mere anarchy is loosed upon the world,
The blood-dimmed tide is loosed, and everywhere 5
The ceremony of innocence is drowned;
The best lack all conviction, while the worst
Are full of passionate intensity.

Surely some revelation is at hand;
Surely the Second Coming is at hand. 10
The Second Coming! Hardly are those words out
When a vast image out of *Spiritus Mundi*
Troubles my sight: somewhere in sands of the desert
A shape with lion body and the head of a man,
A gaze blank and pitiless as the sun, 15
Is moving its slow thighs, while all about it

The Second Coming: a phrase ordinarily used to refer to the prophesied return of Christ to the earth. Yeats, however, expounded in his book A VISION a mystical system which explained history in terms of 2000-year cycles or "gyres." Just as the age of Greek culture had been followed by that of Christianity, so Christianity (its 2000 years now drawing to a conclusion) would end with the coming of a new and entirely different age. 1 *gyre:* 1) the ascending spiral flight of the falcon, 2) the cyclical movement of history. 12 *Spiritus Mundi:* literally, "world-spirit." Yeats used the term to signify the world's collective memory or "collective unconscious."

Reel shadows of the indignant desert birds.
The darkness drops again; but now I know
That twenty centuries of stony sleep
Were vexed to nightmare by a rocking cradle, 20
And what rough beast, its hour come round at last,
Slouches towards Bethlehem to be born?

SAILING TO BYZANTIUM

I

That is no country for old men. The young
In one another's arms, birds in the trees,
—Those dying generations—at their song,
The salmon-falls, the mackerel-crowded seas,
Fish, flesh, or fowl, commend all summer long 5
Whatever is begotten, born, and dies.
Caught in that sensual music all neglect
Monuments of unageing intellect.

II

An aged man is but a paltry thing,
A tattered coat upon a stick, unless 10
Soul clap its hands and sing, and louder sing
For every tatter in its mortal dress,
Nor is there singing school but studying
Monuments of its own magnificence;
And therefore I have sailed the seas and come 15
To the holy city of Byzantium.

III

O sages standing in God's holy fire
As in the gold mosaic of a wall,
Come from the holy fire, perne in a gyre,

Byzantium: an ancient city which became the capital of the Roman Empire in 330 A. D. and was the center of Eastern Christianity in the middle ages (Constantinople was built on its ruins). To Yeats, Byzantium symbolized the peak of spiritual, artistic and intellectual achievement. 1 *That:* Ireland. 19 *perne:* spin (*perne* is an Irish term for spool); *gyre:* see note to "The Second Coming."

And be the singing-masters of my soul. 20
Consume my heart away; sick with desire
And fastened to a dying animal
It knows not what it is; and gather me
Into the artifice of eternity.

IV

Once out of nature I shall never take 25
My bodily form from any natural thing,
But such a form as Grecian goldsmiths make
Of hammered gold and gold enamelling
To keep a drowsy Emperor awake;
Or set upon a golden bough to sing 30
To lords and ladies of Byzantium
Of what is past, or passing, or to come.

27–31: one of the Byzantine emperors had a golden tree in whose branches sang mechanical golden birds.

THE WHEEL

Through winter-time we call on spring,
And through the spring on summer call,
And when abounding hedges ring
Declare that winter's best of all;
And after that there's nothing good 5
Because the spring-time has not come—
Nor know that what disturbs our blood
Is but its longing for the tomb.

YOUTH AND AGE

Much did I rage when young,
Being by the world oppressed,
But now with flattering tongue
It speeds the parting guest.

LEDA AND THE SWAN

A sudden blow: the great wings beating still
Above the staggering girl, her thighs caressed
By the dark webs, her nape caught in his bill,
He holds her helpless breast upon his breast.

How can those terrified vague fingers push   5
The feathered glory from her loosening thighs?
And how can body, laid in that white rush,
But feel the strange heart beating where it lies?

A shudder in the loins engenders there
The broken wall, the burning roof and tower   10
And Agamemnon dead.
                Being so caught up,
So mastered by the brute blood of the air,
Did she put on his knowledge with his power
Before the indifferent beak could let her drop?

Leda and the Swan: Leda was the wife of Tyndareus, king of Sparta, by whom she had a son, Castor, and a daughter, Clytemnestra. She inadvertently attracted the attention of Zeus, who made love to her in the form of a swan; as a result of this union, Leda bore another son and daughter, Pollux and Helen. The union of Leda and Zeus can be taken as the starting-point of the pre-Christian era of classical Greek culture—an event similar in significance to the birth which Yeats foresees as the starting-point of the post-Christian era in "The Second Coming."   10: a reference to the burning of Troy at the end of the Trojan War, which had begun as a result of Paris's abduction of Leda's daughter Helen.   11 *Agamemnon:* husband of Leda's daughter Clytemnestra, who, with her paramour Aegisthus, murdered him upon his return from the Trojan War.

From "A MAN YOUNG AND OLD"

I

First Love

Though nurtured like the sailing moon
In beauty's murderous brood,
She walked awhile and blushed awhile

And on my pathway stood
Until I thought her body bore 5
A heart of flesh and blood.

But since I laid a hand thereon
And found a heart of stone
I have attempted many things
And not a thing is done, 10
For every hand is lunatic
That travels on the moon.

She smiled and that transfigured me
And left me but a lout,
Maundering here, and maundering there, 15
Emptier of thought
Than the heavenly circuit of its stars
When the moon sails out.

II

Human Dignity

Like the moon her kindness is,
If kindness I may call
What has no comprehension in't,
But is the same for all
As though my sorrow were a scene 5
Upon a painted wall.

So like a bit of stone I lie
Under a broken tree.
I could recover if I shrieked
My heart's agony 10
To passing bird, but I am dumb
From human dignity.

III

The Mermaid

A mermaid found a swimming lad,
Picked him for her own,
Pressed her body to his body,
Laughed; and plunging down

Forgot in cruel happiness
That even lovers drown.

THE CHOICE

The intellect of man is forced to choose
Perfection of the life, or of the work,
And if it take the second must refuse
A heavenly mansion, raging in the dark.
When all that story's finished, what's the news? 5
In luck or out the toil has left its mark:
That old perplexity an empty purse,
Or the day's vanity, the night's remorse.

GRATITUDE TO THE UNKNOWN INSTRUCTORS

What they undertook to do
They brought to pass;
All things hang like a drop of dew
Upon a blade of grass.

REMORSE FOR INTEMPERATE SPEECH

I ranted to the knave and fool,
But outgrew that school,
Would transform the part,
Fit audience found, but cannot rule
My fanatic heart. 5

I sought my betters: though in each
Fine manners, liberal speech,
Turn hatred into sport,
Nothing said or done can reach
My fanatic heart. 10

5 *fanatic:* in a note to this poem, Yeats wrote: "I pronounce 'fanatic' in what is, I suppose, the older and more Irish way, so that the last line of each stanza contains but two beats."

Out of Ireland have we come
Great hatred, little room,
Maimed us at the start.
I carry from my mother's womb
A fanatic heart. 15

CRAZY JANE AND THE BISHOP

Bring me to the blasted oak
That I, midnight upon the stroke,
(*All find safety in the tomb.*)
May call down curses on his head
Because of my dear Jack that's dead. 5
Coxcomb was the least he said:
The solid man and the coxcomb.

Nor was he Bishop when his ban
Banished Jack the Journeyman,
(*All find safety in the tomb.*) 10
Nor so much as parish priest,
Yet he, an old book in his fist,
Cried that we lived like beast and beast:
The solid man and the coxcomb.

The Bishop has a skin, God knows, 15
Wrinkled like the foot of a goose,
(*All find safety in the tomb.*)
Nor can he hide in holy black
The heron's bunch upon his back,
But a birch-tree stood my Jack: 20
The solid man and the coxcomb.

Jack had my virginity,
And bids me to the oak, for he
(*All find safety in the tomb.*)
Wanders out into the night 25
And there is shelter under it,
But should that other come, I spit:
The solid man and the coxcomb.

CRAZY JANE TALKS WITH THE BISHOP

I met the Bishop on the road
And much said he and I.
'Those breasts are flat and fallen now,
Those veins must soon be dry;
Live in a heavenly mansion, 5
Not in some foul sty.'

'Fair and foul are near of kin,
And fair needs foul,' I cried.
'My friends are gone, but that's a truth
Nor grave nor bed denied, 10
Learned in bodily lowliness
And in the heart's pride.

'A woman can be proud and stiff
When on love intent;
But Love has pitched his mansion in 15
The place of excrement;
For nothing can be sole or whole
That has not been rent.'

AFTER LONG SILENCE

Speech after long silence; it is right,
All other lovers being estranged or dead,
Unfriendly lamplight hid under its shade,
The curtains drawn upon unfriendly night,
That we descant and yet again descant 5
Upon the supreme theme of Art and Song:
Bodily decrepitude is wisdom; young
We loved each other and were ignorant.

CONSOLATION

O but there is wisdom
In what the sages said;
But stretch that body for a while
And lay down that head
Till I have told the sages 5
Where man is comforted.

How could passion run so deep
Had I never thought
That the crime of being born
Blackens all our lot? 10
But where the crime's committed
The crime can be forgot.

A LAST CONFESSION

What lively lad most pleasured me
Of all that with me lay?
I answer that I gave my soul
And loved in misery,
But had great pleasure with a lad 5
That I loved bodily.

Flinging from his arms I laughed
To think his passion such
He fancied that I gave a soul
Did but our bodies touch, 10
And laughed upon his breast to think
Beast gave beast as much.

I gave what other women gave
That stepped out of their clothes,
But when this soul, its body off, 15
Naked to naked goes,
He it has found shall find therein
What none other knows.

And give his own and take his own
And rule in his own right; 20
And though it loved in misery
Close and cling so tight,
There's not a bird of day that dare
Extinguish that delight.

EDWIN ARLINGTON ROBINSON

[1869–1935]

Edwin Arlington Robinson was born in Head Tide, Maine, and spent his youth in the nearby town of Gardiner, which became the "Tilbury Town" of his poems. He became interested in writing poetry in his boyhood. After attending Harvard for two years (1891–93), he was forced to drop out because of his father's illness and financial difficulties.

Unable to get his verse published in periodicals, Robinson published at his own expense a volume called THE TORRENT AND THE NIGHT BEFORE *(1896). In the following year, much of this book was incorporated with other work in* THE CHILDREN OF THE NIGHT, *which contained, among other poems, "Luke Havergal," "Richard Cory," "Aaron Stark," "Cliff Klingenhagen," "Fleming Helphenstine," "The Clerks," "Erasmus," "Zola," "Calvary," and "L'Envoi."*

In 1898 Robinson went to New York City, where he was to spend the rest of his life (except for summers at the MacDowell Colony at Peterborough, New Hampshire). During his first four years in the city, he worked as a checker in the construction of the New York subway. When CAPTAIN CRAIG *(1902) was published, Robinson's work was called to the attention of President Theodore Roosevelt, who offered Robinson a clerkship in the New York Customs House. Robinson held this position until 1910, when* THE TOWN DOWN THE RIVER *was published. In 1916, Robinson's reputation was firmly established by his volume* THE MAN AGAINST THE SKY.

By this time, Robinson had written almost all of his poems which are widely read today; yet his greatest honors—and the bulk of his creative work—were still before him. This work consisted almost entirely of long narrative poems. In 1917 appeared MERLIN, *the first of his versions of Arthurian legends—the others being* LAUNCELOT *(1920) and* TRISTRAM *(1927). Then came* AVON'S

HARVEST *(1921)*, ROMAN BARTHOLOW *(1923)*, THE MAN WHO DIED TWICE *(1924)*, DIONYSIUS IN DOUBT *(1925)*, CAVENDAR'S HOUSE *(1929)*, THE GLORY OF THE NIGHTINGALES *(1930)*, MATTHIAS AT THE DOOR *(1931)*, NICODEMUS *(1932)*, TALIFER *(1933)*, AMARANTH *(1934), and* KING JASPER *(1935). Robinson was awarded the Pulitzer Prize for poetry three times, in 1921, 1925, and 1927.*

Robinson's COLLECTED POEMS *was published in 1937. His biography was written by Herman Hagedorn (1938) and by Emery Neff (1948); Yvor Winters has written an important critical study (1946). Each of these three books is titled* EDWIN ARLINGTON ROBINSON.

FLAMMONDE

The man Flammonde, from God knows where,
With firm address and foreign air,
With news of nations in his talk
And something royal in his walk,
With glint of iron in his eyes, 5
But never doubt, nor yet surprise,
Appeared, and stayed, and held his head
As one by kings accredited.

Erect, with his alert repose
About him, and about his clothes, 10
He pictured all tradition hears
Of what we owe to fifty years.
His cleansing heritage of taste
Paraded neither want nor waste;
And what he needed for his fee 15
To live, he borrowed graciously.

He never told us what he was,
Or what mischance, or other cause,
Had banished him from better days
To play the Prince of Castaways. 20
Meanwhile he played surpassing well
A part, for most, unplayable;
In fine, one pauses, half afraid
To say for certain that he played.

For that, one may as well forego 25
Conviction as to yes or no;
Nor can I say just how intense
Would then have been the difference
To several, who, having striven
In vain to get what he was given, 30
Would see the stranger taken on
By friends not easy to be won.

Moreover, many a malcontent
He soothed and found munificent;
His courtesy beguiled and foiled 35
Suspicion that his years were soiled;
His mien distinguished any crowd,
His credit strengthened when he bowed;
And women, young and old, were fond
Of looking at the man Flammonde. 40

There was a woman in our town
On whom the fashion was to frown;
But while our talk renewed the tinge
Of a long-faded scarlet fringe,
The man Flammonde saw none of that, 45
And what he saw we wondered at—
That none of us, in her distress,
Could hide or find our littleness.

There was a boy that all agreed
Had shut within him the rare seed 50
Of learning. We could understand,
But none of us could lift a hand.
The man Flammonde appraised the youth,
And told a few of us the truth;
And thereby, for a little gold, 55
A flowered future was unrolled.

There were two citizens who fought
For years and years, and over nought;
They made life awkward for their friends,
And shortened their own dividends. 60

The man Flammonde said what was wrong
Should be made right; nor was it long
Before they were again in line,
And had each other in to dine.

And these I mention are but four 65
Of many out of many more.
So much for them. But what of him—
So firm in every look and limb?
What small satanic sort of kink
Was in his brain? What broken link 70
Withheld him from the destinies
That came so near to being his?

What was he, when we came to sift
His meaning, and to note the drift
Of incommunicable ways 75
That make us ponder while we praise?
Why was it that his charms revealed
Somehow the surface of a shield?
What was it that we never caught?
What was he, and what was he not? 80

How much it was of him we met
We cannot ever know; nor yet
Shall all he gave us quite atone
For what was his, and his alone;
Nor need we now, since he knew best, 85
Nourish an ethical unrest:
Rarely at once will nature give
The power to be Flammonde and live.

We cannot know how much we learn
From those who never will return, 90
Until a flash of unforeseen
Remembrance falls on what has been.
We've each a darkening hill to climb;
And this is why, from time to time
In Tilbury Town, we look beyond 95
Horizons for the man Flammonde.

EROS TURANNOS

She fears him, and will always ask
  What fated her to choose him;
She meets in his engaging mask
  All reasons to refuse him;
But what she meets and what she fears 5
Are less than are the downward years,
Drawn slowly to the foamless weirs
  Of age, were she to lose him.

Between a blurred sagacity
  That once had power to sound him, 10
And Love, that will not let him be
  The Judas that she found him,
Her pride assuages her almost,
As if it were alone the cost.
He sees that he will not be lost, 15
  And waits and looks around him.

A sense of ocean and old trees
  Envelops and allures him;
Tradition, touching all he sees,
  Beguiles and reassures him; 20
And all her doubts of what he says
Are dimmed with what she knows of days—
Till even prejudice delays
  And fades, and she secures him.

The falling leaf inaugurates 25
  The reign of her confusion;
The pounding wave reverberates
  The dirge of her illusion;
And home, where passion lived and died,
Becomes a place where she can hide, 30
While all the town and harbor-side
  Vibrate with her seclusion.

We tell you, tapping on our brows,
  The story as it should be,

Eros Turannos: "Love, the tyrant."

As if the story of a house 35
  Were told, or ever could be;
We'll have no kindly veil between
Her visions and those we have seen,—
As if we guessed what hers have been,
  Or what they are or would be. 40

Meanwhile we do no harm; for they
  That with a god have striven,
Not hearing much of what we say,
  Take what the god has given;
Though like waves breaking it may be, 45
Or like a changed familiar tree,
Or like a stairway to the sea
  Where down the blind are driven.

VETERAN SIRENS

The ghost of Ninon would be sorry now
To laugh at them, were she to see them here,
So brave and so alert for learning how
To fence with reason for another year.

Age offers a far comelier diadem 5
Than theirs; but anguish has no eye for grace,
When time's malicious mercy cautions them
To think awhile of number and of space.

The burning hope, the worn expectancy,
The martyred humor, and the maimed allure, 10
Cry out for time to end his levity,
And age to soften its investiture;

But they, though others fade and are still fair,
Defy their fairness and are unsubdued;
Although they suffer, they may not forswear 15
The patient ardor of the unpursued.

1 *Ninon:* Anne L'Enclos, a Frenchwoman who retained her beauty and wit to a very advanced age. 5 *diadem:* crown. 12 *investiture:* act of investing, as with an office or honor.

Poor flesh, to fight the calendar so long;
Poor vanity, so quaint and yet so brave;
Poor folly, so deceived and yet so strong,
So far from Ninon and so near the grave. 20

THE POOR RELATION

No longer torn by what she knows
And sees within the eyes of others,
Her doubts are when the daylight goes,
Her fears are for the few she bothers.
She tells them it is wholly wrong 5
Of her to stay alive so long;
And when she smiles her forehead shows
A crinkle that had been her mother's.

Beneath her beauty, blanched with pain,
And wistful yet for being cheated, 10
A child would seem to ask again
A question many times repeated;
But no rebellion has betrayed
Her wonder at what she has paid
For memories that have no stain, 15
For triumph born to be defeated.

To those who come for what she was—
The few left who know where to find her—
She clings, for they are all she has;
And she may smile when they remind her, 20
As heretofore, of what they know
Of roses that are still to blow
By ways where not so much as grass
Remains of what she sees behind her.

They stay awhile, and having done 25
What penance or the past requires,
They go, and leave her there alone
To count her chimneys and her spires.
Her lip shakes when they go away,
And yet she would not have them stay; 30

She knows as well as anyone
That Pity, having played, soon tires.

But one friend always reappears,
A good ghost, not to be forsaken;
Whereat she laughs and has no fears 35
Of what a ghost may reawaken,
But welcomes, while she wears and mends
The poor relation's odds and ends,
Her truant from a tomb of years—
Her power of youth so early taken. 40

Poor laugh, more slender than her song
It seems; and there are none to hear it
With even the stopped ears of the strong
For breaking heart or broken spirit.
The friends who clamored for her place, 45
And would have scratched her for her face,
Have lost her laughter for so long
That none would care enough to fear it.

None live who need fear anything
From her, whose losses are their pleasurc; 50
The plover with a wounded wing
Stays not the flight that others measure;
So there she waits, and while she lives,
And death forgets, and faith forgives,
Her memories go foraging 55
For bits of childhood song they treasure.

And like a giant harp that hums
On always, and is always blending
The coming of what never comes
With what has past and had an ending, 60
The City trembles, throbs, and pounds
Outside, and through a thousand sounds
The small intolerable drums
Of Time are like slow drops descending.

Bereft enough to shame a sage 65
And given little to long sighing,
With no illusion to assuage

The lonely changelessness of dying,—
Unsought, unthought-of, and unheard,
She sings and watches like a bird, 70
Safe in a comfortable cage
From which there will be no more flying.

LLEWELLYN AND THE TREE

Could he have made Priscilla share
  The paradise that he had planned,
Llewellyn would have loved his wife
  As well as any in the land.

Could he have made Priscilla cease 5
  To goad him for what God left out,
Llewellyn would have been as mild
  As any we have read about.

Could all have been as all was not,
  Llewellyn would have had no story; 10
He would have stayed a quiet man
  And gone his quiet way to glory.

But howsoever mild he was
  Priscilla was implacable;
And whatsoever timid hopes 15
  He built—she found them, and they fell.

And this went on, with intervals
  Of labored harmony between
Resounding discords, till at last
  Llewellyn turned—as will be seen. 20

Priscilla, warmer than her name,
  And shriller than the sound of saws,
Pursued Llewellyn once too far,
  Not knowing quite the man he was.

The more she said, the fiercer clung 25
  The stinging garment of his wrath;
And this was all before the day
  When Time tossed roses in his path.

Before the roses ever came
  Llewellyn had already risen. 30
The roses may have ruined him,
  They may have kept him out of prison.

And she who brought them, being Fate,
  Made roses do the work of spears,—
Though many made no more of her 35
  Than civet, coral, rouge, and years.

You ask us what Llewellyn saw,
  But why ask what may not be given?
To some will come a time when change
  Itself is beauty, if not heaven. 40

One afternoon Priscilla spoke,
  And her shrill history was done;
At any rate, she never spoke
  Like that again to anyone.

One gold October afternoon 45
  Great fury smote the silent air;
And then Llewellyn leapt and fled
  Like one with hornets in his hair.

Llewellyn left us, and he said
  Forever, leaving few to doubt him; 50
And so, through frost and clicking leaves,
  The Tilbury way went on without him.

And slowly, through the Tilbury mist,
  The stillness of October gold
Went out like beauty from a face. 55
  Priscilla watched it, and grew old.

He fled, still clutching in his flight
  The roses that had been his fall;
The Scarlet One, as you surmise,
  Fled with him, coral, rouge, and all. 60

Priscilla, waiting, saw the change
  Of twenty slow October moons;

36 *civet:* strong perfume; *coral:* i. e., coral jewelry.

And then she vanished, in her turn
To be forgotten, like old tunes.

So they were gone—all three of them, 65
I should have said, and said no more,
Had not a face once on Broadway
Been one that I had seen before.

The face and hands and hair were old,
But neither time nor penury 70
Could quench within Llewellyn's eyes
The shine of his one victory.

The roses, faded and gone by,
Left ruin where they once had reigned;
But on the wreck, as on old shells, 75
The color of the rose remained.

His fictive merchandise I bought
For him to keep and show again,
Then slowly led him from the crush
Of his cold-shouldered fellow men. 80

"And so, Llewellyn," I began—
"Not so," he said; "not so at all:
I've tried the world, and found it good,
For more than twenty years this fall.

"And what the world has left of me 85
Will go now in a little while."
And what the world had left of him
Was partly an unholy guile.

"That I have paid for being calm
Is what you see, if you have eyes; 90
For let a man be calm too long,
He pays for much before he dies.

"Be calm when you are growing old
And you have nothing else to do;
Pour not the wine of life too thin 95
If water means the death of you.

"You say I might have learned at home
The truth in season to be strong?

Not so; I took the wine of life
  To thin, and I was calm too long. 100

"Like others who are strong too late,
  For me there was no going back;
For I had found another speed
  And I was on the other track.

"God knows how far I might have gone 105
  Or what there might have been to see;
But my speed had a sudden end,
  And here you have the end of me."

The end or not, it may be now
  But little farther from the truth 110
To say those worn satiric eyes
  Had something of immortal youth.

He may among the millions here
  Be one; or he may, quite as well,
Be gone to find again the Tree 115
  Of Knowledge, out of which he fell.

He may be near us, dreaming yet
  Of unrepented rouge and coral;
Or in a grave without a name
  May be as far off as a moral. 120

BEWICK FINZER

Time was when his half million drew
  The breath of six per cent;
But soon the worm of what-was-not
  Fed hard on his content;
And something crumbled in his brain 5
  When his half million went.

Time passed, and filled along with his
  The place of many more;
Time came, and hardly one of us
  Had credence to restore, 10
From what appeared one day, the man
  Whom we had known before.

The broken voice, the withered neck,
  The coat worn out with care,
The cleanliness of indigence, 15
  The brilliance of despair,
The fond imponderable dreams
  Of affluence,—all were there.

Poor Finzer, with his dreams and schemes,
  Fares hard now in the race, 20
With heart and eye that have a task
  When he looks in the face
Of one who might so easily
  Have been in Finzer's place.

He comes unfailing for the loan 25
  We give and then forget;
He comes, and probably for years
  Will he be coming yet,—
Familiar as an old mistake,
  And futile as regret. 30

LUKE HAVERGAL

Go to the western gate, Luke Havergal,
There where the vines cling crimson on the wall,
And in the twilight wait for what will come.
The leaves will whisper there of her, and some,
Like flying words, will strike you as they fall; 5
But go, and if you listen she will call.
Go to the western gate, Luke Havergal—
Luke Havergal.

No, there is not a dawn in eastern skies
To rift the fiery night that's in your eyes; 10
But there, where western glooms are gathering,
The dark will end the dark, if anything:
God slays Himself with every leaf that flies,
And hell is more than half of paradise.
No, there is not a dawn in eastern skies— 15
In eastern skies.

Out of a grave I come to tell you this,
Out of a grave I come to quench the kiss
That flames upon your forehead with a glow
That blinds you to the way that you must go. 20
Yes, there is yet one way to where she is,
Bitter, but one that faith may never miss.
Out of a grave I come to tell you this—
To tell you this.

There is the western gate, Luke Havergal, 25
There are the crimson leaves upon the wall.
Go, for the winds are tearing them away,—
Nor think to riddle the dead words they say,
Nor any more to feel them as they fall;
But go, and if you trust her she will call. 30
There is the western gate, Luke Havergal—
Luke Havergal.

THREE QUATRAINS

I

As long as Fame's imperious music rings
  Will poets mock it with crowned words august;
And haggard men will clamber to be kings
  As long as Glory weighs itself in dust.

II

Drink to the splendor of the unfulfilled, 5
  Nor shudder for the revels that are done:
The wines that flushed Lucullus are all spilled,
  The strings that Nero fingered are all gone.

III

We cannot crown ourselves with everything,
  Nor can we coax the Fates for us to quarrel: 10
No matter what we are, or what we sing,
  Time finds a withered leaf in every laurel.

7 *Lucullus:* Roman consul and general, remembered for his wealth and luxury. 8 *Nero:* Roman emperor, famed for his depravity, who is believed to have played a harp while Rome was burning.

THE HOUSE ON THE HILL

They are all gone away,
  The House is shut and still,
There is nothing more to say.

Through broken walls and grey
  The winds blow bleak and shrill: 5
They are all gone away.

Nor is there one today
  To speak them good or ill:
There is nothing more to say.

Why is it then we stray 10
  Around that sunken sill?
They are all gone away,

And our poor fancy-play
  For them is wasted skill:
There is nothing more to say. 15

There is ruin and decay
  In the House on the Hill:
They are all gone away,
There is nothing more to say.

RICHARD CORY

Whenever Richard Cory went down town,
  We people on the pavement looked at him:
He was a gentleman from sole to crown,
  Clean favored, and imperially slim.

And he was always quietly arrayed, 5
  And he was always human when he talked;
But still he fluttered pulses when he said,
  "Good-morning," and he glittered when he walked.

And he was rich—yes, richer than a king,
  And admirably schooled in every grace: 10

In fine, we thought that he was everything
  To make us wish that we were in his place.

So on we worked, and waited for the light,
  And went without the meat, and cursed the bread;
And Richard Cory, one calm summer night, 15
  Went home and put a bullet through his head.

UNCLE ANANIAS

His words were magic and his heart was true,
  And everywhere he wandered he was blessed.
Out of all ancient men my childhood knew
  I choose him and I mark him for the best.
Of all authoritative liars, too, 5
  I crown him loveliest.

How fondly I remember the delight
  That always glorified him in the spring;
The joyous courage and the benedight
  Profusion of his faith in everything! 10
He was a good old man, and it was right
  That he should have his fling.

And often, underneath the apple-trees,
  When we surprised him in the summer time,
With what superb magnificence and ease 15
  He sinned enough to make the day sublime!
And if he liked us there about his knees,
  Truly it was no crime.

All summer long we loved him for the same
  Perennial inspiration of his lies; 20
And when the russet wealth of autumn came,
  There flew but fairer visions to our eyes—
Multiple, tropical, winged with a feathery flame,
  Like birds of paradise.

9 *benedight:* blessed.

So to the sheltered end of many a year 25
He charmed the seasons out with pageantry,
Wearing upon his forehead, with no fear,
The laurel of approved iniquity.
And every child who knew him, far or near,
Did love him faithfully. 30

MINIVER CHEEVY

Miniver Cheevy, child of scorn,
Grew lean while he assailed the seasons;
He wept that he was ever born,
And he had reasons.

Miniver loved the days of old 5
When swords were bright and steeds were prancing.
The vision of a warrior bold
Would set him dancing.

Miniver sighed for what was not,
And dreamed, and rested from his labors; 10
He dreamed of Thebes and Camelot,
And Priam's neighbors.

Miniver mourned the ripe renown
That made so many a name so fragrant:
He mourned Romance, now on the town, 15
And Art, a vagrant.

Miniver loved the Medici,
Albeit he had never seen one:
He would have sinned incessantly
Could he have been one. 20

11 *Thebes:* an ancient city in Egypt, the setting of the great Greek tragedies *Oedipus Rex, Seven Against Thebes,* and *Antigone; Camelot:* legendary town in England at which King Arthur held his court and maintained the Round Table. 12 *Priam:* King of Troy at the time of the Trojan War, the subject of Homer's *Iliad:* father of Paris, who abducted Helen, and of Hector, the Trojan hero. 17 *the Medici:* a great family of medieval Florence, famed for their power, wealth, and their patronage of the arts and literature.

Miniver cursed the commonplace
  And eyed a khaki suit with loathing;
He missed the mediæval grace
  Of iron clothing.

Miniver scorned the gold he sought, 25
  But sore annoyed was he without it;
Miniver thought, and thought, and thought,
  And thought about it.

Miniver Cheevy, born too late,
  Scratched his head and kept on thinking: 30
Miniver coughed, and called it fate,
  And kept on drinking.

FOR A DEAD LADY

No more with overflowing light
Shall fill the eyes that now are faded,
Nor shall another's fringe with night
Their woman-hidden world as they did.
No more shall quiver down the days 5
The flowing wonder of her ways,
Whereof no language may requite
The shifting and the many-shaded.

The grace, divine, definitive,
Clings only as a faint forestalling; 10
The laugh that love could not forgive
Is hushed, and answers to no calling;
The forehead and the little ears
Have gone where Saturn keeps the years;
The breast where roses could not live 15
Has done with rising and with falling.

The beauty, shattered by the laws
That have creation in their keeping,
No longer trembles at applause,

14 *Saturn:* in Roman mythology, the god of agriculture; he became identified with the ancient Greek god Cronus (Time).

Or over children that are sleeping; 20
And we who delve in beauty's lore
Know all that we have known before
Of what inexorable cause
Makes Time so vicious in his reaping.

THE MILL

The miller's wife had waited long,
The tea was cold, the fire was dead;
And there might yet be nothing wrong
In how he went and what he said:
"There are no millers any more," 5
Was all that she had heard him say:
And he had lingered at the door
So long that it seemed yesterday.

Sick with a fear that had no form
She knew that she was there at last; 10
And in the mill there was a warm
And mealy fragrance of the past.
What else there was would only seem
To say again what he had meant;
And what was hanging from a beam 15
Would not have heeded where she went.

And if she thought it followed her,
She may have reasoned in the dark
That one way of the few there were
Would hide her and would leave no mark: 20
Black water smooth above the weir
Like starry velvet in the night,
Though ruffled once, would soon appear
The same as ever to the sight.

THE DARK HILLS

Dark hills at evening in the west,
Where sunset hovers like a sound
Of golden horns that sang to rest

Old bones of warriors under ground,
Far now from all the bannered ways 5
Where flash the legions of the sun,
You fade—as if the last of days
Were fading, and all wars were done.

MR. FLOOD'S PARTY

Old Eben Flood, climbing alone one night
Over the hill between the town below
And the forsaken upland hermitage
That held as much as he should ever know
On earth again of home, paused warily. 5
The road was his with not a native near;
And Eben, having leisure, said aloud,
For no man else in Tilbury Town to hear:

"Well, Mr. Flood, we have the harvest moon
Again, and we may not have many more; 10
The bird is on the wing, the poet says,
And you and I have said it here before.
Drink to the bird." He raised up to the light
The jug that he had gone so far to fill,
And answered huskily: "Well, Mr. Flood, 15
Since you propose it, I believe I will."

Alone, as if enduring to the end
A valiant armor of scarred hopes outworn,
He stood there in the middle of the road
Like Roland's ghost winding a silent horn. 20
Below him, in the town among the trees,
Where friends of other days had honored him,
A phantom salutation of the dead
Rang thinly till old Eben's eyes were dim.

Then, as a mother lays her sleeping child 25
Down tenderly, fearing it may awake,

20 *Roland:* hero of *The Song of Roland,* a medieval romance. When Roland and his warriors are attacked by the Saracens, Roland delays too long in using his horn to summon help from Charlemagne, and he is slain.

He set the jug down slowly at his feet
With trembling care, knowing that most things break;
And only when assured that on firm earth
It stood, as the uncertain lives of men 30
Assuredly did not, he paced away,
And with his hand extended paused again:

"Well, Mr. Flood, we have not met like this
In a long time; and many a change has come
To both of us, I fear, since last it was 35
We had a drop together. Welcome home!"
Convivially returning with himself,
Again he raised the jug up to the light;
And with an acquiescent quaver said:
"Well, Mr. Flood, if you insist, I might. 40

"Only a very little, Mr. Flood—
For auld lang syne. No more, sir; that will do."
So, for the time, apparently it did,
And Eben evidently thought so too;
For soon amid the silver loneliness 45
Of night he lifted up his voice and sang,
Secure, with only two moons listening,
Until the whole harmonious landscape rang—

"For auld lang syne." The weary throat gave out,
The last word wavered; and the song being done, 50
He raised again the jug regretfully
And shook his head, and was again alone.
There was not much that was ahead of him,
And there was nothing in the town below—
Where strangers would have shut the many doors 55
That many friends had opened long ago.

AARON STARK

Withal a meagre man was Aaron Stark,
Cursed and unkempt, shrewd, shrivelled, and morose.
A miser was he, with a miser's nose,
And eyes like little dollars in the dark.

His thin, pinched mouth was nothing but a mark; 5
And when he spoke there came like sullen blows
Through scattered fangs a few snarled words and close,
As if a cur were chary of its bark.

Glad for the murmur of his hard renown,
Year after year he shambled through the town, 10
A loveless exile moving with a staff;
And oftentimes there crept into his ears
A sound of alien pity, touched with tears,—
And then (and only then) did Aaron laugh.

CLIFF KLINGENHAGEN

Cliff Klingenhagen had me in to dine
With him one day; and after soup and meat,
And all the other things there were to eat,
Cliff took two glasses and filled one with wine
And one with wormwood. Then, without a sign 5
For me to choose at all, he took the draught
Of bitterness himself, and lightly quaffed
It off, and said the other one was mine.

And when I asked him what the deuce he meant
By doing that, he only looked at me 10
And smiled, and said it was a way of his.
And though I know the fellow, I have spent
Long time a-wondering when I shall be
As happy as Cliff Klingenhagen is.

5 *wormwood:* a very bitter drink.

FLEMING HELPHENSTINE

At first I thought there was a superfine
Persuasion in his face; but the free glow
That filled it when he stopped and cried, "Hollo!"

Shone joyously, and so I let it shine.
He said his name was Fleming Helphenstine, 5
But be that as it may;—I only know
He talked of this and that and So-and-So,
And laughed and chaffed like any friend of mine.

But soon, with a queer, quick frown, he looked at me,
And I looked hard at him; and there we gazed 10
In a strained way that made us cringe and wince:
Then, with a wordless clogged apology
That sounded half confused and half amazed,
He dodged,—and I have never seen him since.

REUBEN BRIGHT

Because he was a butcher and thereby
Did earn an honest living (and did right)
I would not have you think that Reuben Bright
Was any more a brute than you or I;
For when they told him that his wife must die, 5
He stared at them, and shook with grief and fright,
And cried like a great baby half that night,
And made the women cry to see him cry.

And after she was dead, and he had paid
The singers and the sexton and the rest, 10
He packed a lot of things that she had made
Most mournfully away in an old chest
Of hers, and put some chopped-up cedar boughs
In with them, and tore down the slaughter-house.

DOCTOR OF BILLIARDS

Of all among the fallen from on high,
We count you last and leave you to regain
Your born dominion of a life made vain
By three spheres of insidious ivory.
You dwindle to the lesser tragedy— 5

Content, you say. We call, but you remain.
Nothing alive gone wrong could be so plain,
Or quite so blasted with absurdity.

You click away the kingdom that is yours,
And you click off your crown for cap and bells; 10
You smile, who are still master of the feast,
And for your smile we credit you the least;
But when your false, unhallowed laugh occurs,
We seem to think there may be something else.

10 *cap and bells:* badge of the medieval fool or court jester.

HOW ANNANDALE WENT OUT

"They called it Annandale—and I was there
To flourish, to find words, and to attend:
Liar, physician, hypocrite, and friend,
I watched him; and the sight was not so fair
As one or two that I have seen elsewhere: 5
An apparatus not for me to mend—
A wreck, with hell between him and the end,
Remained of Annandale; and I was there.
"I knew the ruin as I knew the man;
So put the two together, if you can, 10
Remembering the worst you know of me.
Now view yourself as I was, on the spot—
With a slight kind of engine. Do you see?
Like this . . . You wouldn't hang me? I thought not."

ANOTHER DARK LADY

Think not, because I wonder where you fled,
That I would lift a pin to see you there;

Another Dark Lady: the original "dark lady" is the unknown woman whom Shakespeare describes and addresses in some of his sonnets. See Sonnets 127, 130, and 147.

You may, for me, be prowling anywhere,
So long as you show not your little head:
No dark and evil story of the dead 5
Would leave you less pernicious or less fair—
Not even Lilith, with her famous hair;
And Lilith was the devil, I have read.

I cannot hate you, for I loved you then.
The woods were golden then. There was a road 10
Through beeches; and I said their smooth feet showed
Like yours. Truth must have heard me from afar,
For I shall never have to learn again
That yours are cloven as no beech's are.

Lilith: Adam's first wife, according to the Talmud.

AMARYLLIS

Once, when I wandered in the woods alone,
An old man tottered up to me and said,
"Come, friend, and see the grave that I have made
For Amaryllis." There was in the tone
Of his complaint such quaver and such moan 5
That I took pity on him and obeyed,
And long stood looking where his hands had laid
An ancient woman, shrunk to skin and bone.

Far out beyond the forest I could hear
The calling of loud progress, and the bold 10
Incessant scream of commerce ringing clear;
But though the trumpets of the world were glad,
It made me lonely and it made me sad
To think that Amaryllis had grown old.

Amaryllis: a favorite name for the nymph in classical literature: symbol of youth and beauty.

THE CLERKS

I did not think that I should find them there
When I came back again; but there they stood,
As in the days they dreamed of when young blood
Was in their cheeks and women called them fair.
Be sure, they met me with an ancient air,— 5
And yes, there was a shop-worn brotherhood
About them; but the men were just as good,
And just as human as they ever were.

And you that ache so much to be sublime,
And you that feed yourselves with your descent, 10
What comes of all your visions and your fears?
Poets and kings are but the clerks of Time,
Tiering the same dull webs of discontent,
Clipping the same sad alnage of the years.

14 *alnage:* measurement.

THE SHEAVES

Where long the shadows of the wind had rolled,
Green wheat was yielding to the change assigned;
And as by some vast magic undivined
The world was turning slowly into gold.
Like nothing that was ever bought or sold 5
It waited there, the body and the mind;
And with a mighty meaning of a kind
That tells the more the more it is not told.

So in a land where all days are not fair,
Fair days went on till on another day 10
A thousand golden sheaves were lying there,
Shining and still, but not for long to stay—
As if a thousand girls with golden hair
Might rise from where they slept and go away.

ERASMUS

When he protested, not too solemnly,
That for a world's achieving maintenance
The crust of overdone divinity
Lacked aliment, they called it recreance;
And when he chose through his own glass to scan 5
Sick Europe, and reduced, unyieldingly,
The monk within the cassock to the man
Within the monk, they called it heresy.

And when he made so perilously bold
As to be scattered forth in black and white, 10
Good fathers looked askance at him and rolled
Their inward eyes in anguish and affright;
There were some of them did shake at what was told,
And they shook best who knew that he was right.

4 *aliment:* sustenance; *recreance:* unfaithfulness.

ZOLA

Because he puts the compromising chart
Of hell before your eyes, you are afraid;
Because he counts the price that you have paid
For innocence, and counts it from the start,
You loathe him. But he sees the human heart 5
Of God meanwhile, and in His hand was weighed
Your squeamish and emasculate crusade
Against the grim dominion of his art.

Never until we conquer the uncouth
Connivings of our shamed indifference 10
(We call it Christian faith) are we to scan
The racked and shrieking hideousness of Truth
To find, in hate's polluted self-defense
Throbbing, the pulse, the divine heart of man.

CALVARY

Friendless and faint, with martyred steps and slow,
Faint for the flesh, but for the spirit free,
Stung by the mob that came to see the show,
The Master toiled along to Calvary;
We gibed him, as he went, with houndish glee, 5
Till his dimmed eyes for us did overflow;
We cursed his vengeless hands thrice wretchedly,—
And this was nineteen hundred years ago.

But after nineteen hundred years the shame
Still clings, and we have not made good the loss 10
That outraged faith has entered in his name.
Ah, when shall come love's courage to be strong!
Tell me, O Lord—tell me, O Lord, how long
Are we to keep Christ writhing on the cross!

L'ENVOI

Now in a thought, now in a shadowed word,
Now in a voice that thrills eternity,
Ever there comes an onward phrase to me
Of some transcendent music I have heard;
No piteous thing by soft hands dulcimered, 5
No trumpet crash of blood-sick victory,
But a glad strain of some vast harmony
That no brief mortal touch has ever stirred.
There is no music in the world like this,
No character wherewith to set it down, 10
No kind of instrument to make it sing.
No kind of instrument? Ah, yes, there is;
And after time and place are overthrown,
God's touch will keep its one chord quivering.

5 *dulcimered:* played on a dulcimer—an ancient musical instrument.

poem begins in pleasure
and ends in wisdom

ROBERT FROST

[1875-1963]

Robert Frost was born in San Francisco. His father, a descendant of an old New England family, died when Robert was ten; at his death, Robert's mother moved to Lawrence, Massachusetts, where Frost attended high school. He entered Dartmouth, but returned to Lawrence after a few months and went to work in a mill. He was able to sell some of his poems to magazines, and at twenty he married Eleanor White. In 1897, two years after his marriage, he entered Harvard; but after two years, he left school again. During the next eleven years he worked as a teacher, newspaper editor, shoemaker, and farmer.

In 1912, dissatisfied with his inability to gain recognition as a poet in America, Frost sailed with his wife and four children to England. There he met the poets Rupert Brooke and Wilfred Gibson; and there, paradoxically, were published his first two volumes of verse— A BOY'S WILL *(1913) and* NORTH OF BOSTON *(1914).* NORTH OF BOSTON, *which contained such poems as "Mending Wall," "The Death of the Hired Man" and "Home Burial," was reprinted in the United States, and when Frost returned to New Hampshire in 1915 he found himself famous.*

Frost has since divided his time between teaching at various colleges and universities and farming on his Vermont farm. His volumes of verse since NORTH OF BOSTON *include* MOUNTAIN INTERVAL *(1916),* NEW HAMPSHIRE *(1923),* WEST-RUNNING BROOK *(1928),* A FURTHER RANGE *(1936),* A WITNESS TREE *(1942),* A MASQUE OF REASON *(1945),* STEEPLE BUSH *(1947), and* A MASQUE OF MERCY *(1947). He has received the Pulitzer Prize for poetry four times, in 1924, 1931, 1937, and 1943. Frost died in January, 1963.*

A comprehensive edition of the COLLECTED POEMS OF ROBERT FROST *appeared in 1949. Critical studies of his work include Robert P. Tristram Coffin's* NEW POETRY OF NEW ENGLAND: FROST AND ROBINSON *(1938) and L. Thompson's* FIRE AND ICE: THE ART AND THOUGHT OF ROBERT FROST *(1942).*

THE PASTURE

I'm going out to clean the pasture spring;
I'll only stop to rake the leaves away
(And wait to watch the water clear, I may):
I sha'n't be gone long.—You come too.

I'm going out to fetch the little calf 5
That's standing by the mother. It's so young,
It totters when she licks it with her tongue.
I sha'n't be gone long.—You come too.

REVELATION

We make ourselves a place apart
  Behind light words that tease and flout,
But oh, the agitated heart
  Till someone find us really out.

'Tis pity if the case require 5
  (Or so we say) that in the end
We speak the literal to inspire
  The understanding of a friend.

But so with all, from babes that play
  At hide-and-seek to God afar, 10
So all who hide too well away
  Must speak and tell us where they are.

THE TUFT OF FLOWERS

I went to turn the grass once after one
Who mowed it in the dew before the sun.

The dew was gone that made his blade so keen
Before I came to view the levelled scene.

I looked for him behind an isle of trees; 5
I listened for his whetstone on the breeze.

But he had gone his way, the grass all mown,
And I must be, as he had been,—alone,

"As all must be," I said within my heart,
"Whether they work together or apart." 10

But as I said it, swift there passed me by
On noiseless wing a bewildered butterfly,

Seeking with memories grown dim o'er night
Some resting flower of yesterday's delight.

And once I marked his flight go round and round, 15
As where some flower lay withering on the ground.

And then he flew as far as eye could see,
And then on tremulous wing came back to me.

I thought of questions that have no reply,
And would have turned to toss the grass to dry; 20

But he turned first, and led my eye to look
At a tall tuft of flowers beside a brook,

A leaping tongue of bloom the scythe had spared
Beside a reedy brook the scythe had bared.

I left my place to know them by their name, 25
Finding them butterfly weed when I came.

The mower in the dew had loved them thus,
Leaving them to flourish, not for us,

Nor yet to draw one thought of ours to him,
But from sheer morning gladness at the brim. 30

The butterfly and I had lit upon,
Nevertheless, a message from the dawn,

That made me hear the wakening birds around,
And hear his long scythe whispering to the ground,

And feel a spirit kindred to my own; 35
So that henceforth I worked no more alone;

But glad with him, I worked as with his aid,
And weary, sought at noon with him the shade;

And dreaming, as it were, held brotherly speech
With one whose thought I had not hoped to reach. 40

"Men work together," I told him from the heart,
"Whether they work together or apart."

barrier between people

MENDING WALL

Something there is that doesn't love a wall,
That sends the frozen-ground-swell under it,
And spills the upper boulders in the sun;
And makes gaps even two can pass abreast.
The work of hunters is another thing: 5
I have come after them and made repair
Where they have left not one stone on a stone,
But they would have the rabbit out of hiding,
To please the yelping dogs. The gaps I mean,
No one has seen them made or heard them made, 10
But at spring mending-time we find them there.
I let my neighbour know beyond the hill;
And on a day we meet to walk the line
And set the wall between us once again.
We keep the wall between us as we go. 15
To each the boulders that have fallen to each.
And some are loaves and some so nearly balls
We have to use a spell to make them balance:
"Stay where you are until our backs are turned!"
We wear our fingers rough with handling them. 20
Oh, just another kind of out-door game,
One on a side. It comes to little more:
There where it is we do not need the wall:
He is all pine and I am apple orchard.
My apple trees will never get across 25
And eat the cones under his pines, I tell him.
He only says, "Good fences make good neighbours."
Spring is the mischief in me, and I wonder
If I could put a notion in his head:
"*Why* do they make good neighbours? Isn't it 30
Where there are cows? But here there are no cows.

Before I built a wall I'd ask to know
What I was walling in or walling out,
And to whom I was like to give offence.
Something there is that doesn't love a wall, 35
That wants it down." I could say "Elves" to him,
But it's not elves exactly, and I'd rather
He said it for himself. I see him there
Bringing a stone grasped firmly by the top
In each hand, like an old-stone savage armed. 40
He moves in darkness as it seems to me,
Not of woods only and the shade of trees.
He will not go behind his father's saying,
And he likes having thought of it so well
He says again, "Good fences make good neighbours." 45

THE ROAD NOT TAKEN

Two roads diverged in a yellow wood,
And sorry I could not travel both
And be one traveler, long I stood
And looked down one as far as I could
To where it bent in the undergrowth; 5

Then took the other, as just as fair,
And having perhaps the better claim,
Because it was grassy and wanted wear;
Though as for that the passing there
Had worn them really about the same, 10

And both that morning equally lay
In leaves no step had trodden black.
Oh, I kept the first for another day!
Yet knowing how way leads on to way,
I doubted if I should ever come back. 15

I shall be telling this with a sigh
Somewhere ages and ages hence:
Two roads diverged in a wood, and I—
I took the one less traveled by,
And that has made all the difference. 20

A PATCH OF OLD SNOW

There's a patch of old snow in a corner
  That I should have guessed
Was a blow-away paper the rain
  Had brought to rest.

It is speckled with grime as if   5
  Small print overspread it,
The news of a day I've forgotten—
  If I ever read it.

THE COW IN APPLE TIME

Something inspires the only cow of late
To make no more of a wall than an open gate,
And think no more of wall-builders than fools.
Her face is flecked with pomace and she drools
A cider syrup. Having tasted fruit,   5
She scorns a pasture withering to the root.
She runs from tree to tree where lie and sweeten
The windfalls spiked with stubble and worm-eaten.
She leaves them bitten when she has to fly.
She bellows on a knoll against the sky.   10
Her udder shrivels and the milk goes dry.

4 *pomace:* crushed apple-pulp.

THE HILL WIFE

Loneliness

(HER WORD)

One ought not to have to care
  So much as you and I
Care when the birds come round the house
  To seem to say good-bye;

Or care so much when they come back 5
  With whatever it is they sing;
The truth being we are as much
  Too glad for the one thing

As we are too sad for the other here—
  With birds that fill their breasts 10
But with each other and themselves
  And their built or driven nests.

House Fear

Always—I tell you this they learned—
Always at night when they returned
To the lonely house from far away 15
To lamps unlighted and fire gone gray,
They learned to rattle the lock and key
To give whatever might chance to be
Warning and time to be off in flight:
And preferring the out- to the in-door night, 20
They learned to leave the house-door wide
Until they had lit the lamp inside.

The Smile

(HER WORD)

I didn't like the way he went away.
That smile! It never came of being gay.
Still he smiled—did you see him?—I was sure! 25
Perhaps because we gave him only bread
And the wretch knew from that that we were poor.
Perhaps because he let us give instead
Of seizing from us as he might have seized.
Perhaps he mocked at us for being wed, 30
Or being very young (and he was pleased
To have a vision of us old and dead).
I wonder how far down the road he's got.
He's watching from the woods as like as not.

The Oft-Repeated Dream

She had no saying dark enough 35
For the dark pine that kept
Forever trying the window-latch
Of the room where they slept.

The tireless, but ineffectual hands
That with every futile pass 40
Made the great tree seem as a little bird
Before the mystery of glass!

It never had been inside the room,
And only one of the two
Was afraid in an oft-repeated dream 45
Of what the tree might do.

The Impulse

It was too lonely for her there,
And too wild,
And since there were but two of them,
And no child, 50

And work was little in the house,
And she was free,
And followed where he furrowed field,
Or felled tree.

She rested on a log and tossed 55
The fresh chips,
With a song only to herself
On her lips.

And once she went to break a bough
Of black alder. 60
She strayed so far she scarcely heard
When he called her—

And didn't answer—didn't speak—
Or return.
She stood, and then she ran and hid 65
In the fern.

He never found her, though he looked
  Everywhere,
And he asked at her mother's house
  Was she there. 70

Sudden and swift and light as that
  The ties gave,
And he learned of finalities
  Besides the grave.

'OUT, OUT—'

The buzz saw snarled and rattled in the yard
And made dust and dropped stove-length sticks of wood,
Sweet-scented stuff when the breeze drew across it.
And from there those that lifted eyes could count
Five mountain ranges one behind the other 5
Under the sunset far into Vermont.
And the saw snarled and rattled, snarled and rattled,
As it ran light, or had to bear a load.
And nothing happened: day was all but done.
Call it a day, I wish they might have said 10
To please the boy by giving him the half hour
That a boy counts so much when saved from work.
His sister stood beside them in her apron
To tell them 'Supper.' At the word, the saw,
As if to prove saws knew what supper meant, 15
Leaped out at the boy's hand, or seemed to leap—
He must have given the hand. However it was,
Neither refused the meeting. But the hand!
The boy's first outcry was a rueful laugh,
As he swung toward them holding up the hand 20
Half in appeal, half as if to keep
The life from spilling. Then the boy saw all—
Since he was old enough to know, big boy
Doing a man's work, though a child at heart—
He saw all spoiled. 'Don't let him cut my hand off— 25
The doctor, when he comes. Don't let him, sister!'
So. But the hand was gone already.

The doctor put him in the dark of ether.
He lay and puffed his lips out with his breath.
And then—the watcher at his pulse took fright. 30
No one believed. They listened at his heart.
Little—less—nothing!—and that ended it.
No more to build on there. And they, since they
Were not the one dead, turned to their affairs.

FIRE AND ICE

Some say the world will end in fire,
Some say in ice.
From what I've tasted of desire
I hold with those who favor fire.
But if it had to perish twice, 5
I think I know enough of hate
To say that for destruction ice
Is also great
And would suffice.

DUST OF SNOW

The way a crow
Shook down on me
The dust of snow
From a hemlock tree

Has given my heart 5
A change of mood
And saved some part
Of a day I had rued.

THE RUNAWAY

Once when the snow of the year was beginning to fall,
We stopped by a mountain pasture to say "Whose colt?"
A little Morgan had one forefoot on the wall,

The other curled at his breast. He dipped his head
And snorted at us. And then he had to bolt. 5
We heard the miniature thunder where he fled,
And we saw him, or thought we saw him, dim and grey,
Like a shadow against the curtain of falling flakes.
"I think the little fellow's afraid of the snow.
He isn't winter-broken. It isn't play 10
With the little fellow at all. He's running away.
I doubt if even his mother could tell him, 'Sakes,
It's only weather.' He'd think she didn't know!
Where is his mother? He can't be out alone."
And now he comes again with a clatter of stone 15
And mounts the wall again with whited eyes
And all his tail that isn't hair up straight.
He shudders his coat as if to throw off flies.
"Whoever it is that leaves him out so late,
When other creatures have gone to stall and bin, 20
Ought to be told to come and take him in."

STOPPING BY WOODS ON A SNOWY EVENING

Whose woods these are I think I know.
His house is in the village though;
He will not see me stopping here
To watch his woods fill up with snow.

My little horse must think it queer 5
To stop without a farmhouse near
Between the woods and frozen lake
The darkest evening of the year.

He gives his harness bells a shake
To ask if there is some mistake. 10
The only other sound's the sweep
Of easy wind and downy flake.

The woods are lovely, dark and deep.
But I have promises to keep,
And miles to go before I sleep, 15
And miles to go before I sleep.

TO EARTHWARD

Love at the lips was touch
As sweet as I could bear;
And once that seemed too much;
I lived on air

That crossed me from sweet things, 5
The flow of—was it musk
From hidden grapevine springs
Down hill at dusk?

I had the swirl and ache
From sprays of honeysuckle 10
That when they're gathered shake
Dew on the knuckle.

I craved strong sweets, but those
Seemed strong when I was young;
The petal of the rose 15
It was that stung.

Now no joy but lacks salt
That is not dashed with pain
And weariness and fault;
I crave the stain 20

Of tears, the aftermark
Of almost too much love,
The sweet of bitter bark
And burning clove.

When stiff and sore and scarred 25
I take away my hand
From leaning on it hard
In grass and sand,

The hurt is not enough:
I long for weight and strength 30
To feel the earth as rough
To all my length.

ACQUAINTED WITH THE NIGHT

I have been one acquainted with the night.
I have walked out in rain—and back in rain.
I have outwalked the furthest city light.

I have looked down the saddest city lane.
I have passed by the watchman on his beat 5
And dropped my eyes, unwilling to explain.

I have stood still and stopped the sound of feet
When far away an interrupted cry
Came over houses from another street,

But not to call me back or say good-bye; 10
And further still at an unearthly height,
One luminary clock against the sky

Proclaimed the time was neither wrong nor right.
I have been one acquainted with the night.

ONCE BY THE PACIFIC

The shattered water made a misty din.
Great waves looked over others coming in,
And thought of doing something to the shore
That water never did to land before.
The clouds were low and hairy in the skies, 5
Like locks blown forward in the gleam of eyes.
You could not tell, and yet it looked as if
The shore was lucky in being backed by cliff,
The cliff in being backed by continent;
It looked as if a night of dark intent 10
Was coming, and not only a night, an age.
Someone had better be prepared for rage.
There would be more than ocean-water broken
Before God's last *Put out the Light* was spoken.

TWO TRAMPS IN MUD TIME

Out of the mud two strangers came
And caught me splitting wood in the yard.
And one of them put me off my aim
By hailing cheerily "Hit them hard!"
I knew pretty well why he dropped behind 5
And let the other go on a way.
I knew pretty well what he had in mind:
He wanted to take my job for pay.

Good blocks of beech it was I split,
As large around as the chopping block; 10
And every piece I squarely hit
Fell splinterless as a cloven rock.
The blows that a life of self-control
Spares to strike for the common good
That day, giving a loose to my soul, 15
I spent on the unimportant wood.

The sun was warm but the wind was chill.
You know how it is with an April day
When the sun is out and the wind is still,
You're one month on in the middle of May. 20
But if you so much as dare to speak,
A cloud comes over the sunlit arch,
A wind comes off a frozen peak,
And you're two months back in the middle of March.

A bluebird comes tenderly up to alight 25
And fronts the wind to unruffle a plume
His song so pitched as not to excite
A single flower as yet to bloom.
It is snowing a flake: and he half knew
Winter was only playing possum. 30
Except in color he isn't blue,
But he wouldn't advise a thing to blossom.

The water for which we may have to look
In summertime with a witching-wand,
In every wheelrut's now a brook, 35

In every print of a hoof a pond.
Be glad of winter, but don't forget
The lurking frost in the earth beneath
That will steal forth after the sun is set
And show on the water its crystal teeth. 40

The time when most I loved my task
These two must make me love it more
By coming with what they came to ask.
You'd think I never had felt before
The weight of an ax-head poised aloft, 45
The grip on earth of outspread feet.
The life of muscles rocking soft
And smooth and moist in vernal heat.

Out of the woods two hulking tramps
(From sleeping God knows where last night, 50
But not long since in the lumber camps).
They thought all chopping was theirs of right.
Men of the woods and lumberjacks,
They judged me by their appropriate tool.
Except as a fellow handled an ax, 55
They had no way of knowing a fool.

Nothing on either side was said.
They knew they had but to stay their stay
And all their logic would fill my head:
As that I had no right to play 60
With what was another man's work for gain.
My right might be love but theirs was need.
And where the two exist in twain
Theirs was the better right—agreed.

But yield who will to their separation, 65
My object in life is to unite
My avocation and my vocation
As my two eyes make one in sight.
Only where love and need are one,
And the work is play for mortal stakes, 70
Is the deed ever really done
For Heaven and the future's sakes.

DESERT PLACES

Snow falling and night falling fast, oh, fast
In a field I looked into going past,
And the ground almost covered smooth in snow,
But a few weeds and stubble showing last.

The woods around it have it—it is theirs. 5
All animals are smothered in their lairs.
I am too absent-spirited to count;
The loneliness includes me unawares.

And lonely as it is, that loneliness
Will be more lonely ere it will be less— 10
A blanker whiteness of benighted snow,
With no expression, nothing to express.

They cannot scare me with their empty spaces
Between stars—on stars where no human race is.
I have it in me so much nearer home 15
To scare myself with my own desert places.

NEITHER OUT FAR, NOR IN DEEP

The people along the sand
All turn and look one way.
They turn their back on the land.
They look at the sea all day.

As long as it takes to pass 5
A ship keeps raising its hull;
The wetter ground like glass
Reflects a standing gull.

The land may vary more;
But wherever the truth may be— 10
The water comes ashore,
And the people look at the sea.

They cannot look out far.
They cannot look in deep.
But when was that ever a bar 15
To any watch they keep?

A SOLDIER

He is that fallen lance that lies as hurled,
That lies unlifted now, come dew, come rust,
But still lies pointed as it plowed the dust.
If we who sight along it round the world,
See nothing worthy to have been its mark, 5
It is because like men we look too near,
Forgetting that as fitted to the sphere,
Our missiles always make too short an arc.
They fall, they rip the grass, they intersect
The curve of earth, and striking, break their own; 10
They make us cringe for metal-point on stone.
But this we know, the obstacle that checked
And tripped the body, shot the spirit on
Further than target ever showed or shone.

ON A TREE FALLEN ACROSS THE ROAD

(To Hear Us Talk)

The tree the tempest with a crash of wood
Throws down in front of us is not to bar
Our passage to our journey's end for good,
But just to ask us who we think we are

Insisting always on our own way so. 5
She likes to halt us in our runner tracks,
And make us get down in a foot of snow
Debating what to do without an axe.

And yet she knows obstruction is in vain:
We will not be put off the final goal 10

INTO MY OWN

We have it hidden in us to attain,
Not though we have to seize earth by the pole

And, tired of aimless circling in one place,
Steer straight off after something into space.

INTO MY OWN

One of my wishes is that those dark trees,
So old and firm they scarcely show the breeze,
Were not, as 'twere, the merest mask of gloom,
But stretched away unto the edge of doom.

I should not be withheld but that some day 5
Into their vastness I should steal away,
Fearless of ever finding open land,
Or highway where the slow wheel pours the sand.

I do not see why I should e'er turn back,
Or those should not set forth upon my track 10
To overtake me, who should miss me here
And long to know if still I held them dear.

They would not find me changed from him they knew—
Only more sure of all I thought was true.

T. S. ELIOT

[*1888–1965*]

T(homas) S(tearns) Eliot was born in St. Louis, Missouri. His father, a successful business man, and his mother were descendants of old New England families. Eliot was educated in St. Louis and at Harvard, where, as editor of the HARVARD ADVOCATE, *he published some of his own poems. Receiving his A. M. degree at Harvard, he became a graduate student in philosophy; after studying at the Sorbonne in Paris (1911), he returned to Harvard (1912–14), and then went to England to continue his studies at Merton College, Oxford.*

In 1915 Eliot married Vivienne Haigh, an Englishwoman, and settled in London, where he worked as a teacher and bank-clerk. In 1917 he published PRUFROCK AND OTHER OBSERVATIONS *and became editor of the* EGOIST. *He has since served as editor of the* CRITERION *and as a director of the publishing firm of Faber and Faber, Ltd.* THE WASTE LAND, *perhaps the most widely discussed poem of our time, was published in 1922.*

*Eliot's career as a critic began at the same time as his career as a poet; through his criticism and poetry, he has become the greatest single influence on modern poetry. The most dramatic event in both careers occurred in 1927 when, having become a British subject, Eliot declared himself an "Anglo-Catholic in religion, royalist in politics, and classicist in literature." Since that time, his most important poems—*ASH-WEDNESDAY *(1930) and* FOUR QUARTETS *(1939–42)—have been concerned with religious subjects. Eliot's verse plays include* MURDER IN THE CATHEDRAL *(1935),* THE FAMILY REUNION *(1939),* THE COCKTAIL PARTY *(1950), and* THE CONFIDENTIAL CLERK *(1954). In* THE IDEA OF A CHRISTIAN SOCIETY *(1939) and* NOTES TOWARD THE DEFINITION OF CULTURE *(1949) Eliot gave expression to his views on modern society. He received the Nobel Prize for literature in 1948. Eliot died in 1965.*

Eliot's poetry is to be found in THE COMPLETE POEMS AND PLAYS OF T. S. ELIOT *(1952); his most famous critical essays are published in*

SELECTED ESSAYS *(1950). Among the chief critical works on Eliot are F. O. Matthiessen's* THE ACHIEVEMENT OF T. S. ELIOT *(1947);* T. S. ELIOT: A SELECTED CRITIQUE, *edited by Leonard Unger (1948); and Elizabeth Drew's* T. S. ELIOT, THE DESIGN OF HIS POETRY *(1949).*

RHAPSODY ON A WINDY NIGHT

Twelve o'clock.
Across the reaches of the street
Held in a lunar synthesis,
Whispering lunar incantations
Dissolve the floors of memory 5
And all its clear relations
Its divisions and precisions,
Every street lamp that I pass
Beats like a fatalistic drum,
And through the spaces of the dark 10
Midnight shakes the memory
As a madman shakes a dead geranium.

Half-past one,
The street-lamp sputtered,
The street-lamp muttered, 15
The street-lamp said, "Regard that woman
Who hesitates toward you in the light of the door
Which opens on her like a grin.
You see the border of her dress
Is torn and stained with sand, 20
And you see the corner of her eye
Twists like a crooked pin."

The memory throws up high and dry
A crowd of twisted things;
A twisted branch upon the beach 25
Eaten smooth, and polished
As if the world gave up
The secret of its skeleton,
Stiff and white.
A broken spring in a factory yard, 30

3 *lunar:* of the moon.

Rust that clings to the form that the strength has left
Hard and curled and ready to snap.

Half-past two,
The street-lamp said,
"Remark the cat which flattens itself in the gutter, 35
Slips out its tongue
And devours a morsel of rancid butter."
So the hand of the child, automatic,
Slipped out and pocketed a toy that was running along the
quay.
I could see nothing behind that child's eye. 40
I have seen eyes in the street
Trying to peer through lighted shutters,
And a crab one afternoon in a pool,
An old crab with barnacles on his back,
Gripped the end of a stick which I held him. 45

Half-past three,
The lamp sputtered,
The lamp muttered in the dark.
The lamp hummed:
"Regard the moon, 50
La lune ne garde aucune rancune,
She winks a feeble eye,
She smiles into corners.
She smoothes the hair of the grass.
The moon has lost her memory. 55
A washed-out smallpox cracks her face,
Her hand twists a paper rose,
That smells of dust and eau de Cologne,
She is alone
With all the old nocturnal smells 60
That cross and cross across her brain."
The reminiscence comes
Of sunless dry geraniums
And dust in crevices,
Smells of chestnuts in the streets, 65
And female smells in shuttered rooms,

51 *la lune ne garde aucune rancune:* the moon is without rancor—an echo of a line in Jules Laforgue's "Complainte de cette Bonne Lune."

And cigarettes in corridors
And cocktail smells in bars.

The lamp said,
"Four o'clock, 70
Here is the number on the door.
Memory!
You have the key,
The little lamp spreads a ring on the stair.
Mount. 75
The bed is open; the tooth-brush hangs on the wall,
Put your shoes at the door, sleep, prepare for life."

The last twist of the knife.

AUNT HELEN

Miss Helen Slingsby was my maiden aunt,
And lived in a small house near a fashionable square
Cared for by servants to the number of four.
Now when she died there was silence in heaven
And silence at her end of the street. 5
The shutters were drawn and the undertaker wiped his feet—
He was aware that this sort of thing had occurred before.
The dogs were handsomely provided for,
But shortly afterwards the parrot died too.
The Dresden clock continued ticking on the mantelpiece, 10
And the footman sat upon the dining-table
Holding the second housemaid on his knees—
Who had always been so careful while her mistress lived.

COUSIN NANCY

Miss Nancy Ellicott
Strode across the hills and broke them,
Rode across the hills and broke them—
The barren New England hills—
Riding to hounds 5
Over the cow-pasture.

Miss Nancy Ellicott smoked
And danced all the modern dances;
And her aunts were not quite sure how they felt about it,
But they knew that it was modern. 10

Upon the glazen shelves kept watch
Matthew and Waldo, guardians of the faith,
The army of unalterable law.

12 *Matthew and Waldo:* Matthew Arnold, the great British nineteenth-century critic and lecturer, and Ralph Waldo Emerson, the American philosopher and essayist. 13: this line is the concluding line of George Meredith's sonnet "Lucifer in Starlight."

LA FIGLIA CHE PIANGE

O quam te memorem virgo . . .

Stand on the highest pavement of the stair—
Lean on a garden urn—
Weave, weave the sunlight in your hair—
Clasp your flowers to you with a pained surprise—
Fling them to the ground and turn 5
With a fugitive resentment in your eyes:
But weave, weave the sunlight in your hair.

So I would have had him leave,
So I would have had her stand and grieve,
So he would have left 10
As the soul leaves the body torn and bruised,
As the mind deserts the body it has used.
I should find
Some way incomparably light and deft,
Some way we both should understand, 15
Simple and faithless as a smile and shake of the hand.

She turned away, but with the autumn weather
Compelled my imagination many days,

La Figlia Che Piange: the girl who laments. *O quam te memorem virgo:* oh, what shall I call you, girl? (Virgil's *Aeneid,* I, 327).

Many days and many hours:
Her hair over her arms and her arms full of flowers. 20
And I wonder how they should have been together!
I should have lost a gesture and a pose.
Sometimes these cogitations still amaze
The troubled midnight and the noon's repose.

PRELUDES

I

The winter evening settles down
With smell of steaks in passageways.
Six o'clock.
The burnt-out ends of smoky days.
And now a gusty shower wraps 5
The grimy scraps
Of withered leaves about your feet
And newspapers from vacant lots;
The showers beat
On broken blinds and chimney-pots, 10
At the corner of the street
A lonely cab-horse steams and stamps.
And then the lighting of the lamps.

II

The morning comes to consciousness
Of faint stale smells of beer 15
From the sawdust-trampled street
With all its muddy feet that press
To early coffee-stands.
With the other masquerades
That time resumes, 20
One thinks of all the hands
That are raising dingy shades
In a thousand furnished rooms.

III

You tossed a blanket from the bed,
You lay upon your back, and waited; 25

You dozed, and watched the night revealing
The thousand sordid images
Of which your soul was constituted;
They flickered against the ceiling.
And when all the world came back 30
And the light crept up between the shutters
And you heard the sparrows in the gutters,
You had such a vision of the street
As the street hardly understands;
Sitting along the bed's edge, where 35
You curled the papers from your hair,
Or clasped the yellow soles of feet
In the palms of both soiled hands.

IV

His soul stretched tight across the skies
That fade behind a city block, 40
Or trampled by insistent feet
At four and five and six o'clock;
And short square fingers stuffing pipes,
And evening newspapers, and eyes
Assured of certain certainties, 45
The conscience of a blackened street
Impatient to assume the world.

I am moved by fancies that are curled
Around these images, and cling:
The notion of some infinitely gentle 50
Infinitely suffering thing.

Wipe your hand across your mouth, and laugh;
The worlds revolve like ancient women
Gathering fuel in vacant lots.

THE HIPPOPOTAMUS

Similiter et omnes revereantur Diaconos, ut mandatum Jesu Christi; et Episcopum, ut Jesum Christum, existentem filium Patris; Presbyteros autem, ut concilium Dei et conjunctionem Apostolorum. Sine his Ecclesia non vocatur; de quibus suadeo vos sic habeo.

S. Ignatii Ad Trallianos.

And when this epistle is read among you, cause that it be read also in the church of the Laodiceans.

The broad-backed hippopotamus
Rests on his belly in the mud;
Although he seems so firm to us
He is merely flesh and blood.

Flesh and blood is weak and frail, 5
Susceptible to nervous shock;
While the True Church can never fail
For it is based upon a rock.

The hippo's feeble steps may err
In compassing material ends, 10
While the True Church need never stir
To gather in its dividends.

The 'potamus can never reach
The mango on the mango-tree;
But fruits of pomegranate and peach 15
Refresh the Church from over sea.

At mating time the hippo's voice
Betrays inflexions hoarse and odd,
But every week we hear rejoice
The Church, at being one with God. 20

The hippopotamus's day
Is passed in sleep; at night he hunts;
God works in a mysterious way—
The Church can sleep and feed at once.

I saw the 'potamus take wing 25
Ascending from the damp savannas,
And quiring angels round him sing
The praise of God, in loud hosannas.

Similiter et omnes, etc.: "And likewise let all the deacons be reverenced, as commanded by Jesus Christ; and let the bishop be reverenced, as Jesus Christ, the living son of the Father; also let the presbyters be reverenced, as the council of God and the assembly of the apostles. Without these there can be no church; of these things I persuade you as I can." (St. Ignatius' third epistle to the Traillians.) *And when this, etc.:* Colossians 4:16. 26 *savannas:* tropical plains or grasslands.

Blood of the Lamb shall wash him clean
And him shall heavenly arms enfold, 30
Among the saints he shall be seen
Performing on a harp of gold.

He shall be washed as white as snow,
By all the martyr'd virgins kist,
While the True Church remains below 35
Wrapt in the old miasmal mist.

36 *miasmal:* poisonous, pestilential.

WHISPERS OF IMMORTALITY

Webster was much possessed by death
And saw the skull beneath the skin;
And breastless creatures under ground
Leaned backward with a lipless grin.

Daffodil bulbs instead of balls 5
Stared from the sockets of the eyes!
He knew that thought clings round dead limbs
Tightening its lusts and luxuries.

Donne, I suppose, was such another
Who found no substitute for sense, 10
To seize and clutch and penetrate;
Expert beyond experience,

He knew the anguish of the marrow
The ague of the skeleton;
No contact possible to flesh 15
Allayed the fever of the bone.

. . . .

Grishkin is nice: her Russian eye
Is underlined for emphasis;
Uncorseted, her friendly bust
Gives promise of pneumatic bliss. 20

1 *Webster:* John Webster, an Elizabethan playwright whose plays *The White Devil* and *The Duchess of Malfi* have many macabre and grotesque elements. 17 *Grishkin:* a figure symbolic of female sensuality.

The couched Brazilian jaguar
Compels the scampering marmoset
With subtle effluence of cat;
Grishkin has a maisonette;

The sleek Brazilian jaguar 25
Does not in its arboreal gloom
Distil so rank a feline smell
As Grishkin in a drawing room.

And even the Abstract Entities
Circumambulate her charm; 30
But our lot crawls between dry ribs
To keep our metaphysics warm.

30 *circumambulate:* move around.

SWEENEY ERECT

And the trees about me,
Let them be dry and leafless; let the rocks
Groan with continual surges; and behind me
Make all a desolation. Look, look, wenches!

Paint me a cavernous waste shore
Cast in the unstilled Cyclades,
Paint me the bold anfractuous rocks
Faced by the snarled and yelping seas.

And the trees about me, etc.: from Beaumont and Fletcher's *The Maid's Tragedy,* II, ii, 74–77. In the scene in which these lines occur, Aspatia is lamenting her desertion by her lover. Seeing a tapestry of Ariadne lamenting the departure of Theseus, Aspatia asserts that its colors are too bright, and offers herself as the model for another tapestry of Ariadne:

Suppose I stand upon the sea-beach now,
Mine arms thus, and mine hair blown with the wind,
Wild as that desert; and let all about me
Tell that I am forsaken. Do my face
(If thou had'st ever feeling of a sorrow)
Thus, thus, Antiphilia: strive to make me look
Like Sorrow's monument: and the trees about me,
Let them be dry and leafless; let the rocks
Groan with continual surges; and behind me
Make all a desolation. Look, look, wenches! (lines 68–77)

Display me Aeolus above 5
  Reviewing the insurgent gales
Which tangle Ariadne's hair
  And swell with haste the perjured sails.

Morning stirs the feet and hands
  (Nausicaa and Polypheme). 10
Gesture of orang-outang
  Rises from the sheets in steam.

This withered root of knots of hair
  Slitted below and gashed with eyes,
This oval O cropped out with teeth: 15
  The sickle motion from the thighs

Jackknifes upward at the knees
  Then straightens out from heel to hip
Pushing the framework of the bed
  And clawing at the pillow slip. 20

Sweeney addressed full length to shave
  Broadbottomed, pink from nape to base,
Knows the female temperament
  And wipes the suds around his face.

(The lengthened shadow of a man 25
  Is history, said Emerson
Who had not seen the silhouette
  Of Sweeney straddled in the sun.)

Tests the razor on his leg
  Waiting until the shriek subsides. 30

Ariadne, in Greek legend, helped Theseus slay the Minotaur, but was deserted by him on the island of Naxos in the Cyclades, a group of islands in the Aegean sea. 1 *Paint me, etc.:* the first two quatrains paraphrase the passage in *The Maid's Tragedy* from which Eliot took his epigraph. 3 *anfractuous:* full of twists and turns; tortuous. 5 *Aeolus:* Greek god of the winds. 8 *the perjured sails:* the sails of the ships of the departing Theseus, "perjured" because Theseus has been false to Ariadne. 10 *Nausicaa:* the modest and charming princess of the Phaecians, who gives help to Ulysses in the *Odyssey; Polypheme,* Polyphemus, the Cyclops, one-eyed cannibal giant from whom Ulysses escaped by blinding him. Here, the names are applied ironically to Sweeney and his female companion.

The epileptic on the bed
  Curves backward, clutching at her sides.

The ladies of the corridor
  Find themselves involved, disgraced,
Call witness to their principles 35
  And deprecate the lack of taste

Observing that hysteria
  Might easily be misunderstood;
Mrs. Turner intimates
  It does the house no sort of good. 40

But Doris, towelled from the bath,
  Enters padding on broad feet,
Bringing sal volatile
  And a glass of brandy neat.

43 *sal volatile:* smelling salts.

THE LOVE SONG OF J. ALFRED PRUFROCK

S'io credesse che mia risposta fosse
A persona che mai tornasse al mondo,
Questa fiamma staria senza piu scosse.
Ma perciocche giammai di questo fondo
Non torno vivo alcun, s'i'odo il vero,
Senza tema d'infamia ti rispondo.

Let us go then, you and I,
When the evening is spread out against the sky
Like a patient etherized upon a table;
Let us go, through certain half-deserted streets,
The muttering retreats 5
Of restless nights in one-night cheap hotels

S'io credesse, etc.: "If I thought my answer were to one who could ever return to the world, this flame should shake no more [i. e., I would not speak to you]; but since, if what I hear is true, no one ever returned alive from this depth, I answer you without fear of shame." A statement made by a spirit in hell to Dante in the twenty-seventh canto of the *Inferno.*

And sawdust restaurants with oyster-shells:
Streets that follow like a tedious argument
Of insidious intent
To lead you to an overwhelming question. . . 10
Oh, do not ask, "What is it?"
Let us go and make our visit.

In the room the women come and go
Talking of Michelangelo.

The yellow fog that rubs its back upon the window-panes, 15
The yellow smoke that rubs its muzzle on the window-panes,
Licked its tongue into the corners of the evening,
Lingered upon the pools that stand in drains,
Let fall upon its back the soot that falls from chimneys,
Slipped by the terrace, made a sudden leap, 20
And seeing that it was a soft October night,
Curled once about the house, and fell asleep.

And indeed there will be time
For the yellow smoke that slides along the street,
Rubbing its back upon the window-panes; 25
There will be time, there will be time
To prepare a face to meet the faces that you meet;
There will be time to murder and create,
And time for all the works and days of hands
That lift and drop a question on your plate; 30
Time for you and time for me,
And time yet for a hundred indecisions,
And for a hundred visions and revisions,
Before the taking of a toast and tea.

In the room the women come and go 35
Talking of Michelangelo.

And indeed there will be time
To wonder, "Do I dare?" and, "Do I dare?"
Time to turn back and descend the stair,
With a bald spot in the middle of my hair— 40
[They will say: "How his hair is growing thin!"]

29 *works and days:* Hesiod, a Greek poet of the eighth century B.C., wrote a poem on agriculture called *Works and Days.*

My morning coat, my collar mounting firmly to the chin,
My necktie rich and modest, but asserted by a simple pin—
[They will say: "But how his arms and legs are thin!"]
Do I dare 45
Disturb the universe?
In a minute there is time
For decisions and revisions which a minute will reverse.

For I have known them all already, known them all:
Have known the evenings, mornings, afternoons, 50
I have measured out my life with coffee spoons;
I know the voices dying with a dying fall
Beneath the music from a farther room.
So how should I presume?

And I have known the eyes already, known them all— 55
The eyes that fix you in a formulated phrase,
And when I am formulated, sprawling on a pin,
When I am pinned and wriggling on the wall,
Then how should I begin
To spit out all the butt-ends of my days and ways? 60
And how should I presume?

And I have known the arms already, known them all—
Arms that are braceleted and white and bare
[But in the lamplight, downed with light brown hair!]
Is it perfume from a dress 65
That makes me so digress?
Arms that lie along a table, or wrap about a shawl,
And should I then presume?
And how should I begin?

. . . .

Shall I say, I have gone at dusk through narrow streets 70
And watched the smoke that rises from the pipes
Of lonely men in shirt-sleeves, leaning out of windows? . . .

I should have been a pair of ragged claws
Scuttling across the floors of silent seas.

. . . .

And the afternoon, the evening, sleeps so peacefully! 75
Smoothed by long fingers,

Asleep . . . tired . . . or it malingers,
Stretched on the floor, here beside you and me.
Should I, after tea and cakes and ices,
Have the strength to force the moment to its crisis? 80
But though I have wept and fasted, wept and prayed,
Though I have seen my head (grown slightly bald) brought in
    upon a platter,
I am no prophet—and here's no great matter;
I have seen the moment of my greatness flicker,
And I have seen the eternal Footman hold my coat, and snicker, 85
And in short, I was afraid.

And would it have been worth it, after all,
After the cups, the marmalade, the tea,
Among the porcelain, among some talk of you and me,
Would it have been worth while, 90
To have bitten off the matter with a smile,
To have squeezed the universe into a ball
To roll it toward some overwhelming question,
To say: "I am Lazarus, come from the dead,
Come back to tell you all, I shall tell you all"— 95
If one, settling a pillow by her head,
  Should say: "That is not what I meant at all;
  That is not it, at all."

And would it have been worth it, after all,
Would it have been worth while, 100
After the sunsets and the dooryards and the sprinkled streets,
After the novels, after the teacups, after the skirts that trail along
    the floor—

82: John the Baptist's head was delivered to Salome on a platter as her reward for dancing for Herod (Matthew 14:1–11). 92: an allusion to a line in the conclusion of Marvell's "To His Coy Mistress," in which Marvell suggests to his mistress

> Let us roll all our strength and all
> Our sweetness up into one ball,
> And tear our pleasure with rough strife
> Thorough the iron gates of life . . . (lines 41–44)

94 *Lazarus:* could refer to either or both of the two Lazaruses mentioned in the Bible: the beggar Lazarus of Luke 16, who was forbidden to come back from the dead to warn the wealthy sinners of hell; or the Lazarus of John 11, the brother of Mary and Martha, who was brought back to life by Christ.

And this, and so much more?—
It is impossible to say just what I mean!
But as if a magic lantern threw the nerves in patterns on a screen:
Would it have been worth while 106
If one, settling a pillow or throwing off a shawl,
And turning toward the window, should say:
"That is not it at all,
That is not what I meant, at all." 110

. . . .

No! I am not Prince Hamlet, nor was meant to be;
Am an attendant lord, one that will do
To swell a progress, start a scene or two,
Advise the prince; no doubt, an easy tool,
Deferential, glad to be of use, 115
Politic, cautious, and meticulous;
Full of high sentence, but a bit obtuse;
At times, indeed, almost ridiculous—
Almost, at times, the Fool.

I grow old . . . I grow old . . . 120
I shall wear the bottoms of my trousers rolled.
Shall I part my hair behind? Do I dare to eat a peach?
I shall wear white flannel trousers, and walk upon the beach.
I have heard the mermaids singing, each to each.

I do not think that they will sing to me. 125

I have seen them riding seaward on the waves
Combing the white hair of the waves blown back
When the wind blows the water white and black.

We have lingered in the chambers of the sea
By sea-girls wreathed with seaweed red and brown 130
Till human voices wake us, and we drown.

113 *progress:* journey of a royal personage. 117 *high sentence:* wise speech. 121: at the time when Eliot wrote this poem, "rolled" (cuffed) trousers were a new fashion.

picture of an empty man, full of indecision, so will only drift through life

emptyness in modern world

THE HOLLOW MEN

Mistah Kurtz—he dead.

A penny for the Old Guy

I

We are the hollow men
We are the stuffed men
Leaning together
Headpiece filled with straw. Alas!
Our dried voices, when 5
We whisper together
Are quiet and meaningless
As wind in dry grass
Or rats' feet over broken glass
In our dry cellar 10

Shape without form, shade without color,
Paralysed force, gesture without motion;

Those who have crossed
With direct eyes, to death's other Kingdom
Remember us—if at all—not as lost 15
Violent souls, but only
As the hollow men
The stuffed men.

II

Eyes I dare not meet in dreams
In death's dream kingdom 20
These do not appear:
There, the eyes are

Mistah Kurtz—he dead: a quotation from Joseph Conrad's story "The Heart of Darkness." In the story, this statement announces to the narrator and his companions the death of the central character, an ambitious and imaginative European who has destroyed himself in his venture into the heart of the African darkness. *A penny for the Old Guy:* a phrase which English children traditionally cry out in the streets on Guy Fawkes day, in request for money with which to buy fireworks to burn effigies of the seventeenth-century traitor Guy Fawkes.

Sunlight on a broken column
There, is a tree swinging
And voices are 25
In the wind's singing
More distant and more solemn
Than a fading star.

Let me be no nearer
In death's dream kingdom 30
Let me also wear
Such deliberate disguises
Rat's coat, crowskin, crossed staves
In a field
Behaving as the wind behaves 35
No nearer—

Not that final meeting
In the twilight kingdom

III

This is the dead land
This is cactus land 40
Here the stone images
Are raised, here they receive
The supplication of a dead man's hand
Under the twinkle of a fading star.

Is it like this 45
In death's other kingdom
Waking alone
At the hour when we are
Trembling with tenderness
Lips that would kiss 50
Form prayers to broken stone.

IV

The eyes are not here
There are no eyes here

33 *Rat's coat, crowskin, crossed staves:* a reference to a scarecrow, with possibly an additional ironic reference to the crossed weapons which frequently appear (against a "field") on coats of arms.

In this valley of dying stars
In this hollow valley 55
This broken jaw of our lost kingdoms

In this last of meeting places
We grope together
And avoid speech
Gathered on this beach of the tumid river 60

Sightless, unless
The eyes reappear
As the perpetual star
Multifoliate rose
Of death's twilight kingdom 65
The hope only
Of empty men.

V

Here we go round the prickly pear
Prickly pear, prickly pear
Here we go round the prickly pear 70
At five o'clock in the morning.

Between the idea
And the reality
Between the motion
And the act 75
Falls the shadow
For Thine is the Kingdom.

Between the conception
And the creation
Between the emotion 80
And the response
Falls the Shadow
Life is very long.

Between the desire
And the spasm 85
Between the potency
And the existence
Between the essence

And the descent
Falls the Shadow. 90
For Thine is the Kingdom.

For Thine is
Life is
For Thine is the

This is the way the world ends 95
This is the way the world ends
This is the way the world ends
Not with a bang but a whimper.

ANIMULA

'Issues from the hand of God, the simple soul'
To a flat world of changing lights and noise,
To light, dark, dry or damp, chilly or warm;
Moving between the legs of tables and of chairs,
Rising or falling, grasping at kisses and toys, 5
Advancing boldly, sudden to take alarm,
Retreating to the corner of arm and knee,
Eager to be reassured, taking pleasure
In the fragrant brilliance of the Christmas tree,
Pleasure in the wind, the sunlight and the sea; 10
Studies the sunlit pattern on the floor
And running stags around a silver tray;
Confounds the actual and the fanciful,
Content with playing-cards and kings and queens,
What the fairies do and what the servants say. 15
The heavy burden of the growing soul
Perplexes and offends more, day by day;
Week by week, offends and perplexes more
With the imperatives of 'is and seems'

1: Eliot's condensation of a passage from the sixteenth canto of Dante's *Purgatorio:* "From the hands of Him who loves her before she is, there issues like a little child that plays, with weeping and laughter, the simple soul, that knows nothing except that, come from the hands of a glad creator, she turns willingly to everything that delights her."

And may and may not, desire and control. 20
The pain of living and the drug of dreams
Curl up the small soul in the window seat
Behind the *Encyclopedia Britannica*.
Issues from the hand of time the simple soul
Irresolute and selfish, misshapen, lame, 25
Unable to fare forward or retreat,
Fearing the warm reality, the offered good,
Denying the importunity of the blood,
Shadow of its own shadows, spectre in its own gloom,
Leaving disordered papers in a dusty room; 30
Living first in the silence after the viaticum.

Pray for Guiterriez, avid of speed and power,
For Boudin, blown to pieces,
For this one who made a great fortune,
And that one who went in his own way. 35
Pray for Floret, by the boarhound slain between the yew trees,
Pray for us now and at the hour of our birth.

31 *viaticum:* the Communion or Eucharist given to one who is dying or in danger of death. 32–36 *Guiterriez, Boudin, Floret:* So far as can be determined, these are "made-up" names, not identifiable with genuine persons. 37: an inverted echo of the line from the prayer, "Pray for us sinners now and at the hour of our death."

JOURNEY OF THE MAGI

'A cold coming we had of it,
Just the worst time of the year
For a journey, and such a long journey:
The ways deep and the weather sharp,
The very dead of winter.' 5

1–5: in these lines Eliot paraphrases a passage from a sermon delivered by Lancelot Andrewes in 1622: "It was no summer progress. A cold coming they had of it at this time of the year, just the worst time of the year to take a journey, and specially a long journey in. The ways deep, the weather sharp, the days short, the sun farthest off, *in solstitio brumali,* 'the very dead of winter.' "

And the camels galled, sore-footed, refractory,
Lying down in the melting snow.
There were times we regretted
The summer palaces on slopes, the terraces,
And the silken girls bringing sherbet. 10
Then the camel men cursing and grumbling
And running away, and wanting their liquor and women,
And the night-fires going out, and the lack of shelters,
And the cities hostile and the towns unfriendly
And the villages dirty and charging high prices: 15
A hard time we had of it.
At the end we preferred to travel all night,
Sleeping in snatches,
With the voices singing in our ears, saying
That this was all folly. 20
Then at dawn we came down to a temperate valley,
Wet, below the snow line, smelling of vegetation;
With a running stream and a water-mill beating the darkness,
And three trees on the low sky,
And an old white horse galloped away in the meadow. 25
Then we came to a tavern with vine-leaves over the lintel,
Six hands at an open door dicing for pieces of silver,
And feet kicking the empty wine-skins.
But there was no information, and so we continued
And arrived at evening, not a moment too soon 30
Finding the place; it was (you may say) satisfactory.

All this was a long time ago, I remember,
And I would do it again, but set down
This set down
This: were we led all that way for 35
Birth or Death? There was a Birth, certainly,
We had evidence and no doubt. I had seen birth and death,
But had thought they were different; this Birth was
Hard and bitter agony for us, like Death, our death.
We returned to our places, these Kingdoms, 40
But no longer at ease here, in the old dispensation,
With an alien people clutching their gods.
I should be glad of another death.

MACAVITY: THE MYSTERY CAT

Macavity's a Mystery Cat: he's called the Hidden Paw—
For he's the master criminal who can defy the Law.
He's the bafflement of Scotland Yard, the Flying Squad's despair:
For when they reach the scene of crime—*Macavity's not there!*

Macavity, Macavity, there's no-one like Macavity, 5
He's broken every human law, he breaks the law of gravity.
His powers of levitation would make a fakir stare,
And when you reach the scene of crime—*Macavity's not there!*
You may seek him in the basement, you may look up in the air—
But I tell you once and once again, *Macavity's not there!* 10

Macavity's a ginger cat, he's very tall and thin;
You would know him if you saw him, for his eyes are sunken in.
His brow is deeply lined with thought, his head is highly domed;
His coat is dusty from neglect, his whiskers are uncombed.
He sways his head from side to side, with movements like a snake; 15
And when you think he's half asleep, he's always wide awake.

Macavity, Macavity, there's no-one like Macavity,
For he's a fiend in feline shape, a monster of depravity.
You may meet him in a by-street, you may see him in the square—
But when a crime's discovered, then *Macavity's not there!* 20

He's outwardly respectable. (They say he cheats at cards.)
And his footprints are not found in any file of Scotland Yard's.
And when the larder's looted, or the jewel-case is rifled,
Or when the milk is missing, or another Peke's been stifled,
Or the greenhouse glass is broken, and the trellis past repair— 25
Ay, there's the wonder of the thing! *Macavity's not there!*

And when the Foreign Office find a Treaty's gone astray,
Or the Admiralty lose some plans and drawings by the way,
There may be a scrap of paper in the hall or on the stair—
But it's useless to investigate—*Macavity's not there!* 30
And when the loss has been disclosed, the Secret Service say:
'It *must* have been Macavity!'—but he's a mile away.
You'll be sure to find him resting, or a-licking of his thumbs,
Or engaged in doing complicated long division sums.

Macavity, Macavity, there's no-one like Macavity, 35
There never was a Cat of such deceitfulness and suavity.
He always has an alibi, and one or two to spare:
At whatever time the deed took place—MACAVITY WASN'T THERE!
And they say that all the Cats whose wicked deeds are
widely known
(I might mention Mungojerrie, I might mention Griddlebone) 40
Are nothing more than agents for the Cat who all the time
Just controls their operations: the Napoleon of Crime!

INDEX OF FIRST LINES